245 MONEY MAKING STOCK CHART SETUPS

Profiting from

SWING TRADING

SASHA EVDAKOV

INTRODUCTION

Thank you for joining me in your miraculous journey in learning more about the stock market. The market can be a tricky place if you are in the beginning stages of your journey, but it is something that I believe anyone can use to enhance their life.

Whether you want to make a couple of hundred dollars on the side and worry less about your financials or you want to build a nest egg for retirement – the stock market can help you achieve these things if you put the time, effort, and energy to learn how to use it to your advantage.

Some people see the market as an evil scheme, where stress is created, huge fortunes lost, and lives ruined! For me, I see beauty in the market. I see the opportunities that can be created and I've seen what's possible.

However, before you become profitable in the markets you have to go through an enormous amount of study time ahead of you. I think if you relate a stock trader to a doctor – I believe the time and effort involved is similar. Your study time may consist of eight years of gruesome nights until you become profitable. It's kind of like going to college, then medical school, and then shadowing a doctor for ten years. After all this time, energy, and money that you invest – you finally get a chance to start your career.

You have to remember that a tennis player isn't created overnight. It takes years for them to become great. After practicing ten or more years on the tennis court, then they may become a professional and win their million dollar tournaments. This is similar to the stock market. Little victories and tournaments do come. If you are looking for the big wins right from the beginning your thinking process is incorrect and you should adjust it quickly or else you will be disappointed.

Unfortunately many people think that the market is a quick way to riches. "Trade stocks and make a fortune by next week" is what many think or hear from advertisements. The sad part is, over the years I have seen more traders become broke than a swarm of wasps dropping dead after being sprayed with pesticide. This is because they listen to the advertisements and hype brought on by the media.

The good news is that if you put the time and effort into studying, building experience, and start trading slowly you can eventually become profitable to the point where your life will be different than it is today. You can experience life in a whole new way. You will have less financial stress and you can have more time-freedom if you structure your life accordingly.

However, to become profitable you will need to work on not only the outer game of trading such as risk management, money management, and learning the technicals, but also your inner game. The inner game includes things such as staying determined, being patient, and persistent. At times you have to be willing to do things that may be uncomfortable for you and make changes in your habits (such as something as simple as waking up earlier).

As for me, I first got into the stock market when I was about 14 years old. Although I had heard about stocks previously, it was because of my mom that I became interested in stocks.

At the time she worked as a private health care nurse to older patients in Florida and they were always watching their stocks and checking their investments. Slowly after about five years of watching the markets with her patients my mom decided to try trading herself.

I helped her open the account since she was not very computer savvy and then I would execute the trades, but she would tell me the stocks to buy or sell.

Our first year was very profitable! It surprised me even at my young age. We were lucky more than experienced as stocks were going through a bull market run. We traded one stock in particular – where we made a few hundred dollars of profit weekly. It was a good feeling making an extra $1,000 a month!

After some time, I took the reins into my own hands. I got the investment capital to trade from working on my digital design business. After about six months of isolated gains I hit a critical part in my trading. I lost over $16,000 in about 16 minutes!!! It was a biotech company and it proved to me that I had no clue what the heck I was doing. I decided to take a moment to step back and try to figure out what happened. From then on I took the next 7+ years to study everything I could get my hands on and slowly made my way back to the market (I think it takes a major experience to realize how fast you can lose money in the markets).

Since that time I put many personal disciplines in place and created my own trading system. I decided to help other people out from the knowledge that I learned when I started my educational business. Stock market education was expensive and I wanted to give everyone the opportunity to learn what I had learnt over the last 10+ years.

So that's my goal for you. Learn what you can and then make it in your own. Make your money work for you! Think of each dollar as a little worker that is out there working for your future.

WHAT THIS BOOK IS ABOUT AND TIPS ON USING IT

This book is different than most stock market books. It isn't a story in the sense of what happened to me in my life and how you can profit using what I learnt. It is a story about the price movement of companies and the way I would trade them.

This book was created to build your muscle memory just like you would in tennis. For you to be able to hit the ball properly, powerfully, correctly, and easily you need to train to do this continually the right way.

The same concept applies to many other sports. If you want to have a great jump shot in basketball, you need to practice shooting. If you want to have a great slap shot then you need to build up the right muscles to help you.

If you want to learn to predict chart patterns better, then you need to study chart patterns and build your brain muscles to spot various trends. This is what this book focuses on. It is designed to build up your technical awareness in stocks so that you can make great decisions in the stock market based on chart data focusing in on the three primary things which are price action, behavior, and volume.

- **Price action** is the price. It is where the price is at for the stock.

- **Behavior** is how the stock is moving. It is a bit difficult to interpret behavior in a book versus a live market. Think of behavior as if a stock is pausing for too long, not acting right, highs keep getting rejected, or the stock is acting sluggish.

- **Volume** is just volume. I tend to use volume because it is a leading indicator versus a lagging indicator. Think of volume as the amount of people exchanging shares of stock or voting for the company. If there is a surge, spike, or pop in volume this means more people are exchanging stock.

Putting all three of these concepts together along with patterns is when you can grasp all the pieces of the puzzle. If you do not have all the components, this does not mean you cannot trade the stock, but if you have all the pieces the probability of your prediction has a higher rate of success. That's what this business is all about – probabilities. You want as many things in your favor as possible because it creates a greater chance of success.

Low probability of success: For example a stock continues to break higher on lighter volume and volume continues to dry up this is a bad sign. Even though the stock may be moving higher in a few weeks things can take a turn. Sometimes these things take time to develop, but eventually they come more often than not.

Again, this does not mean you cannot trade a stock moving to the upside with lower volume, but just have tighter stops or exit points and be prepared for a sudden pull back at any time.

High probability of success: If a stock has been moving well to the upside at a 30 to 40 degree angle and then it consolidates (or moves sideways for 6 weeks) this creates a healthy base. Once this stock starts breaking out of the consolidation pattern with 5x the normal volume it is a great opportunity to enter. Everything is in alignment and the signs are there. This doesn't mean the stock will run up forever, but it does mean you have a higher probability of success from the breaking point.

Some common terminology that I use throughout this book to mark notes on the charts are a way to communicate what I am thinking as I look at the stock chart. Remember that not every opportunity will be a 100% successful so you want to always follow your own risk management and money management plan.

As you start reading the charts you should understand the ways that I refer to some things on the charts and how you should think about them. I tried to used simplified terms on the charts so they are not over crowded; here are some additional tips on how to think of these scenarios that you will come across:

- **Early entry point**: the early entry point could be a place you nibble or get in early. It is usually not the safest place to enter because either there is low volume or there was not a great chart pattern or consolidation prior to the break. However you can still enter at this point just use tight stops or be very cautious if the stock starts to pull back once you enter.

- **Entry point (Safer entry point)**: The regular entry point, or the safer entry point, is the recommended place to enter a stock if you are more risk averse. It is the appropriate and better place to enter as more pieces of the puzzle are in alignment. The volume might be greater, there might have been a consolidation period, or the stock could be clearing recent highs.

- **Sell some into strength**: You should always be selling part of your stock into strength. The more accelerated a move is (the faster it is) the more you should be selling since you should assume a stock will come back and retest earlier levels. Even though I mention at times on the charts "sell into strength" you should be doing this constantly and more often than when I mention. Especially if you added to a position, you should start looking for an opportunity to reduce risk once a stock goes in your favor (even if it is just a little bit).

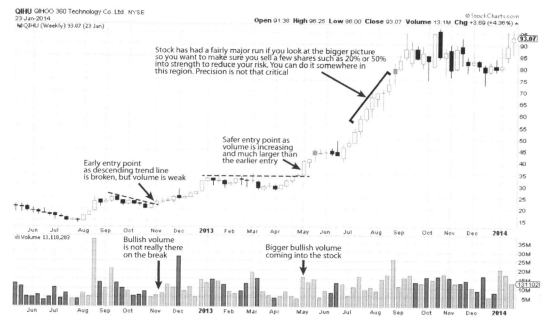

- **Retesting support**: Stocks like to come back down and retest support. This is normally healthy and at times it can be an opportunity to add to your position after the stock starts its move back to the upside. When a stock comes back to test its previous support you want to make sure it comes back on lighter volume and bounces on heavier volume. If a stock is coming down fast with heavy volume then chances are it will blow past the previous support or resistance line.

- **Confluence**: Confluence is a meeting point. Often times in stocks they will not hit lines of support, resistance, or trend lines perfectly. It takes a little bit of wiggle room for everyone to get on board and meet. Just like when you meet a friend at 6:00 pm for dinner it is rarely perfect. Always give stocks a little bit of room of a few pennies to confirm the move is real (otherwise the stock may quickly reverse as you could be buying stocks when you should be short selling them).

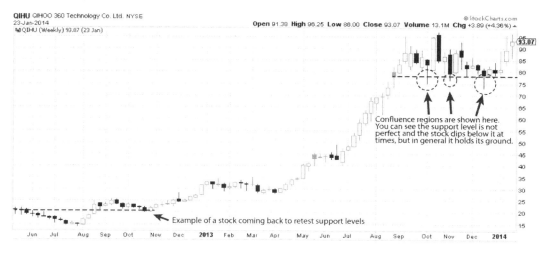

- **Gaps**: Gaps happen often on daily charts and they are not rare to see. When gaps do happen you should be extra careful as gaps typically fill. If a stock does have a great pop that has gapped up, this does not mean you should not buy it – instead if it appears like an opportunity use the highest part of the stock as a stop. However, once the stock starts breaking down back into the gap then prepare for the gap to be filled (or go back down to where it gapped up from).

- **Healthy trend lines**: Typically you will see me mark trend lines as healthy trend lines, accelerated, or super accelerated trend lines. Healthy trend lines have a nice angle to the move. They are not too fast. A healthy movement to the stock gives it an opportunity to consolidate, build patterns, and bases. Healthy trend lines are more sustainable and longer lasting unfortunately they are slower moving. On the upside, their pull backs are less violent. As a side note, you can always draw a healthy trend line at about a 40 degree angle and see how fast a stock should be moving even if it is not hitting those points as it will give you an idea of what would be healthy.

- **Accelerated trend lines**: Accelerated trend lines are trend lines that move at a steep angle. They are trend lines that move faster than healthier trend lines probably over a 50 degree angle or more. If the angle looks too steep to pedal a bike on, then it is probably an accelerated trend line. Although they do feel great when you are in them as a long trader since they move nice and fast unfortunately, these trend lines usually have harsh or rash pull backs and can even pull back to a healthy trend line level.

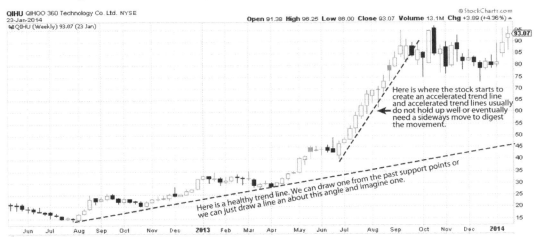

- **Safe exit point**: The safe exit point is the place where you can get out of the stock since it shows some sign of caution. It is also an area where you can sell some more shares to reduce your risk. If you had a great run so far in your stock investment, you don't mind a slight pull back, and you are willing to risk it then you can hold a stock for a bit longer until true danger comes. The reason for the safe exit point is sometimes it appears like an exit, whereas other times a stock is just doing a natural and healthy pull back.

- **Exit here**: The exit here point is definitely an exit point. This is the area where you should get rid of 100% of your holdings because the signs are there such as a bearish engulfing pattern, huge bearish volume, the stock is breaking a healthy trend line, or it is showing you some kind of weakness.

- **Volume rising (volume increasing):** Volume rising or increasing is a sign that volume is picking up over the last few bars. This means that it is becoming bigger. You need to watch whether the volume is getting bigger to the down side (bearish volume is rising) or bullish volume is rising. If bearish volume (sometimes called down volume or negative volume) is rising then this is a bad sign. If bullish or positive volume is rising then this is a good sign.

- **Volume pop, spike, and surge:** A volume pop, spike, or surge is usually a huge movement in volume. This again can be bullish volume or bearish volume. When looking at these huge spikes or surges they are usually double or triple what the normal volume is. Often they are great points to enter or exit and give you a sign. When looking at the weekly chart sometimes these surges or spikes happen on earnings when a stock gaps up and this is when you need to be careful and follow the tips I mentioned regarding gaps.

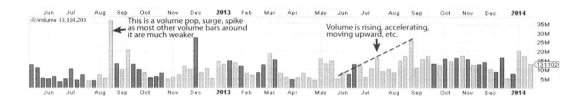

- **Volume cluster:** A cluster of volume is a group of volume bars that are of the same stature meaning either mostly all bearish or all bullish. Cluster of volume can help confirm the move or shows what people think of the stock. Remember that stocks eventually like to balance back out so if it is too heavy on one side eventually things reverse.

- **Looking at chart time frames:** Many times I will show you the weekly charts in this book, however you need to be looking at multiple chart frames. Look at the monthly chart or yearly chart to see the picture. This will tell you where the stock has been and where is it going. Look for setup opportunities then on weekly and zoom in on the daily if they are difficult to see. Once you have your trend lines in place or patterns marked wait for the break. In other words you should trade off the weekly or daily for finding your successful swing point entries. This ensures the run is sustained for some time. When looking at the chart you can watch the 15 minute or 30 minute ticks to place your order to double check the behavior is acting properly. However remember that you are still trading off the weekly or the daily as they create stronger support and resistance lines.

If you are still struggling with understanding the concepts in this book, I highly recommend you read my book "Start Trading Stocks" which you can find on Amazon or get my video course "Stock Trading Foundation" (the green one) which covers important basic setups for charts, when to enter stocks based on technical data, discusses volume, gaps, and more! It is over 3 hours long and packed with an abundance of information.

TRADING DISCLAIMER

Sasha Evdakov or Rise2Learn, LLC are NOT licensed financial advisers (here in after will be referred to as Rise2Learn). Nothing contained in our material (hereinafter referred to as media) is intended to be or construed to be as financial advice. All information on any media is not intended as investment, tax, accounting, or legal advice. Nor is it an offer or endorsement or recommendation of any company, security, or fund.

TRADING INVOLVES RISK AND IS NOT SUITABLE FOR ALL INVESTORS

Online trading has inherent risk due to system response and access times that may vary due to market conditions, system performance, and other factors. An investor should understand these and additional risks before trading. While implied volatility represents the consensus of the marketplace as to the future level of stock price volatility or probability of researching a specific price point, there is no guarantee that this forecast will be correct.

Content, research, tools, and stock or option symbols are for entertainment, educational, and illustrative purposes only and do not imply a recommendation or solicitation to buy or sell a particular security or to engage in any particular investment strategy. The projections or other information regarding the likelihood of various investment outcomes are hypothetical in nature, and are not guarantees of future results.

You agree that all content including all media under Rise2Learn, LLC along with its materials are proprietary rights and that their use is restricted by the terms of this agreement. Use of the content, media, or material, for any purpose without written permission from Rise2Learn, LLC is strictly prohibited. You further agree that you will not create derivate works of this media, material or products offered by Rise2Learn, LLC.

Rise2Learn does not guarantee or promise any income or particular result from your use of the information contained herein. Rise2Learn, LLC assumes no responsibility or liability for issues, errors, or omissions in the information in our media.

DAMAGES AND LIABILITIES

Rise2Learn will not be liable for any incidental, indirect, direct, punitive, consequential, special, exemplary, or other damages including, but not limited to, loss of revenue or income, pain and suffering, emotional distress, or similar damages even if Rise2Learn has been advised of the possibility of such damages.

In no event will the collective liability to any party (regardless of the form of action, whether in contract, tort, or otherwise) exceed the greater of $100 or the amount you have paid to Rise2Learn for the information product, service, seminar, or media out of which liability arose. Under no circumstances will Rise2Learn be liable for any loss or damage caused by your reliance on the information contained herein.

It is your responsibility to evaluate the accuracy, completeness, or usefulness of any information, advice, opinion, or other content contained in any media presented by Rise2Learn. Please seek the advice of professionals, as appropriate, regarding the evaluation of any specific information, advice, opinion, or content, or media.

COPYRIGHT NOTICE

This book is copyright. I love spreading knowledge in the world, educating other people, and helping others achieve their potential. You are welcome to cite things from this book however please give credit back to me or my website http://tradersfly.com or http://sashaevdakov.com.

If you have any questions regarding the copyright or would like to use parts of it on your website, presentation, just contact me from my stock trading website http://tradersfly.com or my personal website http://sashaevdakov.com

COPYRIGHT FROM THE LAWYERS

Okay, enough with that. Let's get into some stock market tips!

QuiCk RESOuRCES

Before you get too far I just want to give you a few handful resources that I use. All of these resources can be easily found on my website at:

http://www.tradersfly.com : Free Stock Trading Lessons. There is even a place where you can get access to my critical charts. Critical charts are the stock charts that I'm watching in the current market conditions. If you are aiming to study the current market and stock charts in today's market conditions then I highly recommend it. I usually try to post a few times a week.

Just visit www.tradersfly.com as there are a plethora of articles, videos, and resources to learn from. Most of them are free!

If you decide to take your trading to the next level and want to accelerate your education I have created in depth video training materials that are unlike any others on the market. Take a look at my parent company:

http://www.rise2learn.com that has all my training products listed.

SPECial TnaNkS TO STOCkCnaRTS.COm

I wanted to give my gratitude and a special thank you to stockcharts.com and their team for allowing me to use their charts throughout this book. Without them, this book would not be possible!

With that being said… let's get rolling!

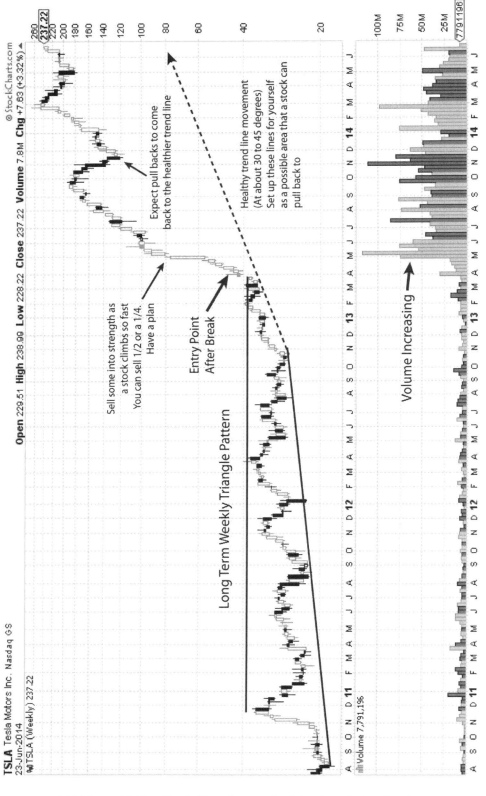

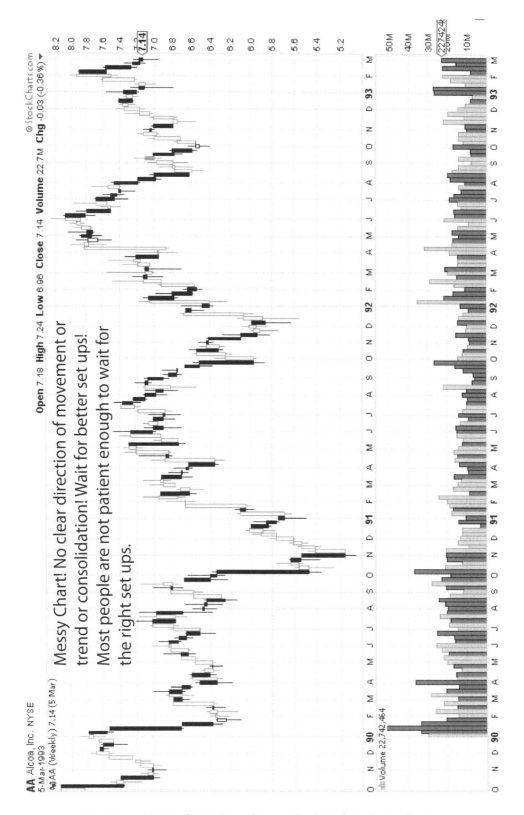

Messy Chart! No clear direction of movement or
trend or consolidation! Wait for better set ups!

Most people are not patient enough to wait for
the right set ups.

16

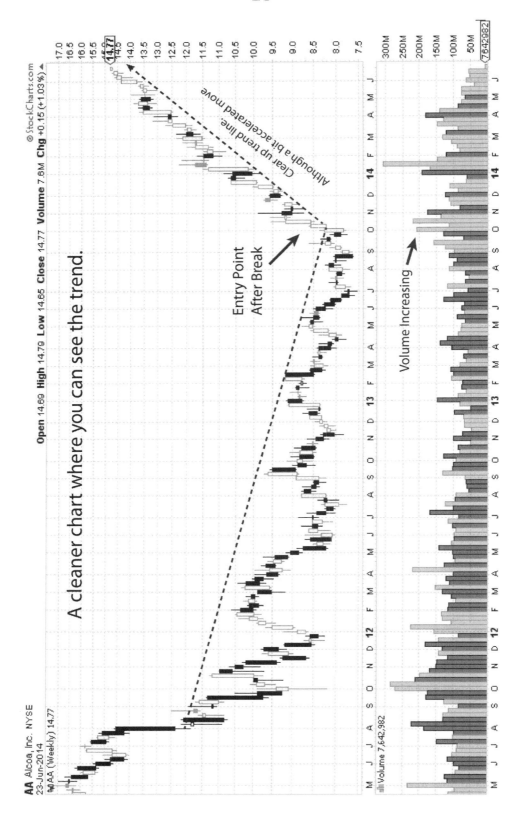

A cleaner chart where you can see the trend.

AA Alcoa, Inc. NYSE
23-Jun-2014
Open 14.69 High 14.79 Low 14.65 Close 14.77 Volume 7.8M Chg +0.15 (+1.03%)
© StockCharts.com

Clear up trend line.
Although a bit accelerated move

Entry Point After Break

Volume Increasing

245 Money Making Stock Chart Setups: Profiting from Swing Trading

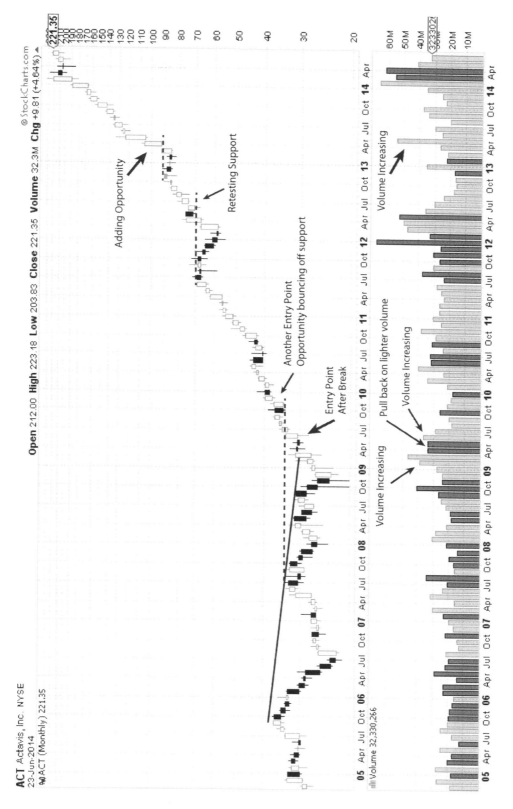

245 Money Making Stock Chart Setups: Profiting from Swing Trading

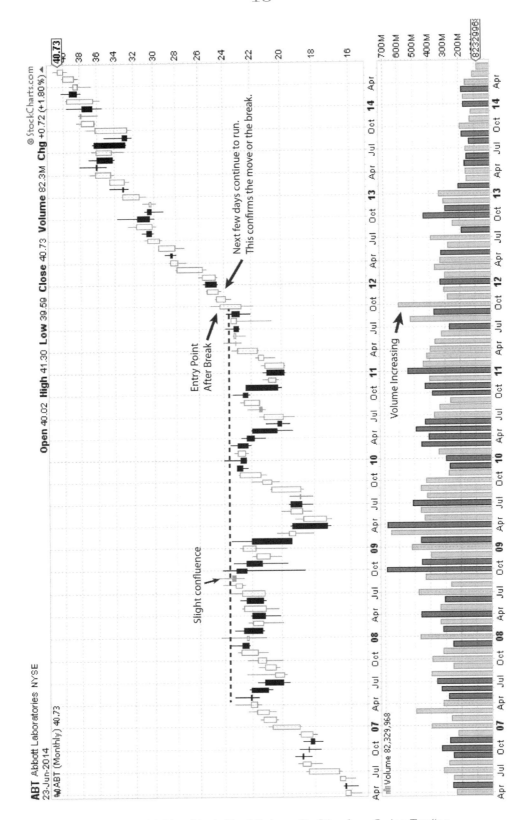

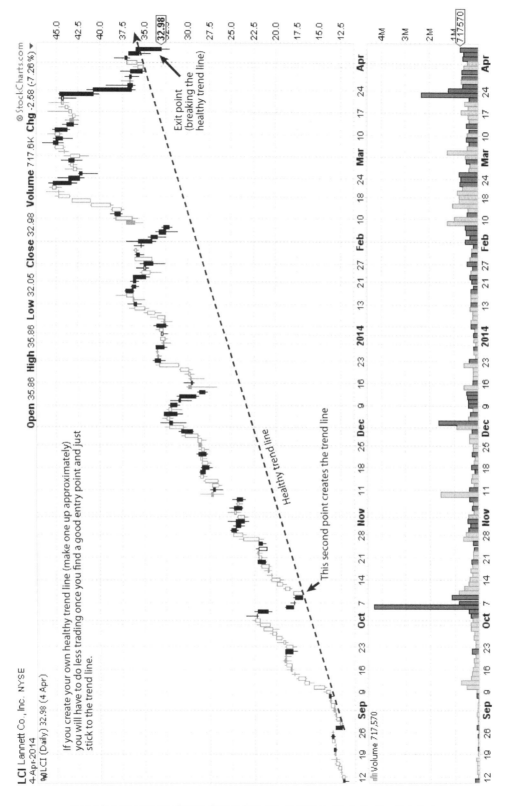

LCI Lannett Co., Inc. NYSE
4-Apr-2014
Open 35.86 High 35.86 Low 32.05 Close 32.98 Volume 717.6K Chg -2.58 (-7.26%) ▼
© StockCharts.com
◆LCI (Daily) 32.98 (4 Apr)

If you create your own healthy trend line (make one up approximately)
you will have to do less trading once you find a good entry point and just
stick to the trend line.

Exit point
(breaking the
healthy trend line)

Healthy trend line

This second point creates the trend line

dln Volume 717,570

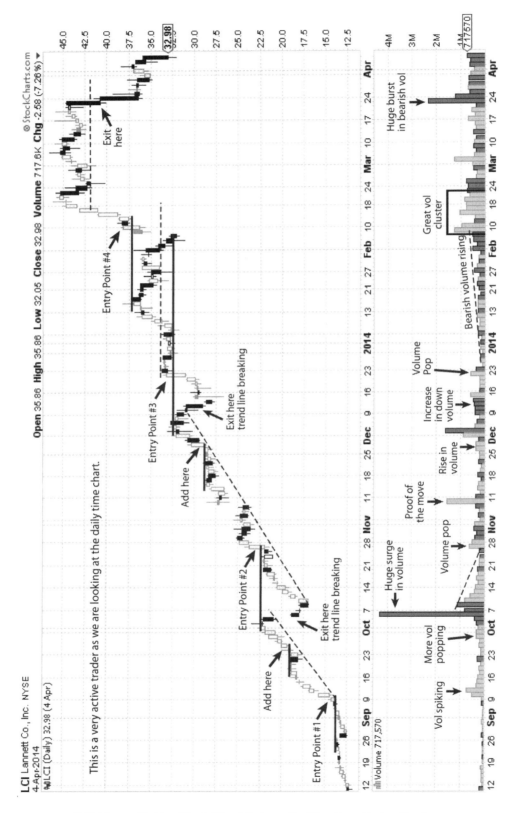

LCI Lannett Co., Inc. NYSE
4-Apr-2014
◆LCI (Daily) 32.98 (4 Apr)

Open 35.86 **High** 35.86 **Low** 32.05 **Close** 32.98 **Volume** 717.6K **Chg** -2.58 (-7.26%) ▼

® StockCharts.com

This is a very active trader as we are looking at the daily time chart.

Entry Point #4

Entry Point #3

Add here

Exit here
trend line breaking

Exit here

Entry Point #2

Add here

Exit here
trend line breaking

Entry Point #1

Huge burst
in bearish vol

Great vol
cluster

Bearish volume rising

Volume
Pop

Increase
in down
volume

Rise in
volume

Proof of
the move

Volume pop

Huge surge
in volume

More vol
popping

Vol spiking

ıllıl Volume 717,570

245 Money Making Stock Chart Setups: Profiting from Swing Trading

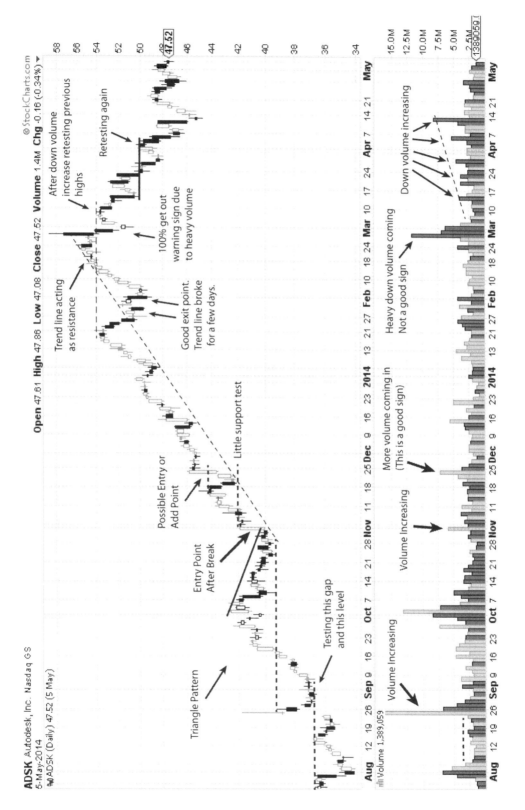

ADSK Autodesk, Inc. Nasdaq GS
5-May-2014
ADSK (Daily) 47.52 (5 May)

Open 47.61 High 47.88 Low 47.08 Close 47.52 Volume 1.4M Chg -0.16 (-0.34%) ▼

© StockCharts.com

47.52

After down volume
increase retesting previous
highs

Retesting again

100% get out
warning sign due
to heavy volume

Trend line acting
as resistance

Good exit point.
Trend line broke
for a few days.

Possible Entry or
Add Point

Little support test

Entry Point
After Break

Testing this gap
and this level

Triangle Pattern

Volume 1,389,059

Volume Increasing

Volume Increasing

More volume coming in
(This is a good sign)

Volume Increasing

Heavy down volume coming
Not a good sign

Down volume increasing

1389059

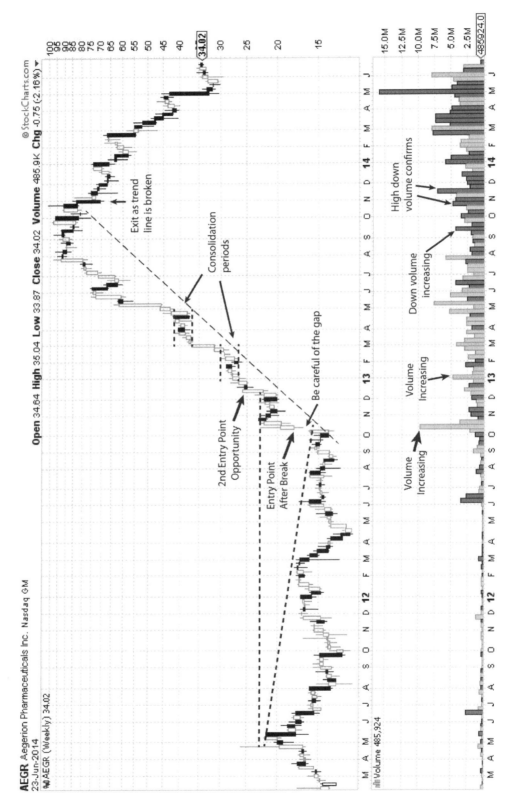

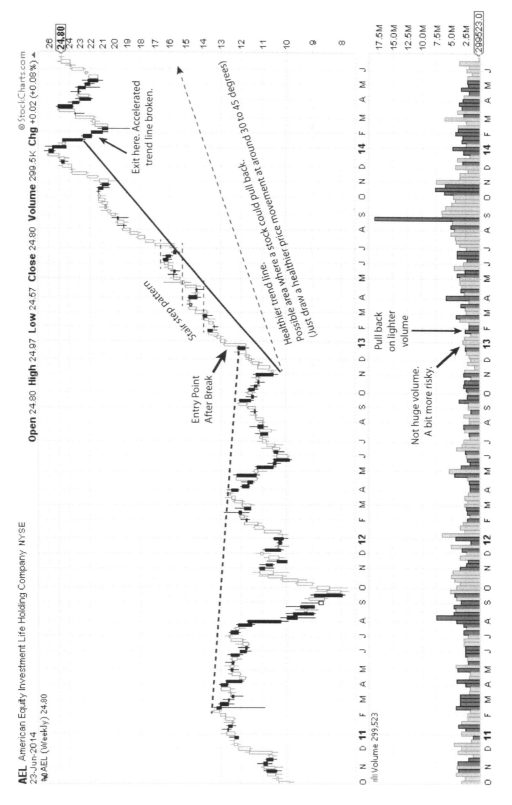

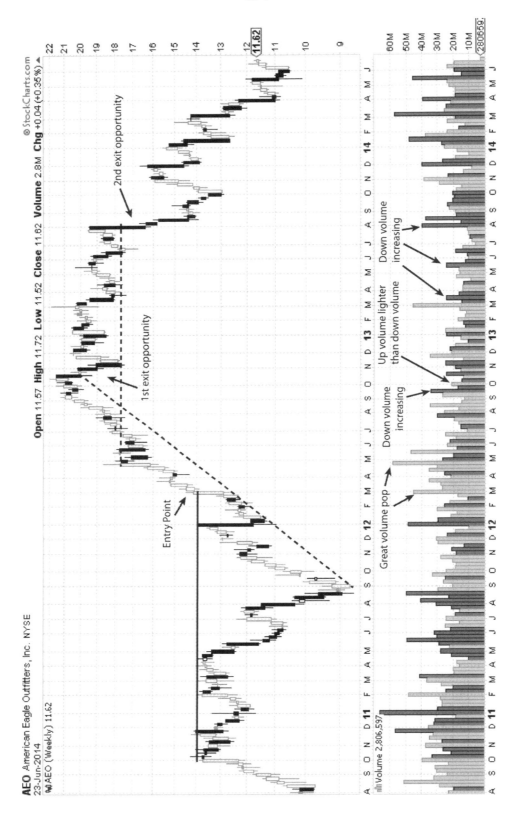

245 Money Making Stock Chart Setups: Profiting from Swing Trading

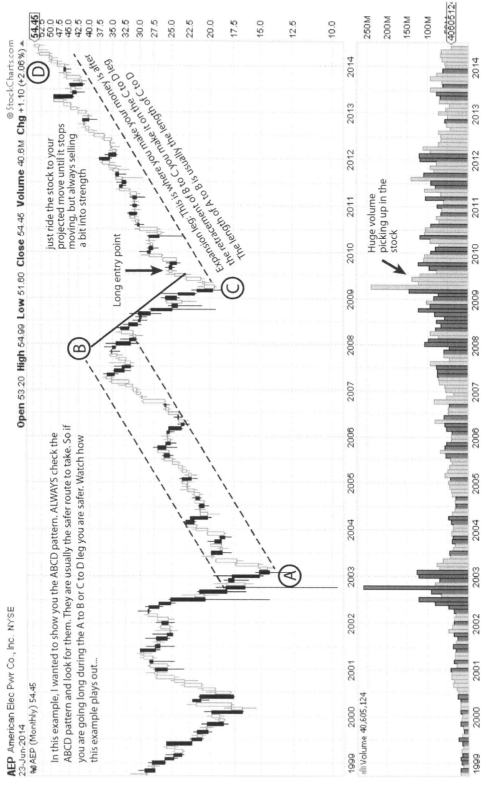

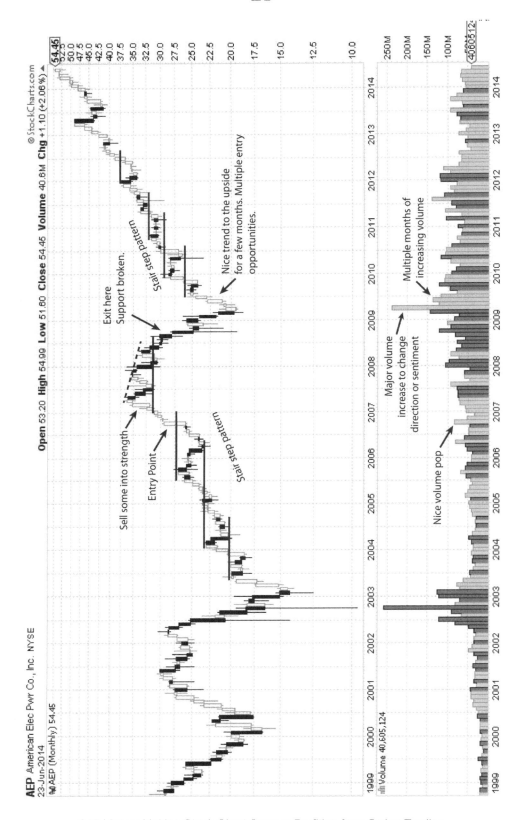

245 Money Making Stock Chart Setups: Profiting from Swing Trading

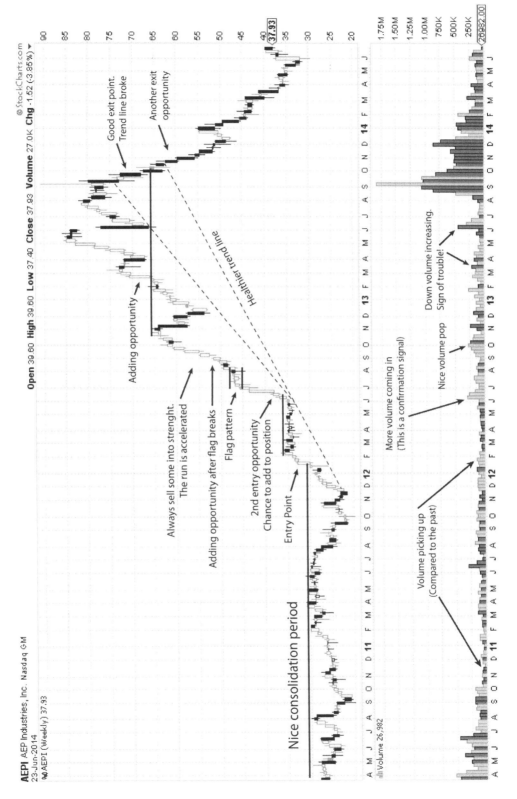

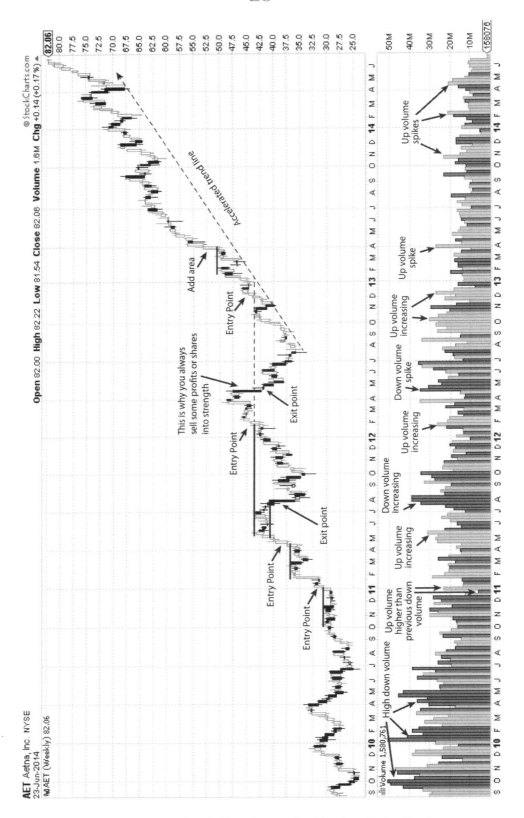

245 Money Making Stock Chart Setups: Profiting from Swing Trading

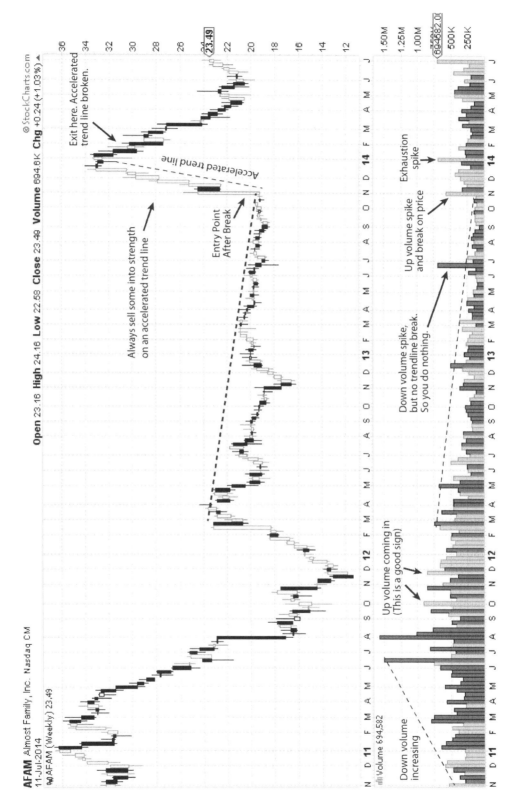

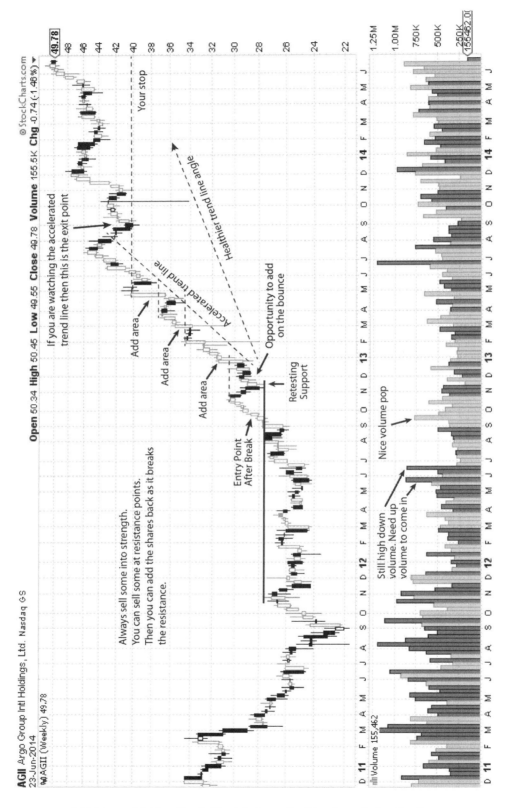

245 Money Making Stock Chart Setups: Profiting from Swing Trading

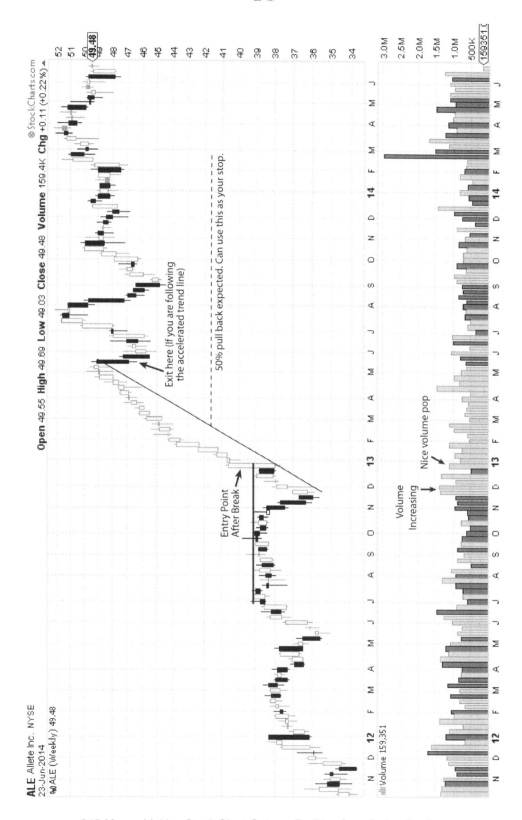

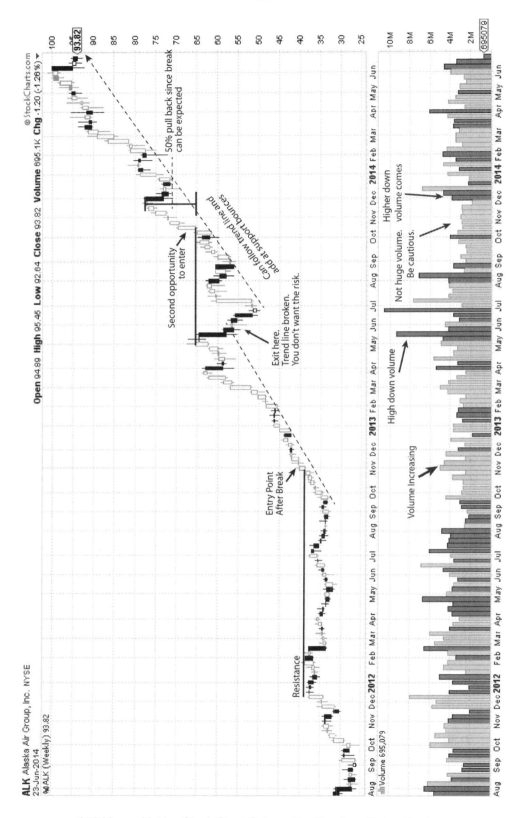

245 Money Making Stock Chart Setups: Profiting from Swing Trading

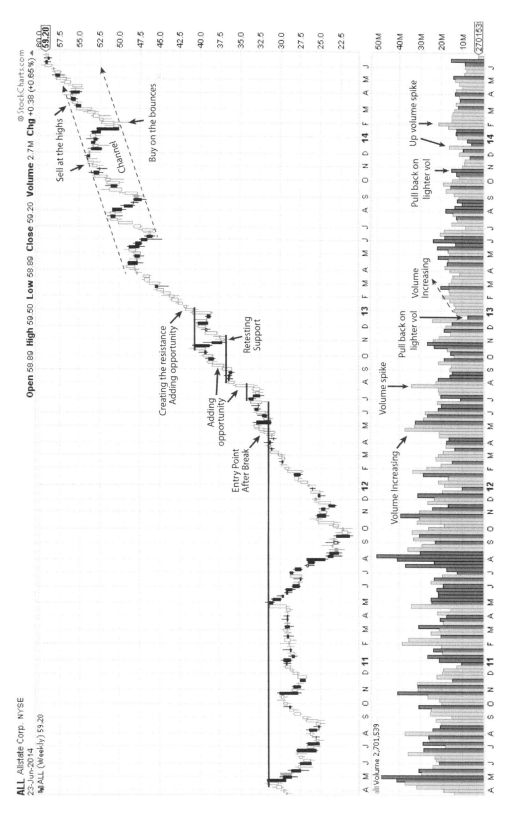

ALL Allstate Corp. NYSE
23-Jun-2014
ᴅᴅ ALL (Weekly) 59.20

Open 58.89 **High** 59.50 **Low** 58.89 **Close** 59.20 **Volume** 2.7M **Chg** +0.38 (+0.65%) ▲

© StockCharts.com

245 Money Making Stock Chart Setups: Profiting from Swing Trading

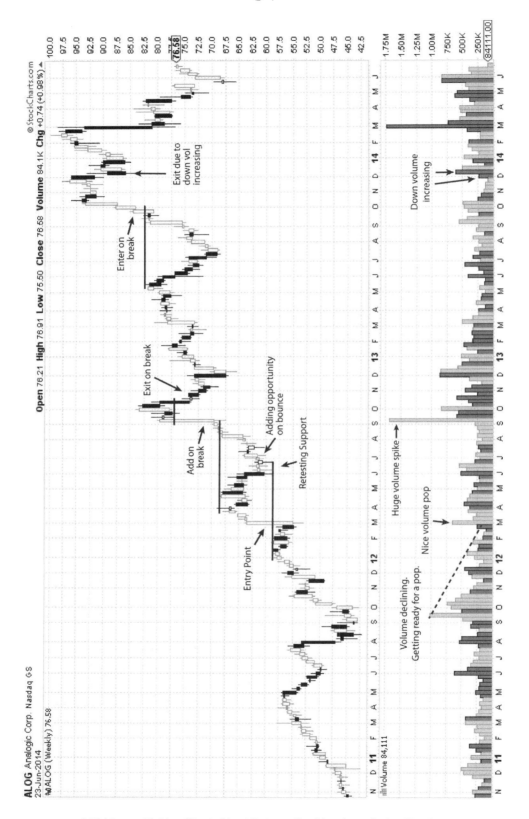

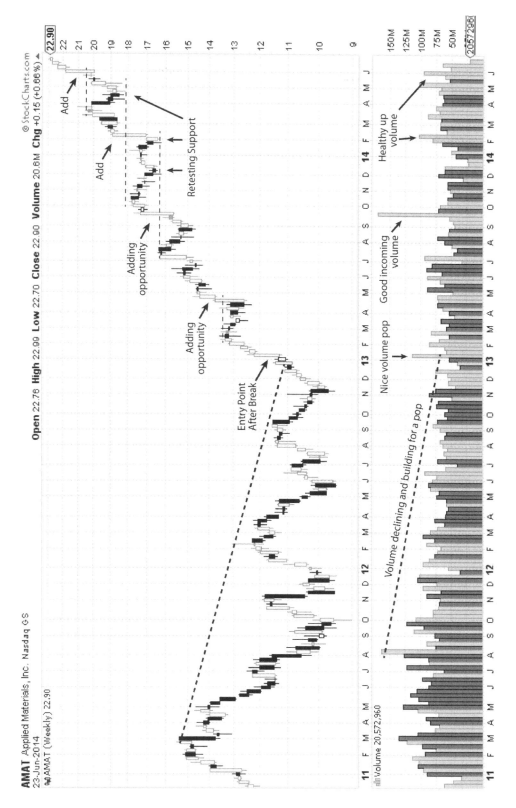

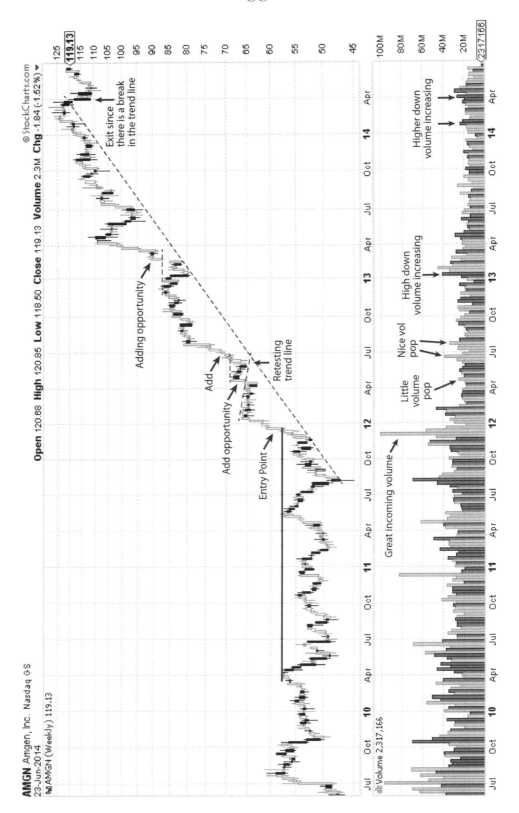

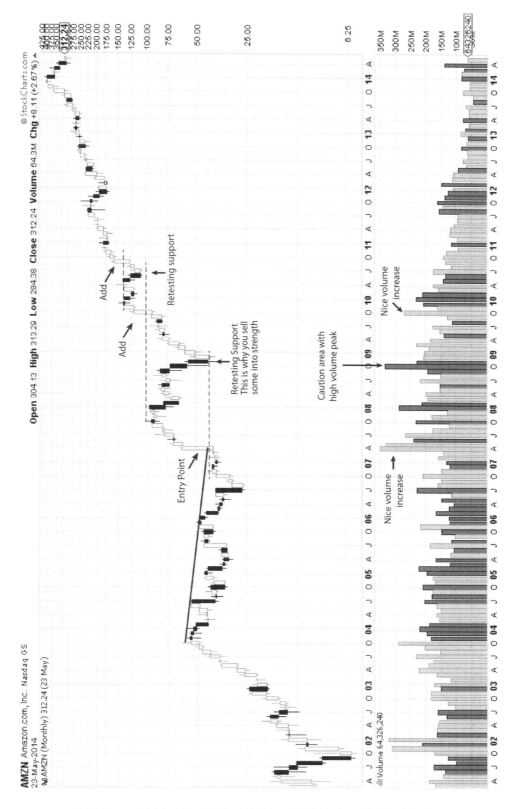

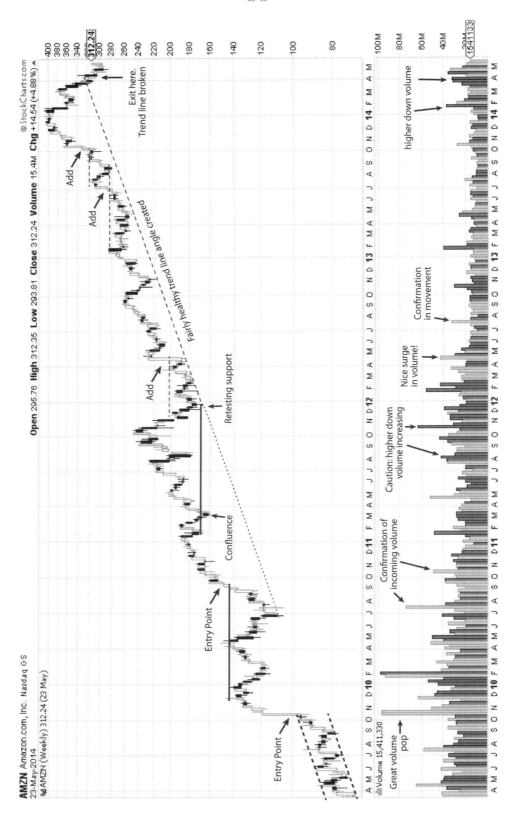

245 Money Making Stock Chart Setups: Profiting from Swing Trading

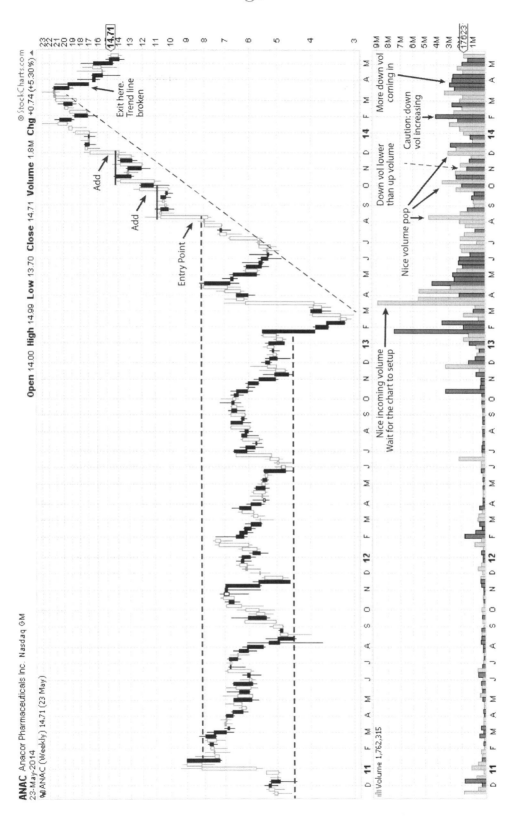

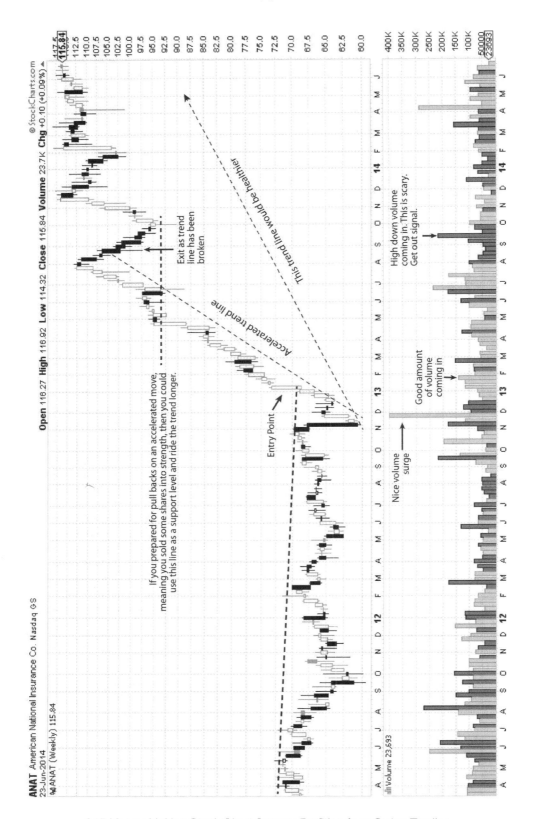

245 Money Making Stock Chart Setups: Profiting from Swing Trading

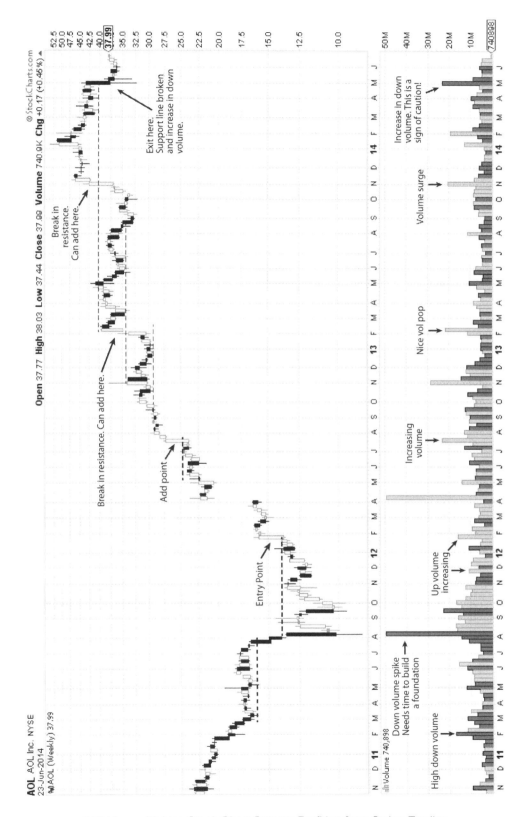

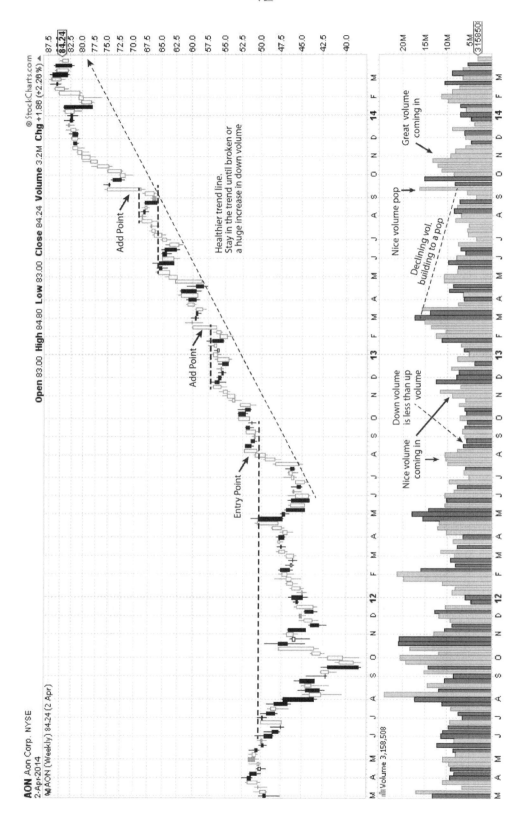

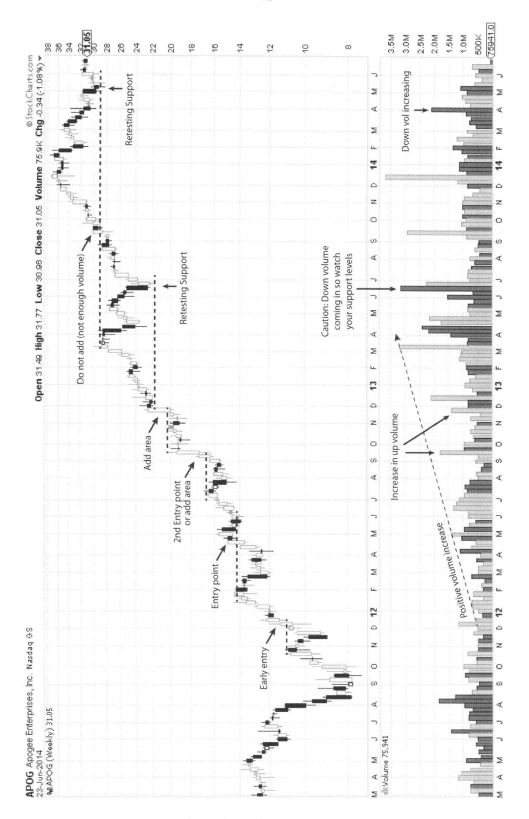

245 Money Making Stock Chart Setups: Profiting from Swing Trading

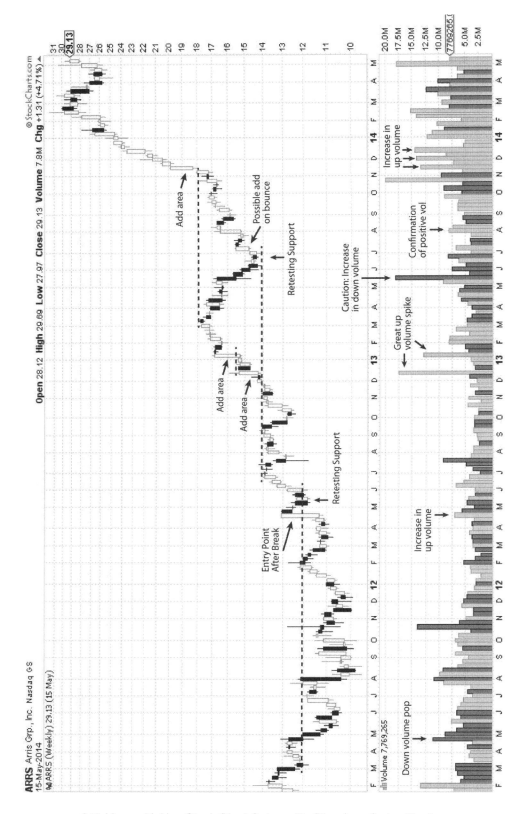

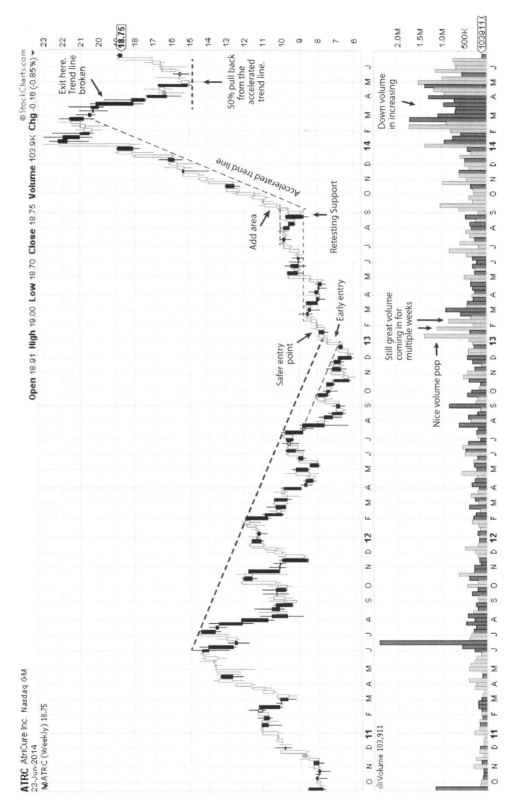

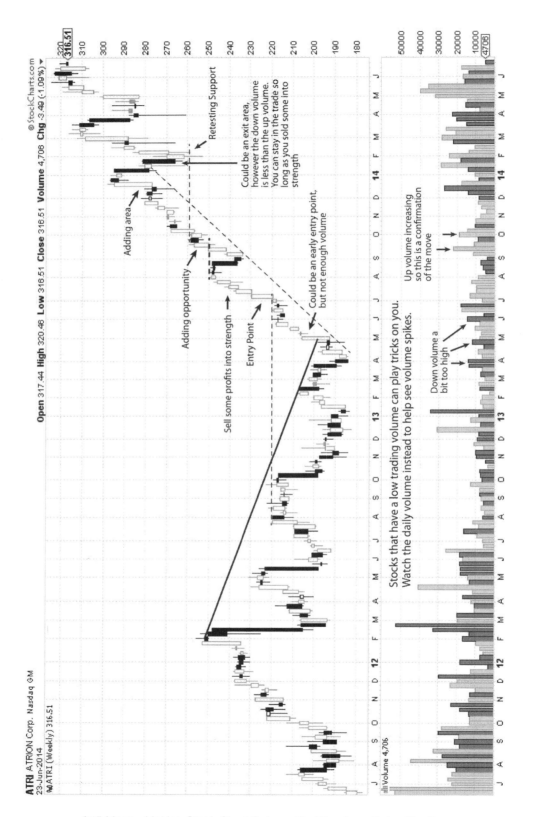

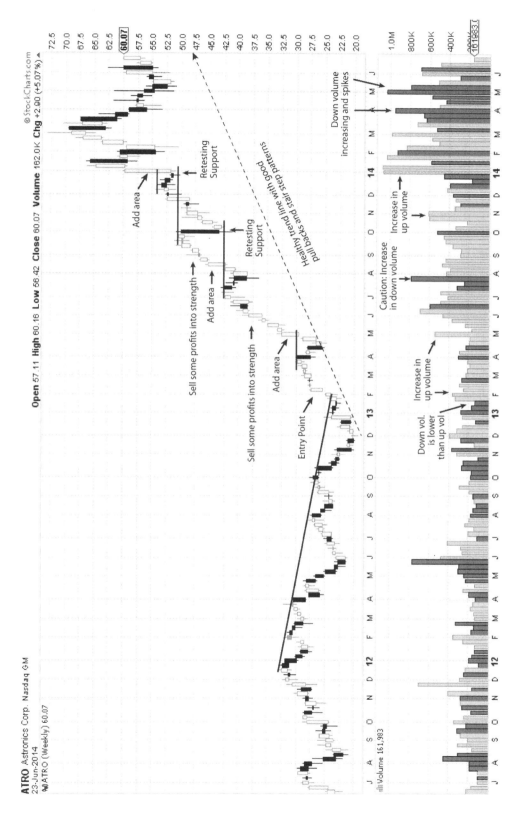

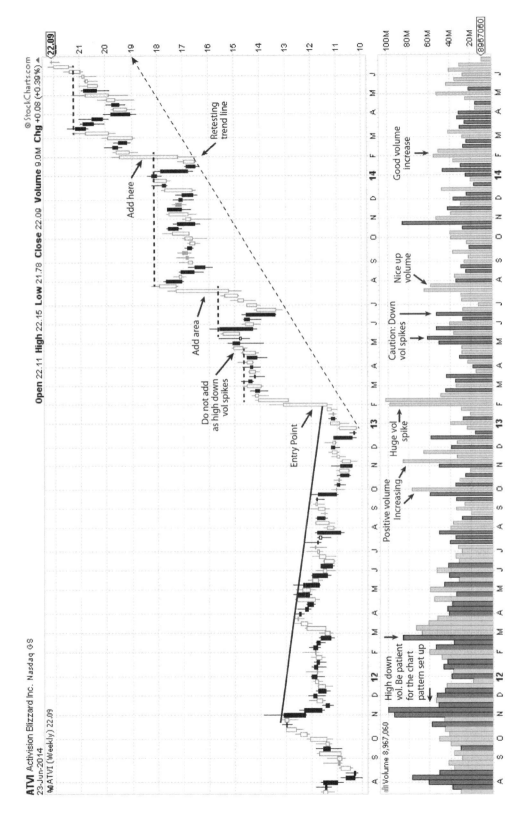

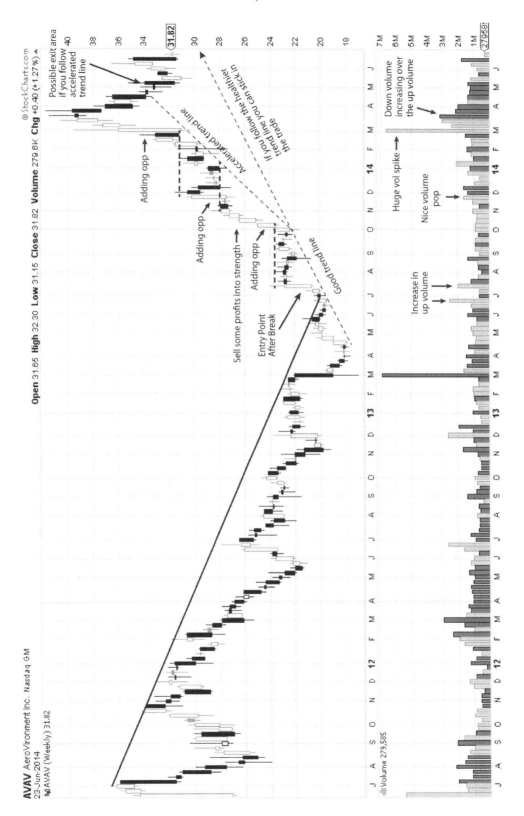

AVAV AeroVironment Inc. Nasdaq GM
23-Jun-2014
W AVAV (Weekly) 31.82

Open 31.65 **High** 32.30 **Low** 31.15 **Close** 31.82 **Volume** 279.8K **Chg** +0.40 (+1.27%) ▲

© StockCharts.com

245 Money Making Stock Chart Setups: Profiting from Swing Trading

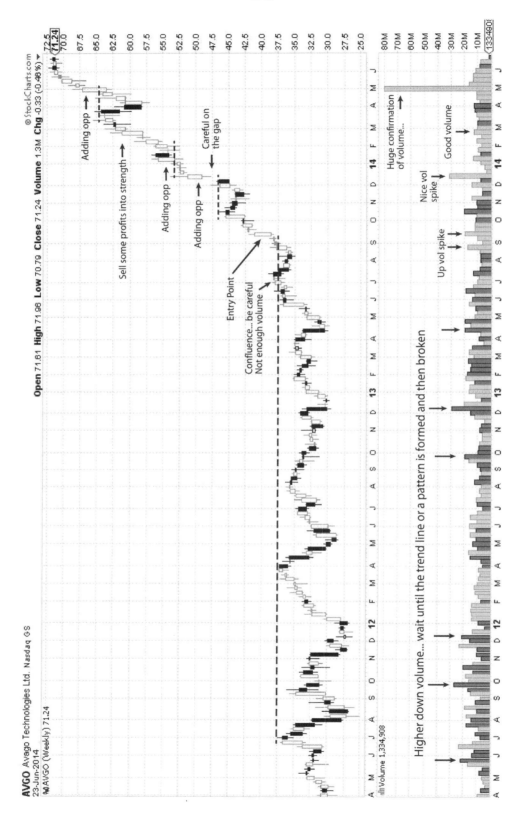

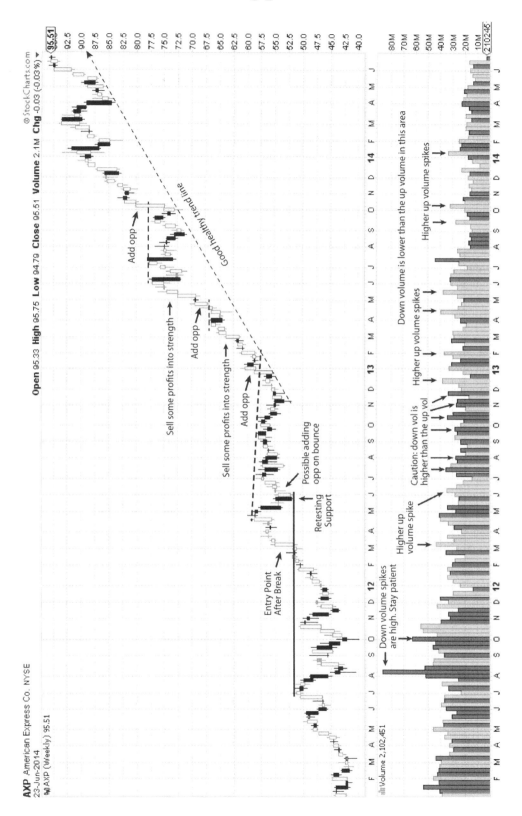

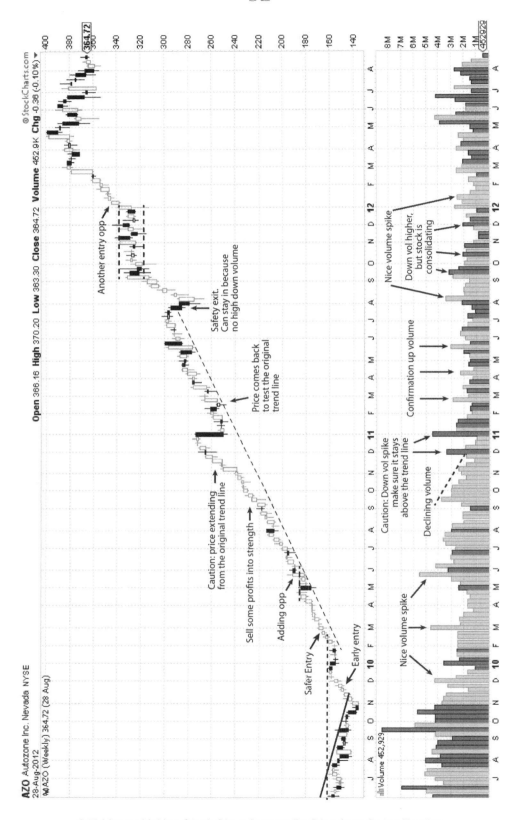

245 Money Making Stock Chart Setups: Profiting from Swing Trading

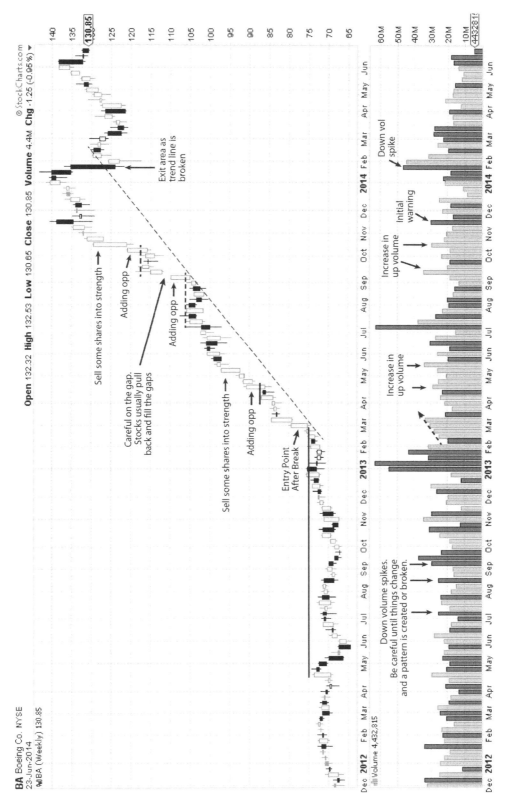

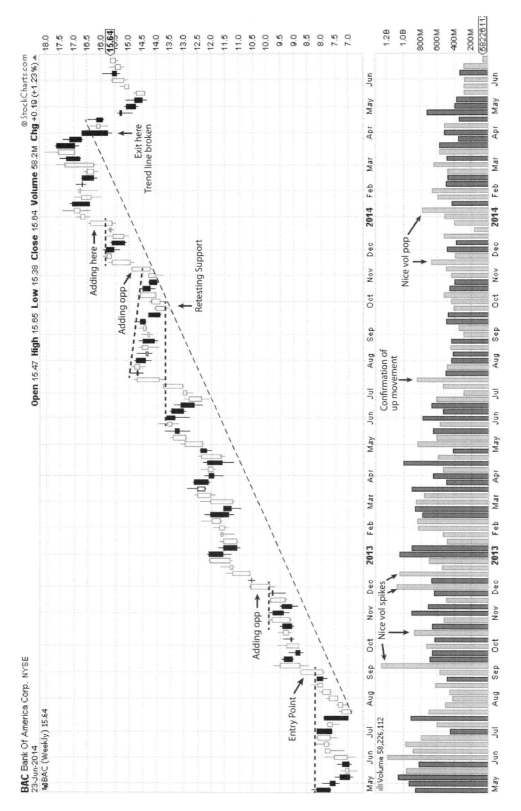

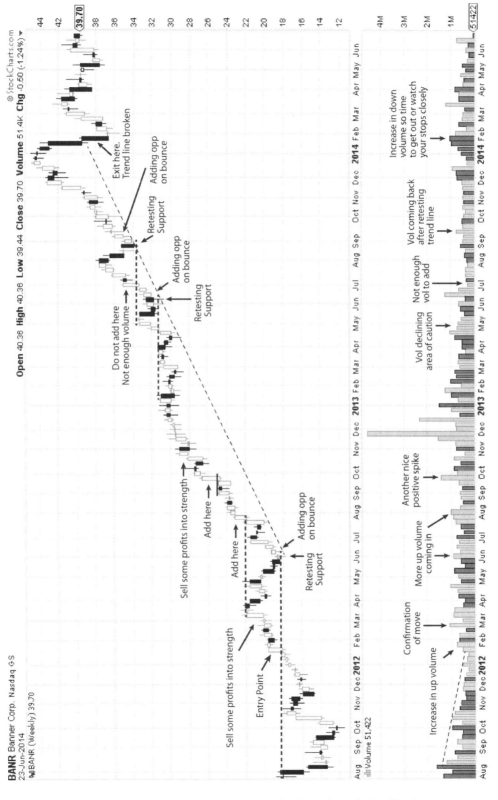

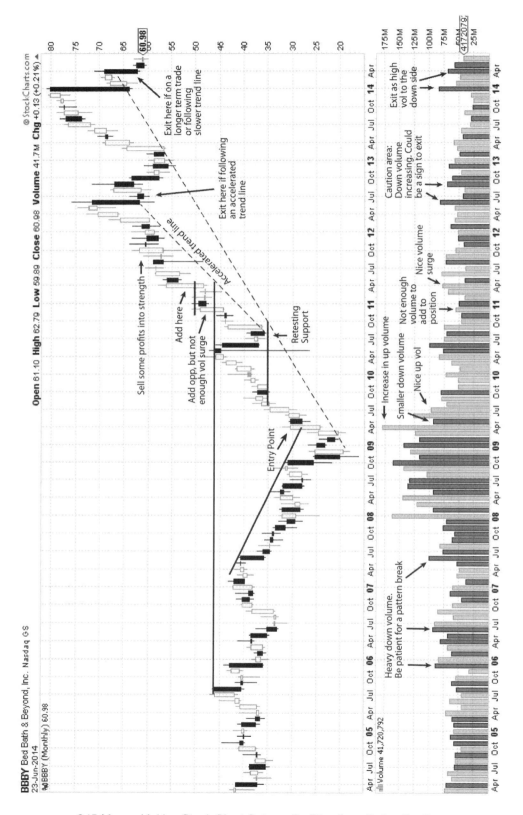

57

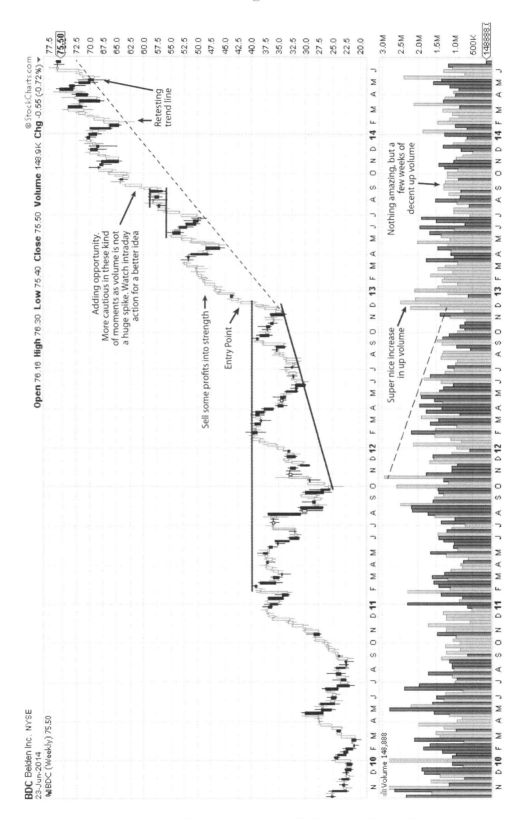

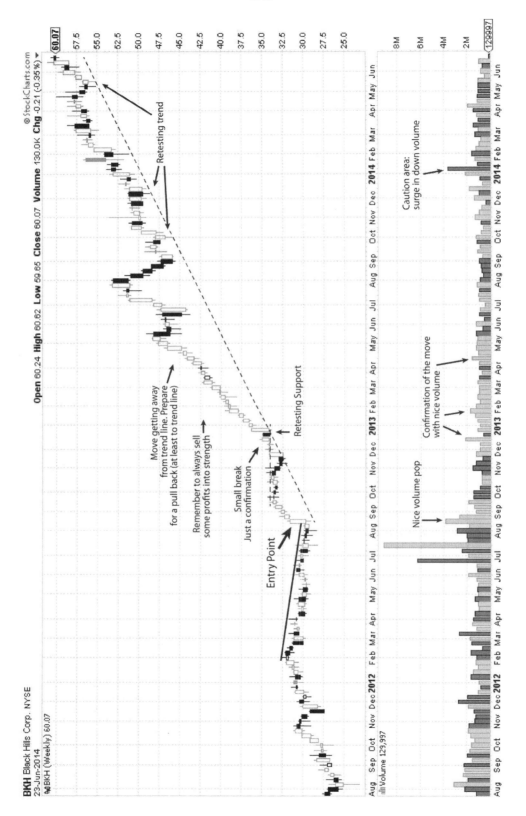

BKH Black Hills Corp. NYSE
23-Jun-2014
☑BKH (Weekly) 60.07

Open 60.24 High 60.82 Low 59.85 Close 60.07 Volume 130.0K Chg -0.21 (-0.35%) ▼

© StockCharts.com

Retesting trend

Move getting away
from trend line. Prepare
for a pull back (at least to trend line)

Remember to always sell
some profits into strength

Small break
Just a confirmation

Retesting Support

Entry Point

Volume 129,997

Caution area:
surge in down volume

Confirmation of the move
with nice volume

Nice volume pop

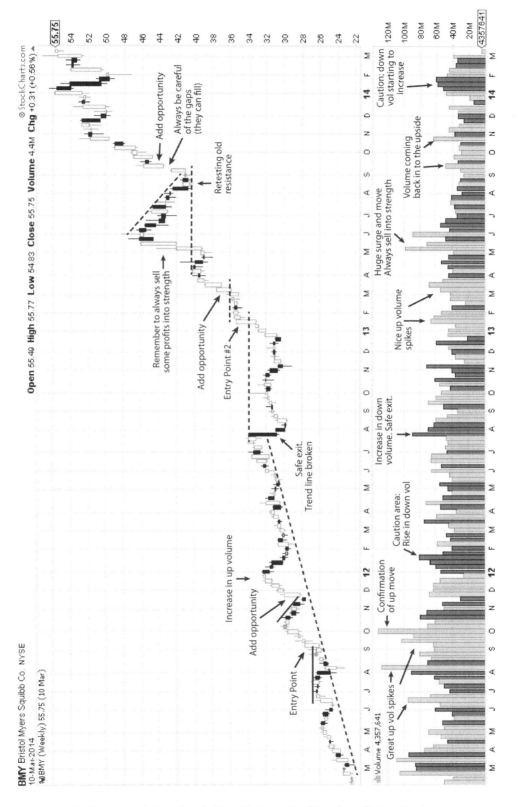

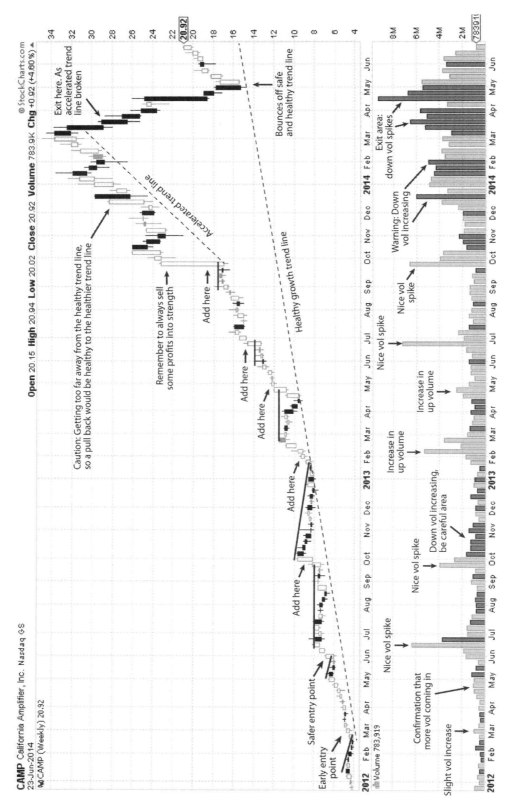

245 Money Making Stock Chart Setups: Profiting from Swing Trading

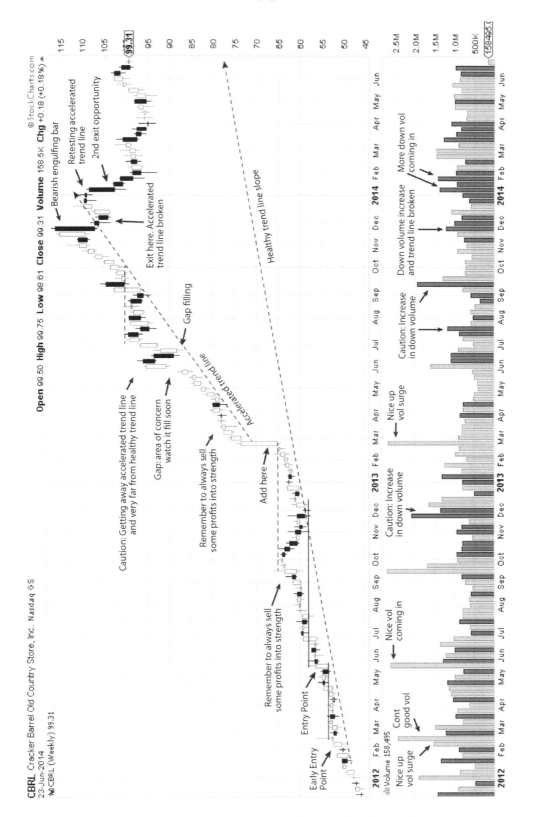

CBRL Cracker Barrel Old Country Store, Inc. Nasdaq GS
23-Jun-2014
*W·CBRL (Weekly) 99.31

Open 99.50 High 99.75 Low 98.81 Close 99.31 Volume 158.5K Chg +0.18 (+0.18%) ▲

@StockCharts.com

Bearish engulfing bar

Retesting accelerated trend line

2nd exit opportunity

Exit here. Accelerated trend line broken

Caution: Getting away accelerated trend line and very far from healthy trend line

Gap: area of concern watch it fill soon

Gap filling

Remember to always sell some profits into strength

Healthy trend line slope

Accelerated trend line

Add here

Remember to always sell some profits into strength

Entry Point

Early Entry Point

Volume 158,495

Nice vol coming in

More down vol coming in

Down volume increase and trend line broken

Caution: Increase in down volume

Nice up vol surge

Caution: Increase in down volume

Nice vol coming in

Cont good vol

Nice up vol surge

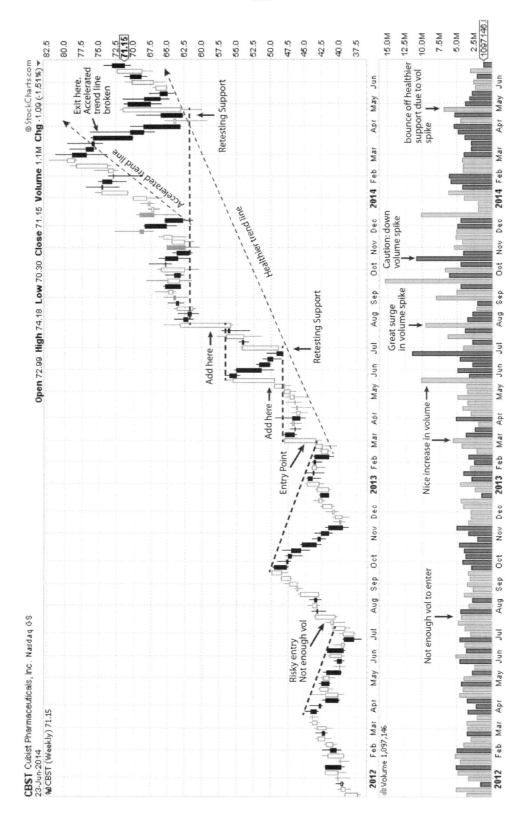

245 Money Making Stock Chart Setups: Profiting from Swing Trading

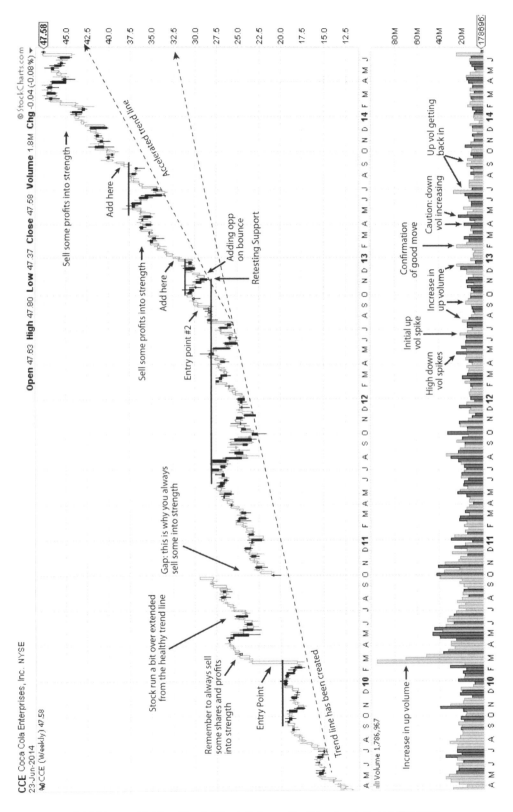

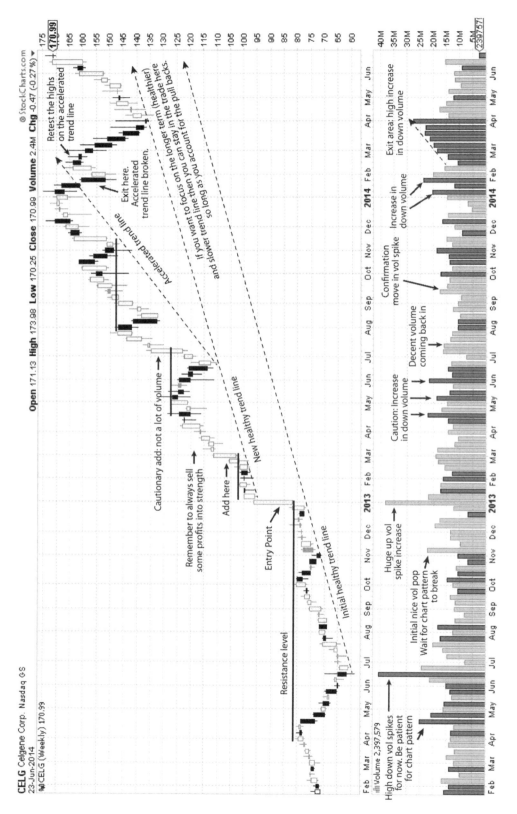

CELG Celgene Corp. Nasdaq GS
23-Jun-2014
Open 171.13 High 173.98 Low 170.25 Close 170.99 Volume 2.4M Chg -0.47 (-0.27%) ▼
®StockCharts.com
170.99
W CELG (Weekly) 170.99
175
170.99

Retest the highs on the accelerated trend line

Exit here.
Accelerated trend line broken.

Accelerated trend line

If you want to focus on the longer term trade here (healthier)
so long as you account for the pull backs.

If you want to focus on the longer trend line then you can stay in the trade
and slower trend line

Cautionary add: not a lot of volume

Remember to always sell some profits into strength

Add here

New healthy trend line

Entry Point

Initial healthy trend line

Resistance level

Exit area: high increase in down volume

Increase in down volume

Confirmation move in vol spike

Decent volume coming back in

Caution: Increase in down volume

Huge up vol spike increase

Initial nice vol pop
Wait for chart pattern to break

High down vol spikes for now. Be patient for chart pattern

ili Volume 2,397,579

245 Money Making Stock Chart Setups: Profiting from Swing Trading

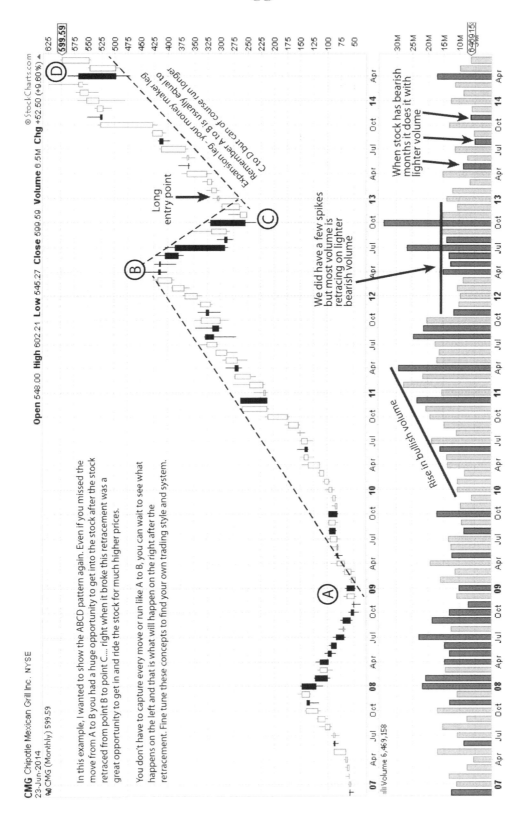

CMG Chipotle Mexican Grill Inc. NYSE
23-Jun-2014
W CMG (Monthly) 599.59

Open 548.00 **High** 602.21 **Low** 545.27 **Close** 599.59 **Volume** 6.5M **Chg** +52.50 (+9.60%) ▲

@ StockCharts.com

In this example, I wanted to show the ABCD pattern again. Even if you missed the move from A to B you had a huge opportunity to get into the stock after the stock retraced from point B to point C.... right when it broke this retracement was a great opportunity to get in and ride the stock for much higher prices.

You don't have to capture every move or run like A to B, you can wait to see what happens on the left and that is what will happen on the right after the retracement. Fine tune these concepts to find your own trading style and system.

Expansion leg - your money maker leg
Remember A to B is usually equal to
C to D but can of course run longer

Long
entry point

We did have a few spikes
but most volume is
retracing on lighter
bearish volume

Rise in bullish volume

When stock has bearish
months it does it with
lighter volume

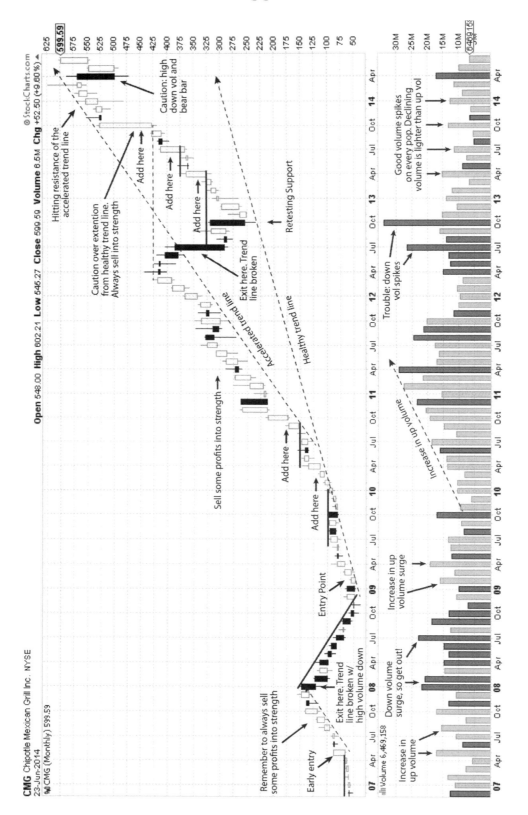

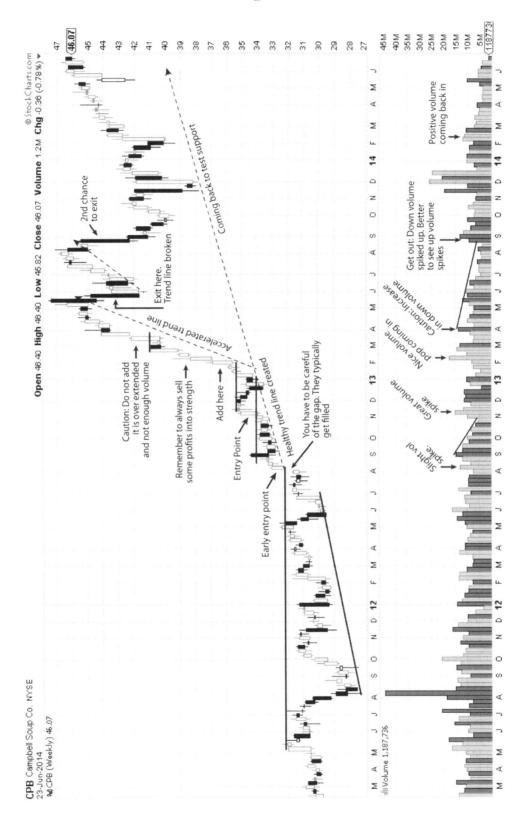

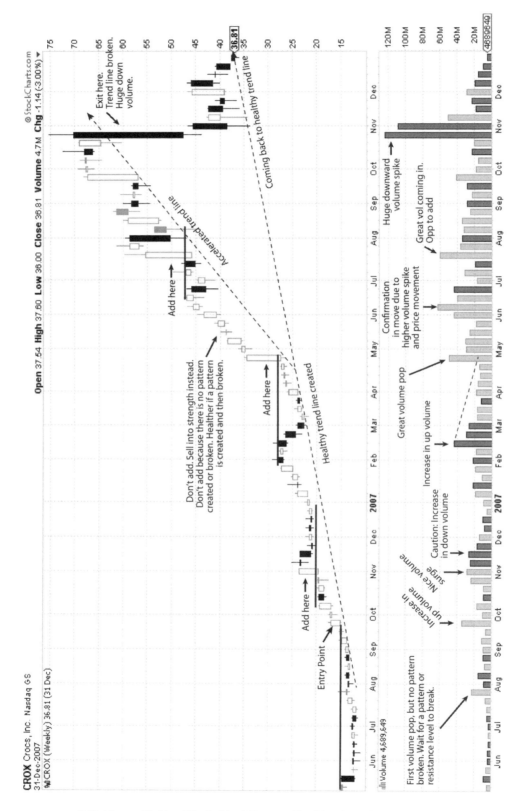

CROX Crocs, Inc. Nasdaq GS
31-Dec-2007
Open 37.54 High 37.80 Low 36.00 Close 36.81 Volume 4.7M Chg -1.14 (-3.00%)

W CROX (Weekly) 36.81 (31 Dec)   © StockCharts.com

Exit here.
Trend line broken.
Huge down
volume.

Coming back to healthy trend line

Accelerated trend line

Add here

Don't add. Sell into strength instead.
Don't add because there is no pattern
created or broken. Healther if a pattern
is created and then broken.

Add here

Healthy trend line created

Add here

Entry Point

Volume 4,689,649

Huge downward
volume spike

Great vol coming in.
Opp to add

Confirmation
in move due to
higher volume spike
and price movement

Great volume pop

Increase in up volume

Caution: Increase
in down volume

Nice volume
surge

Increase in
up volume

First volume pop, but no pattern
broken. Wait for a pattern or
resistance level to break.

245 Money Making Stock Chart Setups: Profiting from Swing Trading

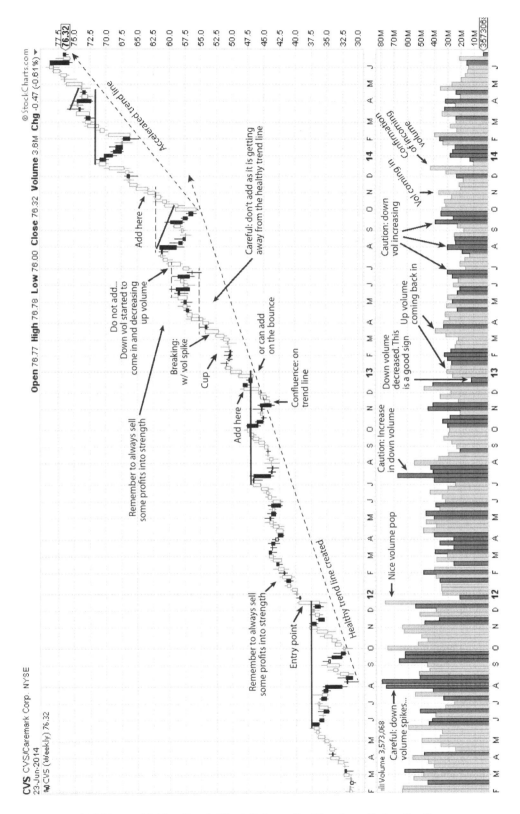

245 Money Making Stock Chart Setups: Profiting from Swing Trading

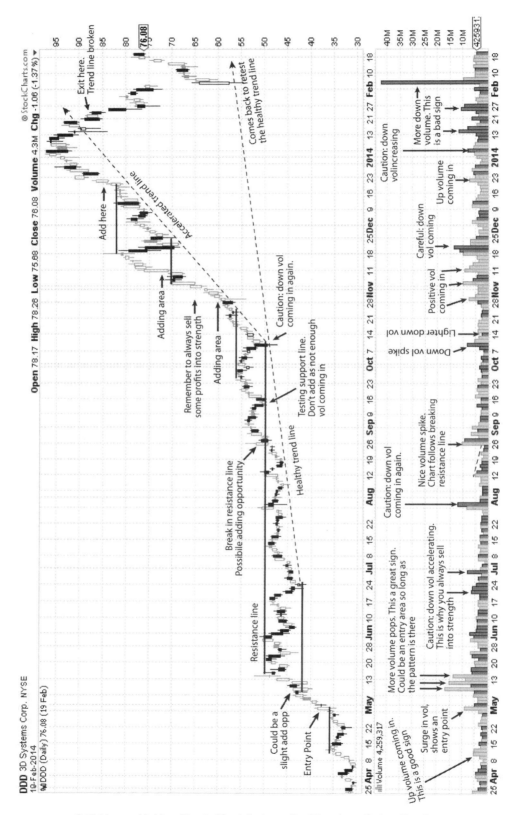

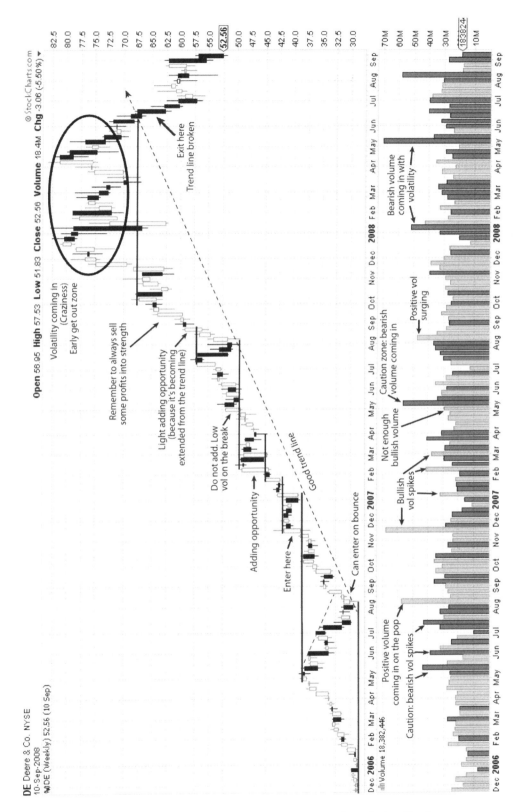

72

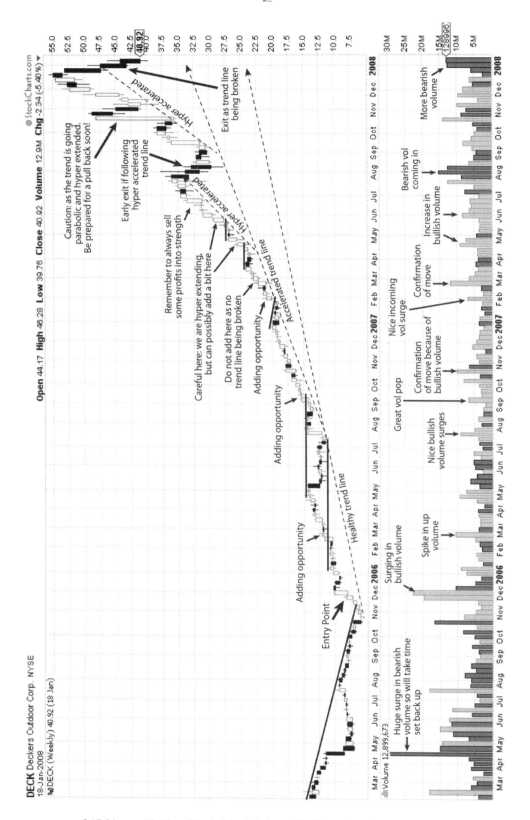

245 Money Making Stock Chart Setups: Profiting from Swing Trading

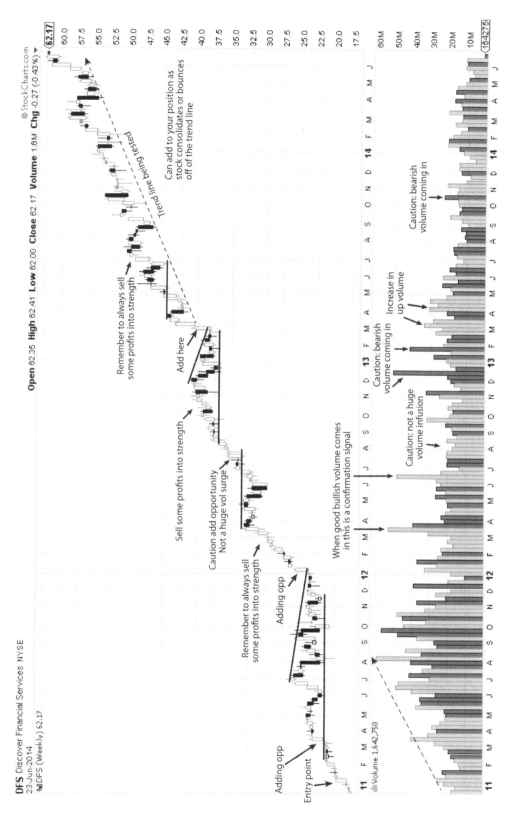

245 Money Making Stock Chart Setups: Profiting from Swing Trading

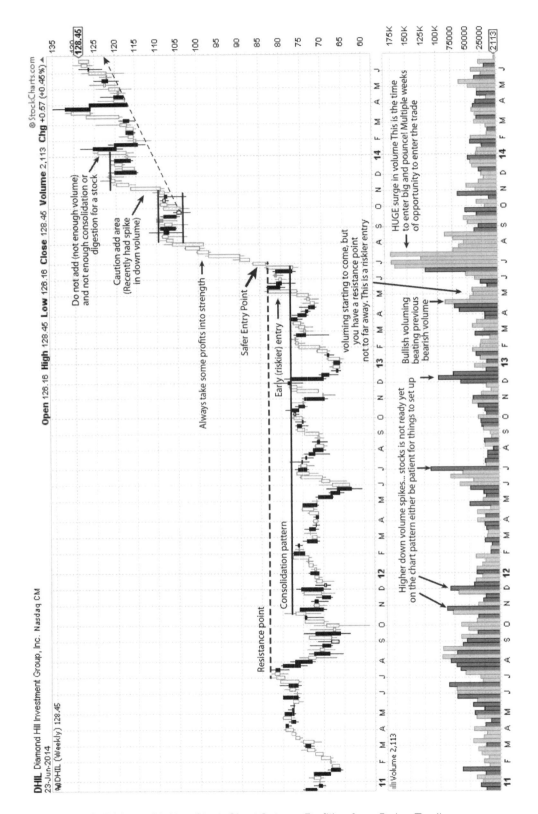

DHIL Diamond Hill Investment Group, Inc. Nasdaq CM
23-Jun-2014
⋈DHIL (Weekly) 128.45

Open 126.16 High 128.45 Low 128.16 Close 128.45 Volume 2,113 Chg +0.57 (+0.45%) ▲

© StockCharts.com

128.45

Do not add (not enough volume) and not enough consolidation or digestion for a stock

Caution add area (Recently had spike in down volume)

Always take some profits into strength

Safer Entry Point

Early (riskier) entry

Resistance point

Consolidation pattern

voluming starting to come, but you have a resistance point not to far away. This is a riskier entry

HUGE surge in volume This is the time to enter big and pounce! Multiple weeks of opportunity to enter the trade

Bullish voluming beating previous bearish volume

Higher down volume spikes... stocks is not ready yet on the chart pattern either be patient for things to set up

Volume 2,113

2113

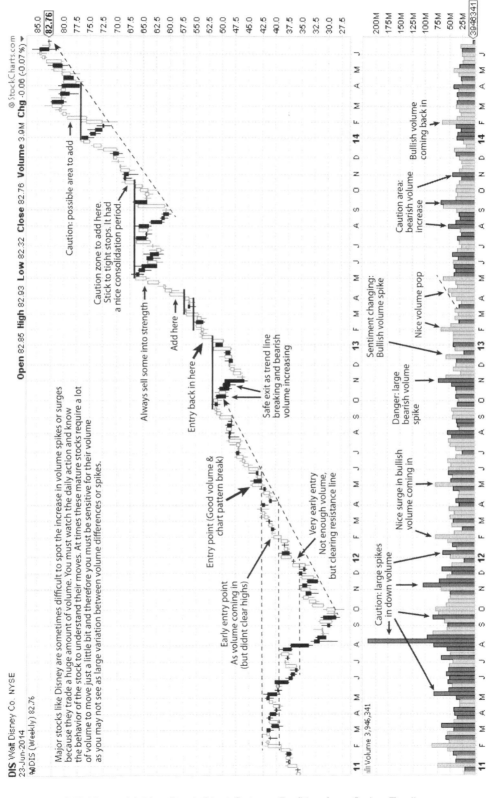

DIS Walt Disney Co. NYSE
23-Jun-2014
●WDIS (Weekly) 82.76

Open 82.85 **High** 82.93 **Low** 82.32 **Close** 82.76 **Volume** 3.9M **Chg** -0.06 (-0.07%) ▼

ⓦ StockCharts.com

Major stocks like Disney are sometimes difficult to spot the increase in volume spikes or surges because they trade a huge amount of volume. You must watch the daily action and know the behavior of the stock to understand their moves. At times these mature stocks require a lot of volume to move just a little bit and therefore you must be sensitive for their volume as you may not see as large variation between volume differences or spikes.

Caution: possible area to add

Caution zone to add here.
Stick to tight stops. It had
a nice consolidation period.

Always sell some into strength

Add here →

Entry back in here

Safe exit as trend line
breaking and bearish
volume increasing

Entry point (Good volume &
chart pattern break)

Early entry point
As volume coming in
(but didnt clear highs)

Very early entry
Not enough volume,
but clearing resistance line

Caution: large spikes
in down volume

Nice surge in bullish
volume coming in

Danger: large
bearish volume
spike

Sentiment changing:
Bullish volume spike

Nice volume pop

Caution area:
bearish volume
increase

Bullish volume
coming back in

Volume 3,946,341

85.0
82.76
80.0
77.5
75.0
72.5
70.0
67.5
65.0
62.5
60.0
57.5
55.0
52.5
50.0
47.5
45.0
42.5
40.0
37.5
35.0
32.5
30.0
27.5

200M
175M
150M
125M
100M
75M
50M
25M
3946341

11 F M A M J J A S O N D 12 F M A M J J A S O N D 13 F M A M J J A S O N D 14 F M A M J

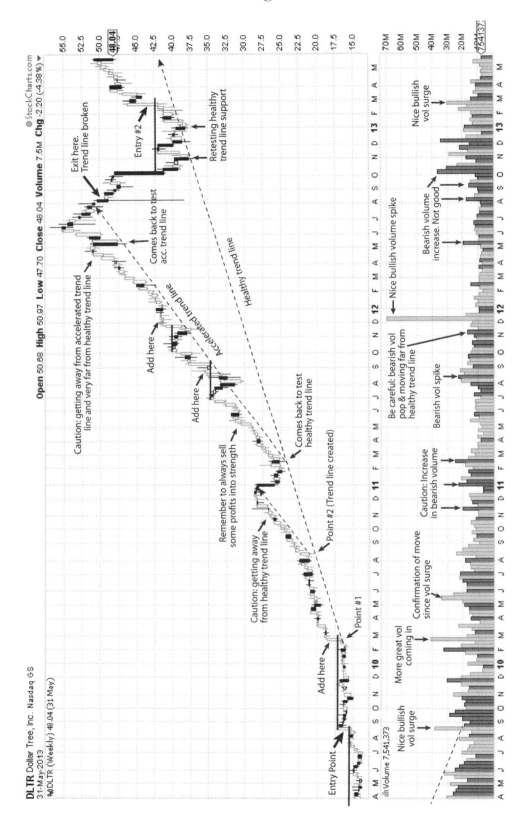

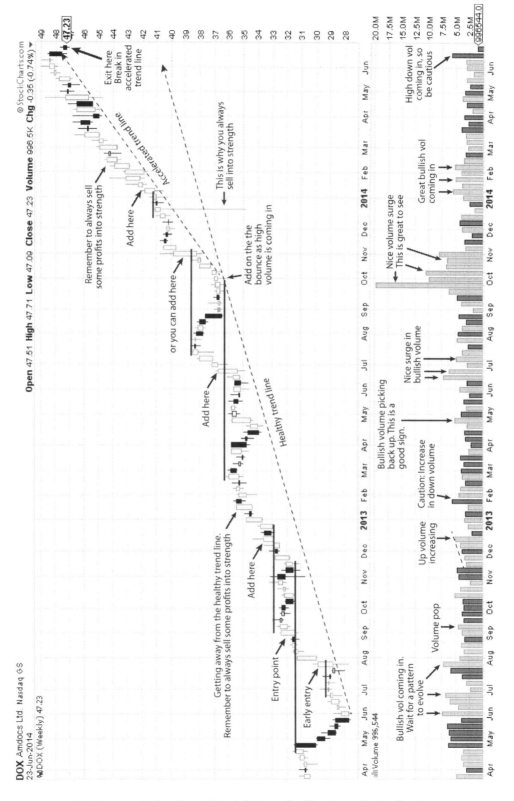

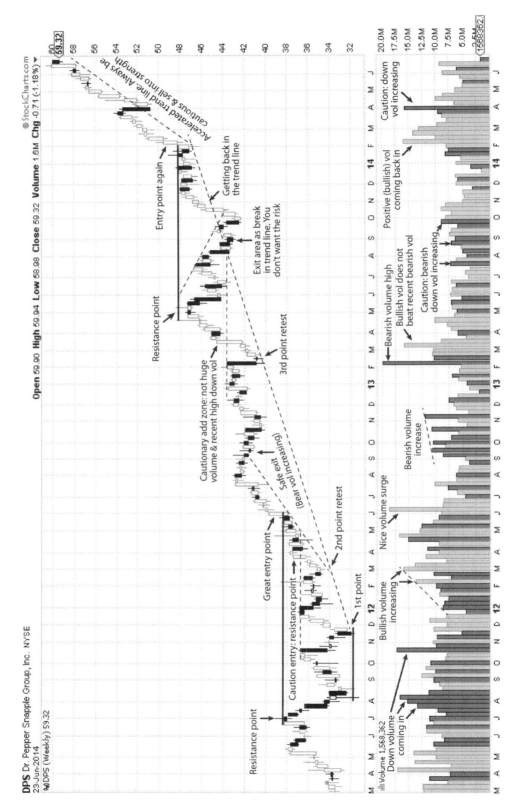

DPS Dr. Pepper Snapple Group, Inc. NYSE
23-Jun-2014
W DPS (Weekly) 59.32

Open 59.90 High 59.94 Low 58.98 Close 59.32 Volume 1.6M Chg -0.71 (-1.18%) ▼

@ StockCharts.com

Accelerated trend line. Always be
cautious & sell into strength

Entry point again

Getting back in
the trend line

Exit area as break
in trend line. You
don't want the risk

Resistance point

3rd point retest

Cautionary add zone: not huge
volume & recent high down vol

Safe exit

(Bear vol increasing)

2nd point retest

Great entry point

Caution entry: resistance point

1st point

Resistance point

Caution: down
vol increasing

Positive (bullish) vol
coming back in

Bearish volume high
Bullish vol does not
beat recent bearish vol

Caution: bearish
down vol increasing

Bearish volume
increase

Nice volume surge

Bullish volume
increasing

Volume 1,568,362
Down volume
coming in

1,568,362

20.0M
17.5M
15.0M
12.5M
10.0M
7.5M
5.0M

245 Money Making Stock Chart Setups: Profiting from Swing Trading

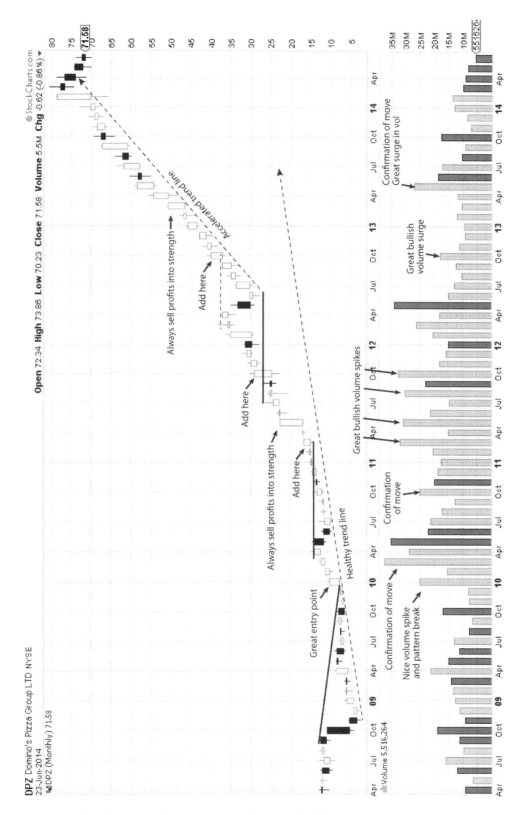

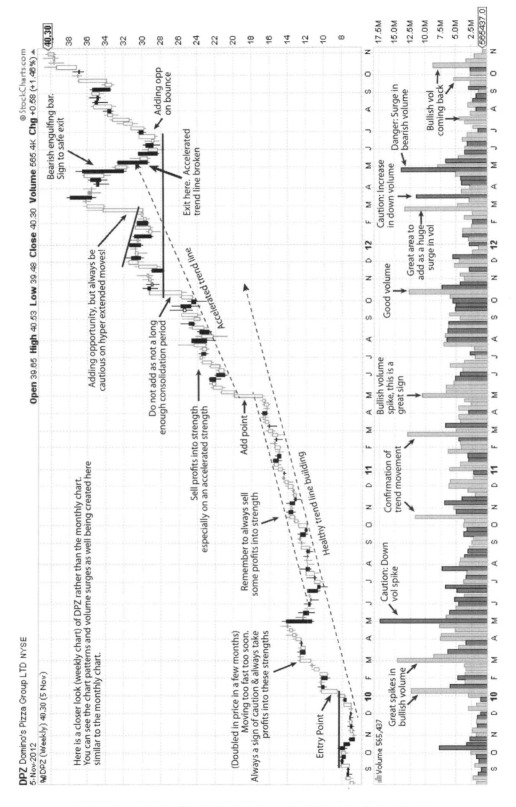

DPZ Domino's Pizza Group LTD NYSE
5-Nov-2012
Open 39.85 **High** 40.53 **Low** 39.48 **Close** 40.30 **Volume** 565.4K **Chg** +0.58 (+1.46%) ▲

W DPZ (Weekly) 40.30 (5 Nov)
40.30
© StockCharts.com

Here is a closer look (weekly chart) of DPZ rather than the monthly chart.
You can see the chart patterns and volume surges as well being created here similar to the monthly chart.

Bearish engulfing bar.
Sign to safe exit

Adding opp on bounce

Adding opportunity, but always be cautious on hyper extended moves!

Exit here. Accelerated trend line broken

Do not add as not a long enough consolidation period

Accelerated trend line

Sell profits into strength especially on an accelerated strength

Add point

Remember to always sell some profits into strength

Healthy trend line building

(Doubled in price in a few months)
Moving too fast too soon.
Always a sign of caution & always take profits into these strengths

Entry Point

Volume 565,437

Volume panel:

Danger: Surge in bearish volume

Caution: Increase in down volume

Good volume

Great area to add as a huge surge in vol

Bullish volume spike, this is a great sign

Confirmation of trend movement

Caution: Down vol spike

Great spikes in bullish volume

Bullish vol coming back

565437.0

245 Money Making Stock Chart Setups: Profiting from Swing Trading

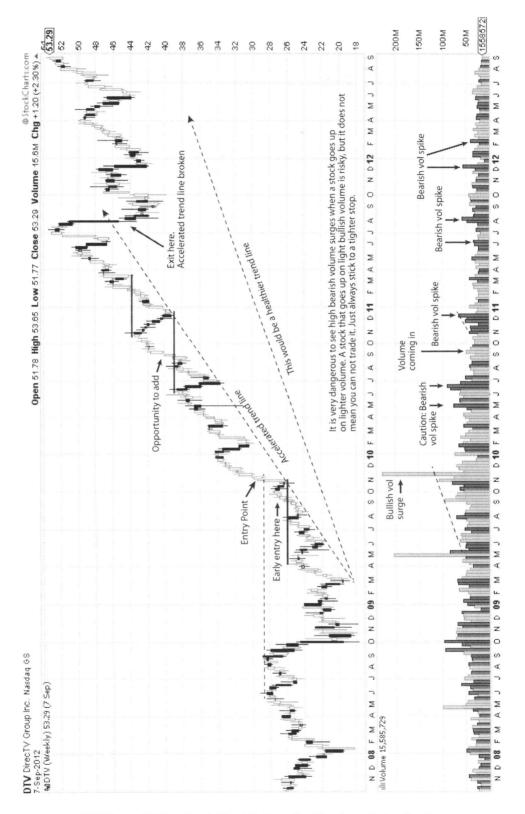

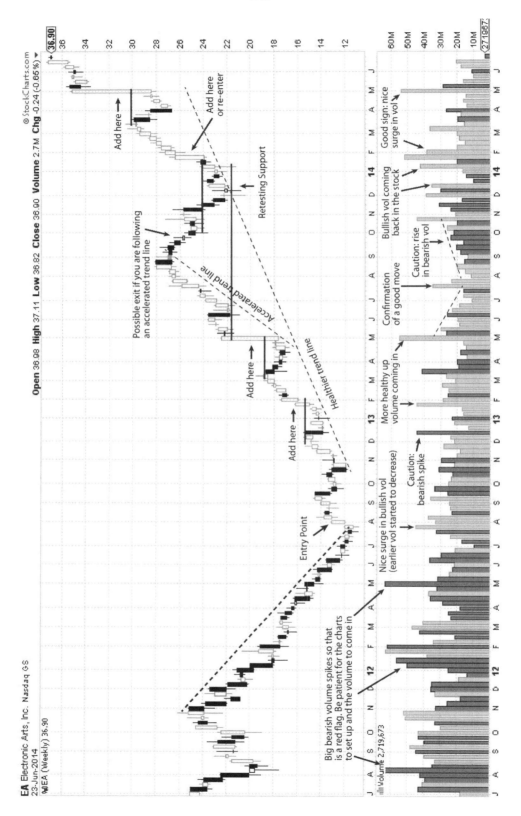

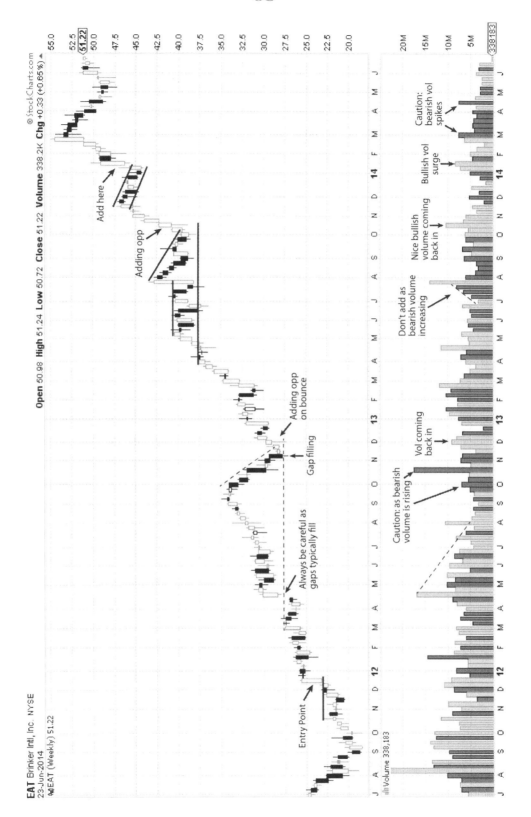

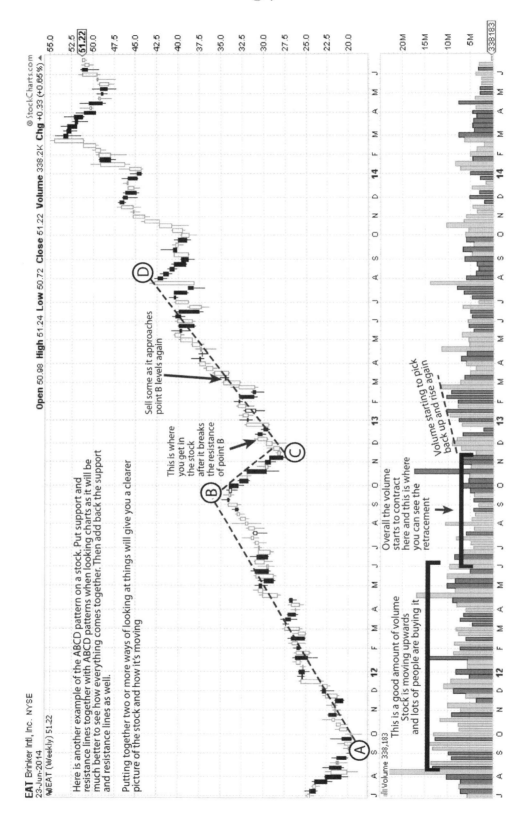

EAT Brinker Intl, Inc. NYSE
23-Jun-2014
♦EAT (Weekly) 51.22

Open 50.98 **High** 51.24 **Low** 50.72 **Close** 51.22 **Volume** 338.2K **Chg** +0.33 (+0.65%) ▲

©StockCharts.com

Here is another example of the ABCD pattern on a stock. Put support and resistance lines together with ABCD patterns when looking charts as it will be much better to see how everything comes together. Then add back the support and resistance lines as well.

Putting together two or more ways of looking at things will give you a clearer picture of the stock and how it's moving

This is where you get in the stock after it breaks the resistance of point B

Sell some as it approaches point B levels again

This is a good amount of volume Stock is moving upwards and lots of people are buying it

Overall the volume starts to contract here and this is where you can see the retracement

Volume starting to pick back up and rise again

◔ Volume 338,183

245 Money Making Stock Chart Setups: Profiting from Swing Trading

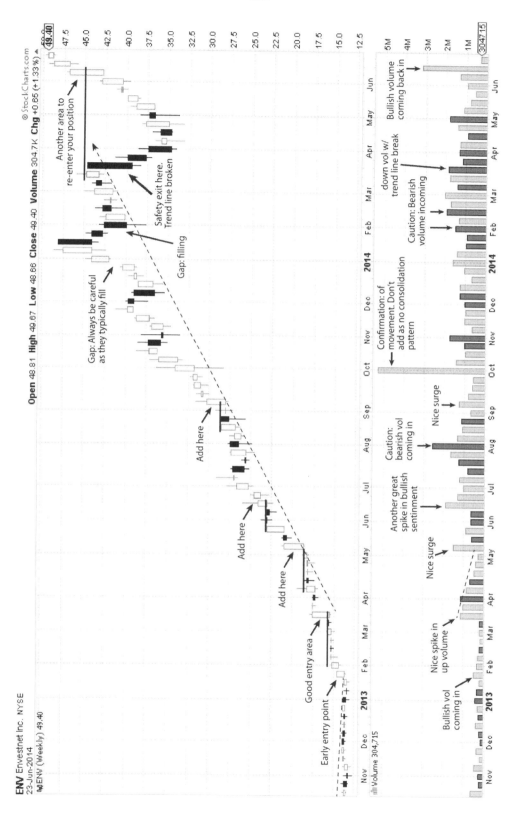

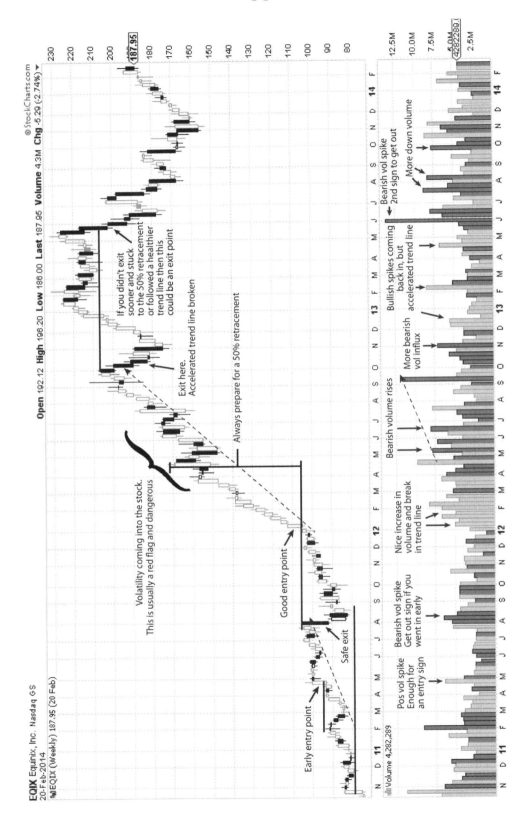

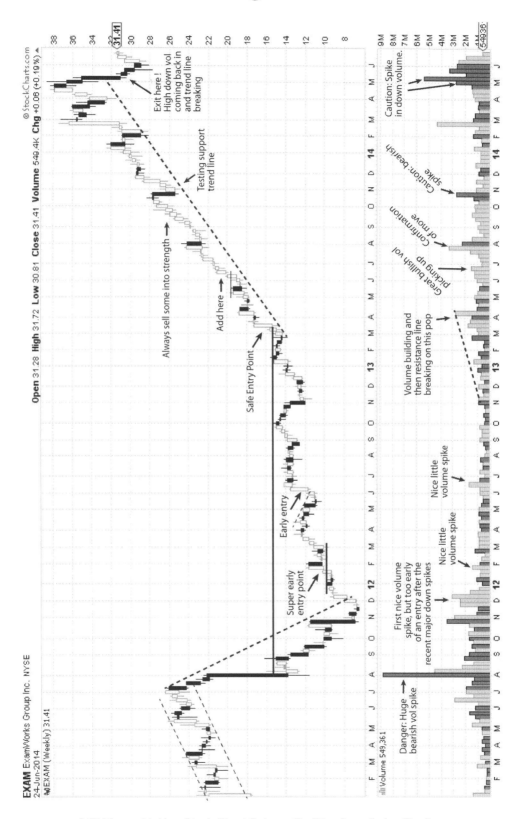

EXAM ExamWorks Group Inc. NYSE
24-Jun-2014
ⁿⁱEXAM (Weekly) 31.41

Open 31.28 High 31.72 Low 30.81 Close 31.41 Volume 549.4K Chg +0.06 (+0.19%) ▲

© StockCharts.com

31.41

38
36
34
32
30
28
26
24
22
20
18
16
14
12
10
8

Exit here !
High down vol
coming back in
and trend line
breaking

Testing support
trend line

Always sell some into strength

Add here

Safe Entry Point

Early entry

Super early
entry point

F M A M J J A S O N D 12 F M A M J J A S O N D 13 F M A M J J A S O N D 14 F M A M J

ⁱⁱⁱVolume 549,361

Danger: Huge
bearish vol spike

First nice volume
spike, but too early
of an entry after the
recent major down spikes

Nice little
volume spike

Nice little
volume spike

Volume building and
then resistance line
breaking on this pop

Great bullish vol
picking up

Confirmation
of move

Caution: bearish
spike

Caution: Spike
in down volume.

9M
8M
7M
6M
5M
4M
3M
2M

549,36

F M A M J J A S O N D 12 F M A M J J A S O N D 13 F M A M J J A S O N D 14 F M A M J

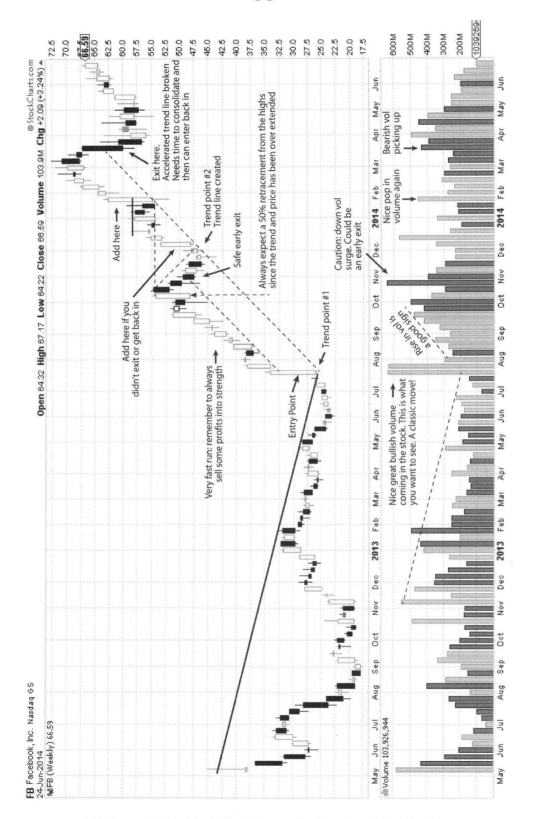

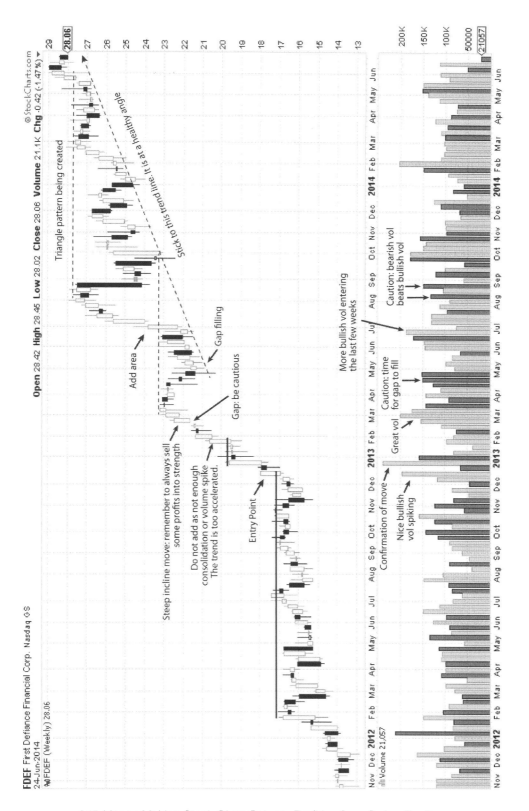

FDEF First Defiance Financial Corp. Nasdaq GS
24-Jun-2014
Open 28.42 **High** 28.45 **Low** 28.02 **Close** 28.06 **Volume** 21.1K **Chg** -0.42 (-1.47%) ▼
Ⓦ FDEF (Weekly) 28.06

© StockCharts.com

Triangle pattern being created

Stick to this trend line. It is at a healthy angle

Add area

Gap filling

Gap: be cautious

Steep incline move: remember to always sell some profits into strength

Do not add as not enough consolidation or volume spike. The trend is too accelerated.

Entry Point

More bullish vol entering the last few weeks

Caution: bearish vol beats bullish vol

Caution: time for gap to fill

Great vol

Confirmation of move

Nice bullish vol spiking

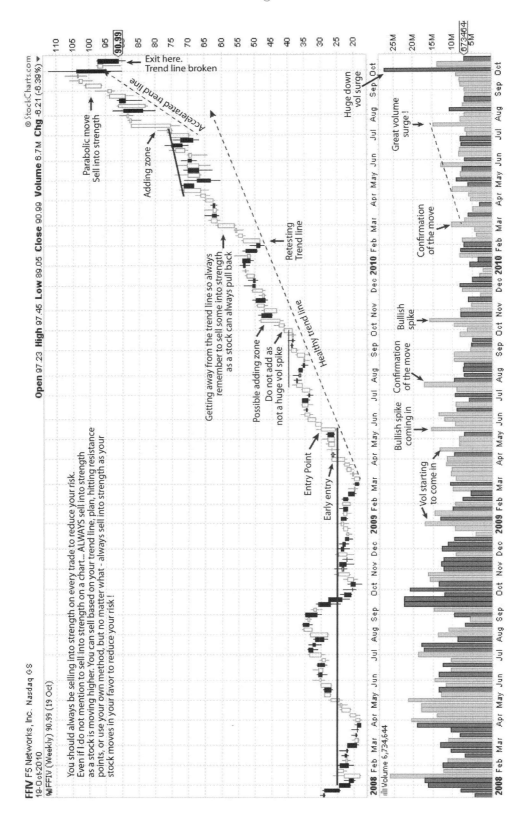

FFIV F5 Networks, Inc. Nasdaq GS
19-Oct-2010
Open 97.23 **High** 97.45 **Low** 89.05 **Close** 90.99 **Volume** 6.7M **Chg** -6.21 (-6.39%) ▼
© StockCharts.com
W FFIv (Weekly) 90.99 (19 Oct)

You should always be selling into strength on every trade to reduce your risk.
Even if I do not mention to sell into strength on a chart... ALWAYS sell into strength
as a stock is moving higher. You can sell based on your trend line, plan, hitting resistance
points, or use your own method, but no matter what - always sell into strength as your
stock moves in your favor to reduce your risk!

Exit here.
Trend line broken

Parabolic move
Sell into strength

Accelerated trend line

Adding zone

Getting away from the trend line so always
remember to sell some into strength
as a stock can always pull back

Retesting
Trend line

Possible adding zone

Do not add as
not a huge vol spike

Healthy trend line

Entry Point

Early entry

Huge down
vol surge

Great volume
surge!

Confirmation
of the move

Bullish
spike

Confirmation
of the move

Bullish spike
coming in

Vol starting
to come in

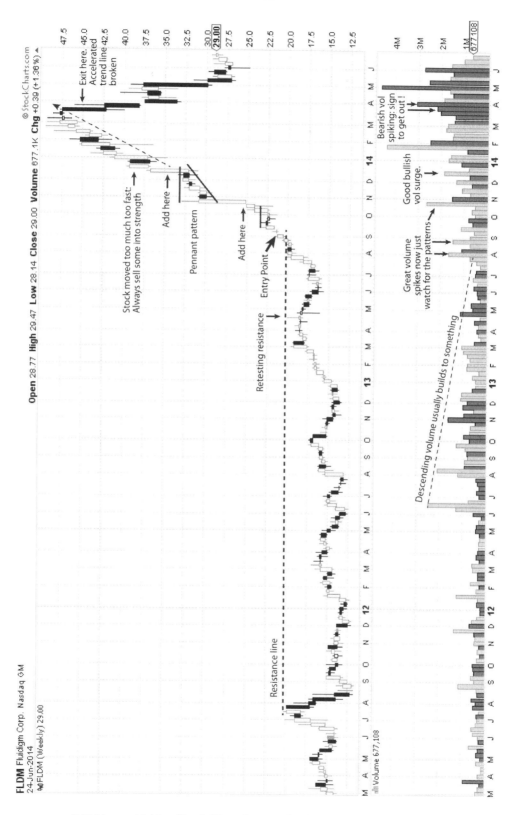

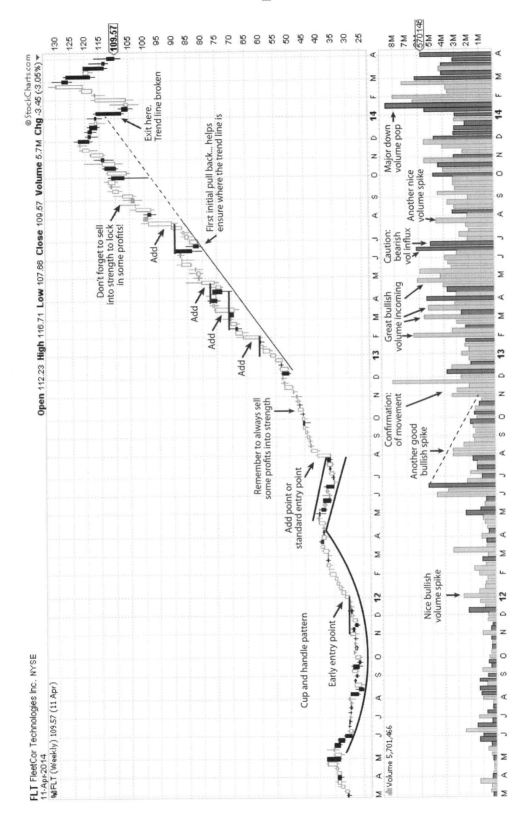

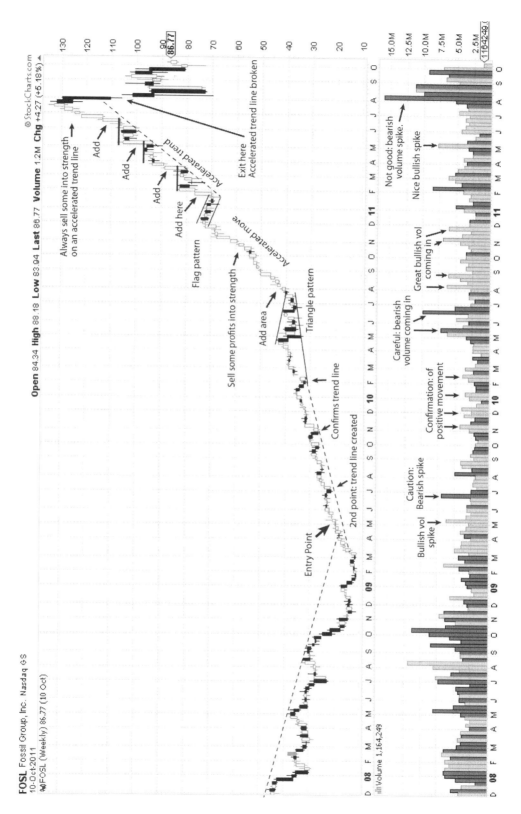

FOSL Fossil Group, Inc. Nasdaq GS
10-Oct2011
FOSL (Weekly) 86.77 (10 Oct)

Open 84.34 High 88.18 Low 83.94 Last 86.77 Volume 1.2M Chg +4.27 (+5.18%) ▲

© StockCharts.com

Always sell some into strength
on an accelerated trend line

Add
Add
Add
Add here
Accelerated trend

Exit here
Accelerated trend line broken

Flag pattern
Accelerated move
Sell some profits into strength

Add area
Triangle pattern
Confirms trend line
2nd point: trend line created
Entry Point

Volume 1,164,249

Not good: bearish
volume spike.
Nice bullish spike

Great bullish vol
coming in

Careful: bearish
volume coming in

Confirmation: of
positive movement

Caution:
Bearish spike

Bullish vol
spike

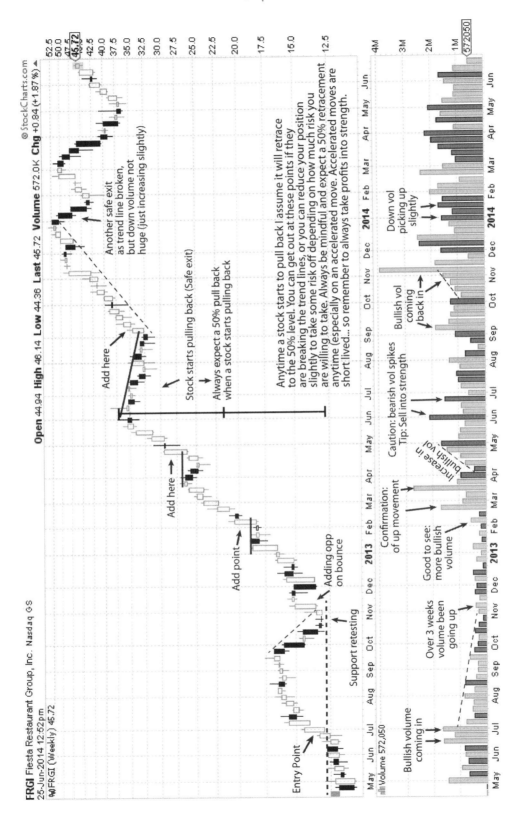

FRGI Fiesta Restaurant Group, Inc. Nasdaq GS

25-Jun-2014 12:52pm

W FRGI (Weekly) 45.72

Open 44.94 High 46.14 Low 44.36 Last 45.72 **Volume** 572.0K **Chg** +0.84 (+1.87%) ▲

© StockCharts.com

45.72

Another safe exit as trend line broken, but down volume not huge (just increasing slightly)

Add here

Stock starts pulling back (Safe exit)

Always expect a 50% pull back when a stock starts pulling back

Anytime a stock starts to pull back I assume it will retrace to the 50% level. You can get out at these points if they are breaking the trend lines, or you can reduce your position slightly to take some risk off depending on how much risk you are willing to take. Always be mindful and expect a 50% retracement anytime (especially on an accelerated move. Accelerated moves are short-lived... so remember to always take profits into strength.

Add here

Add point

Adding opp on bounce

Support retesting

Entry Point

Volume 572,050

Bullish volume coming in

Over 3 weeks volume been going up

Good to see: more bullish volume

Confirmation: of up movement

Increase in bullish vol

Caution: bearish vol spikes
Tip: Sell into strength

Bullish vol coming back in

Down vol picking up slightly

572,050

245 Money Making Stock Chart Setups: Profiting from Swing Trading

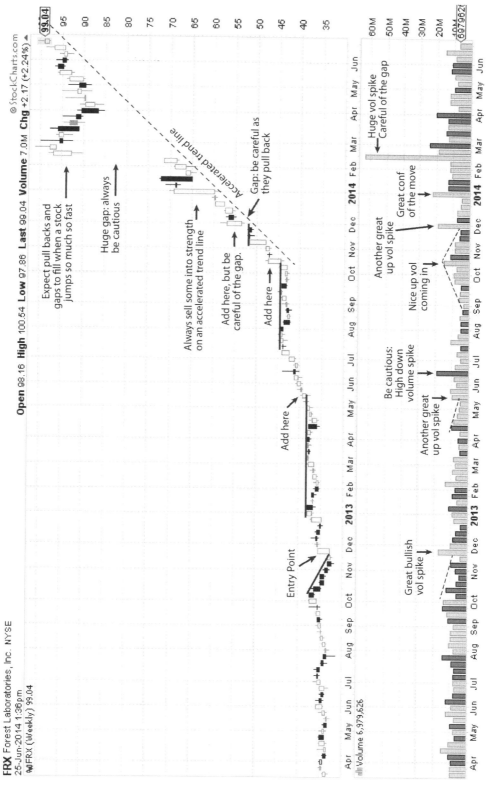

FRX Forest Laboratories, Inc. NYSE
25-Jun-2014 1:36pm
W FRX (Weekly) 99.04

Open 98.16 High 100.54 Low 97.88 Last 99.04 Volume 7.0M Chg +2.17 (+2.24%) ▲

© StockCharts.com

99.04

Accelerated trend line

Expect pull backs and
gaps to fill when a stock
jumps so much so fast

Huge gap: always
be cautious

Always sell some into strength
on an accelerated trend line

Add here, but be
careful of the gap.

Add here

Gap: be careful as
they pull back

Entry Point

Add here

Volume 6,979,626

Great bullish
vol spike

Be cautious:
High down
volume spike

Another great
up vol spike

Nice up vol
coming in

Another great
up vol spike

Great conf
of the move

Huge vol spike
Careful of the gap

6979626

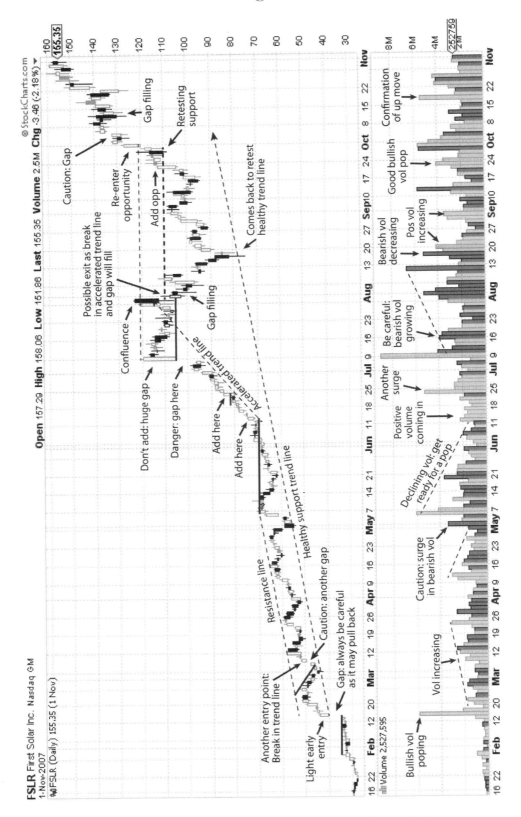

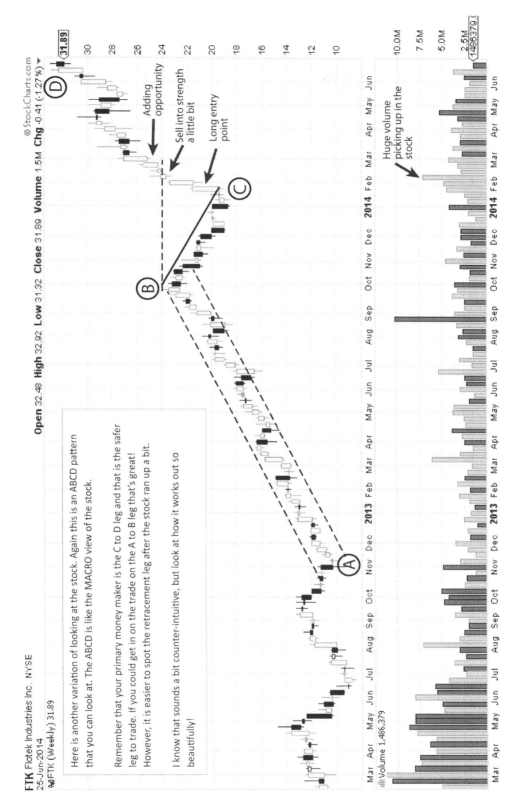

FTK Flotek Industries Inc. NYSE
25-Jun-2014
© StockCharts.com
Open 32.48 High 32.92 Low 31.32 Close 31.89 Volume 1.5M Chg -0.41 (-1.27%) ▼
W FTK (Weekly) 31.89

Here is another variation of looking at the stock. Again this is an ABCD pattern that you can look at. The ABCD is like the MACRO view of the stock.

Remember that your primary money maker is the C to D leg and that is the safer leg to trade. If you could get in on the trade on the A to B leg that's great! However, it is easier to spot the retracement leg after the stock ran up a bit.

I know that sounds a bit counter-intuitive, but look at how it works out so beautifully!

Adding opportunity

Sell into strength a little bit

Long entry point

Huge volume picking up in the stock

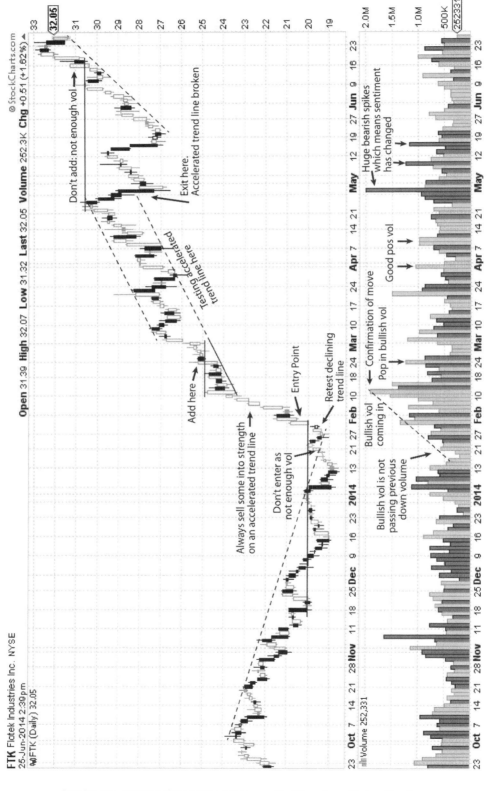

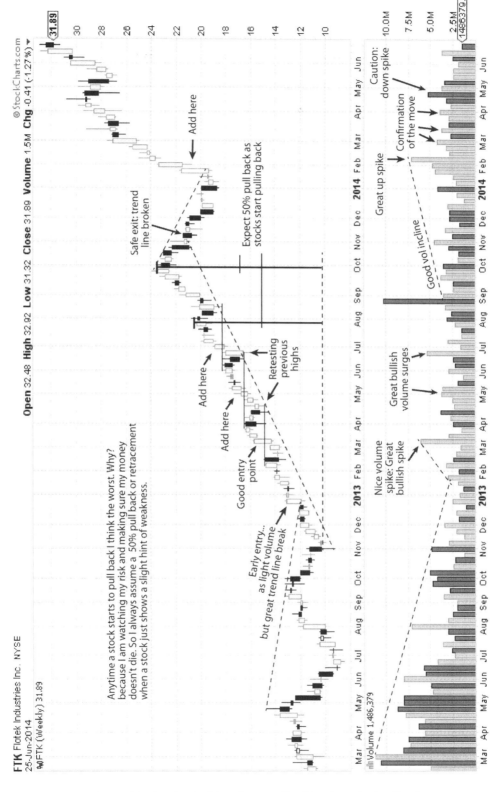

FTK Flotek Industries Inc. NYSE
25-Jun-2014
◆FTK (Weekly) 31.89

Open 32.48 High 32.92 Low 31.32 Close 31.89 Volume 1.5M Chg -0.41 (-1.27%) ▼

© StockCharts.com

Anytime a stock starts to pull back I think the worst. Why? because I am watching my risk and making sure my money doesn't die. So I always assume a 50% pull back or retracement when a stock just shows a slight hint of weakness.

Add here

Safe exit: trend line broken

Expect 50% pull back as stocks start pulling back

Add here

Add here

Retesting previous highs

Good entry point

Early entry... but great trend line break

Volume 1,486,379

Caution: down spike

Confirmation of the move

Great up spike

Good vol incline

Great bullish volume surges

Nice volume spike: Great bullish spike

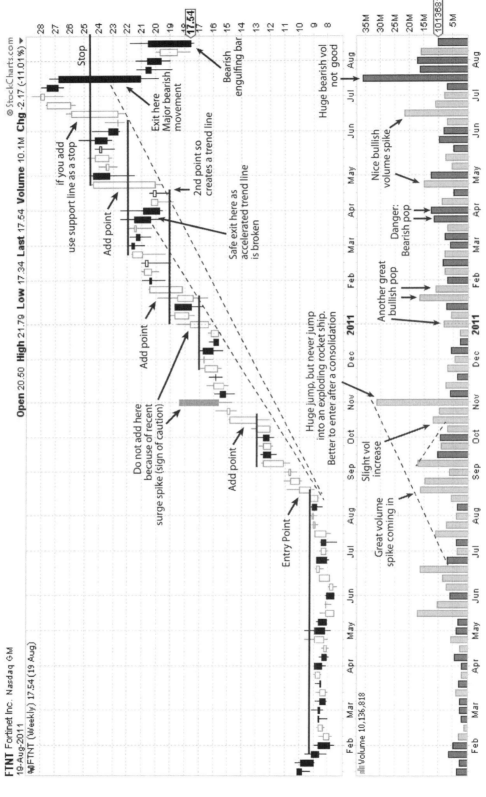

FTNT Fortinet Inc. Nasdaq GM
19-Aug-2011
FTNT (Weekly) 17.54 (19 Aug)

Open 20.50 High 21.79 Low 17.34 Last 17.54 Volume 10.1M Chg -2.17 (-11.01%) ▼

© StockCharts.com

Stop

if you add
use support line as a stop

Add point

Exit here
Major bearish
movement

Bearish
engulfing bar

2nd point so
creates a trend line

Safe exit here as
accelerated trend line
is broken

Huge bearish vol
not good

Add point

Do not add here
because of recent
surge spike (sign of caution)

Add point

Huge jump, but never jump
into an exploding rocket ship.
Better to enter after a consolidation

Entry Point

Nice bullish
volume spike

Danger:
Bearish pop

Another great
bullish pop

Slight vol
increase

Great volume
spike coming in

Volume 10,136,818

101368

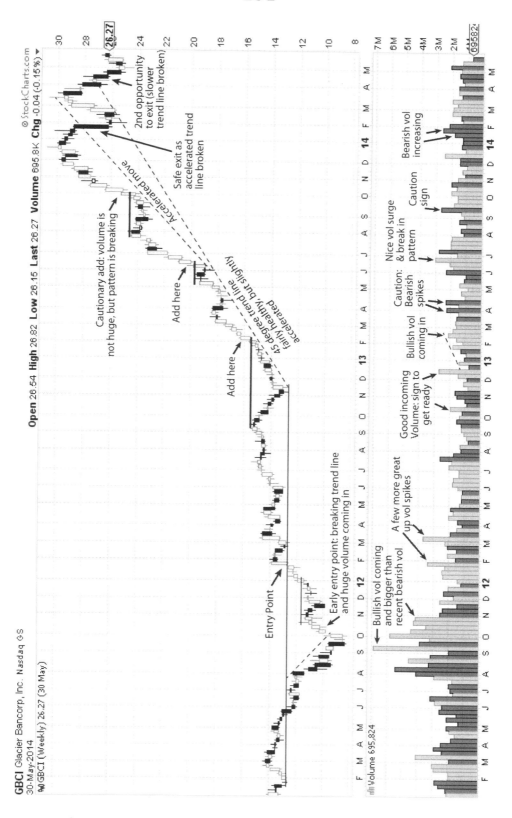

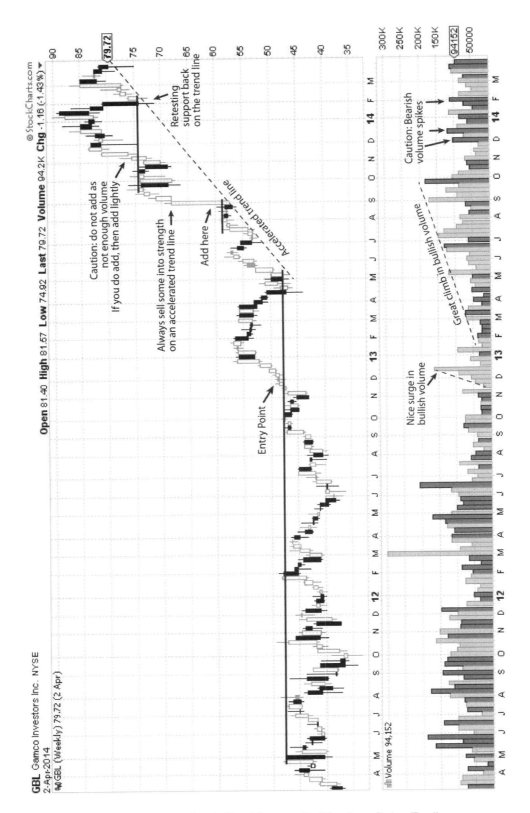

GBL Gamco Investors Inc. NYSE
2-Apr-2014

Open 81.40 High 81.57 Low 74.92 Last 79.72 Volume 94.2K Chg -1.18 (-1.43%) ▼

© StockCharts.com

W GBL (Weekly) 79.72 (2 Apr)

Retesting
support back
on the trend line

Caution: do not add as
not enough volume
If you do add, then add lightly

Always sell some into strength
on an accelerated trend line →

Add here →

Accelerated trend line

Entry Point

Caution: Bearish
volume spikes

Great climb in bullish volume

Nice surge in
bullish volume

Volume 94,152

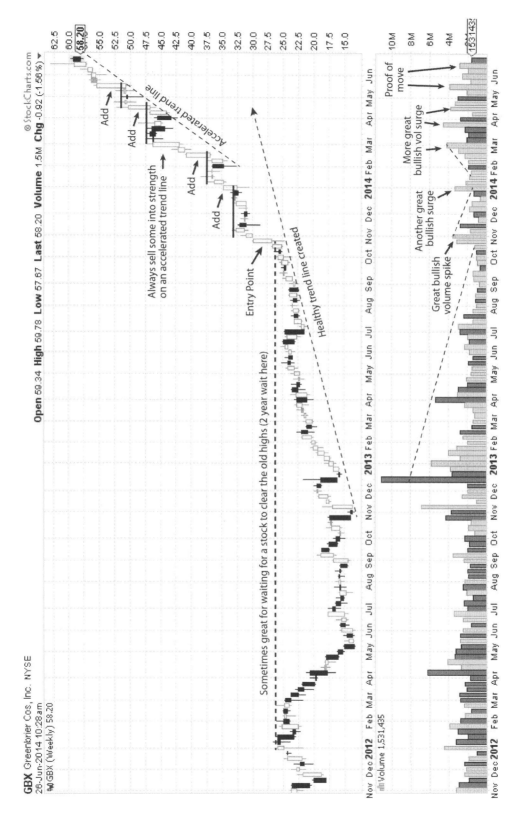

GBX Greenbrier Cos, Inc. NYSE
26-Jun-2014 10:28am
Open 59.34 **High** 59.78 **Low** 57.67 **Last** 58.20 **Volume** 1.5M **Chg** -0.92 (-1.56%) ▼

© StockCharts.com

Add

Add

Always sell some into strength on an accelerated trend line

Add

Add

Accelerated trend line

Entry Point

Healthy trend line created

Sometimes great for waiting for a stock to clear the old highs (2 year wait here)

Proof of move

More great bullish vol surge

Another great bullish surge

Great bullish volume spike

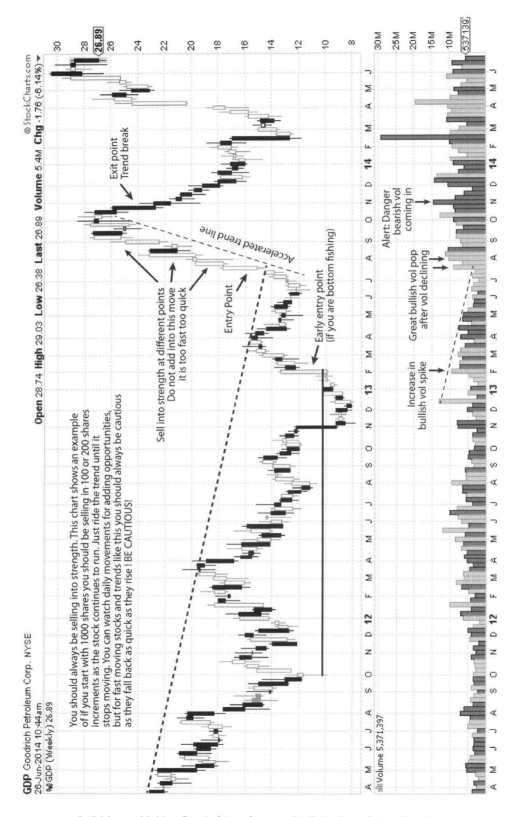

GDP Goodrich Petroleum Corp. NYSE
26-Jun-2014 10:44am
₩)GDP (Weekly) 26.89

Open 28.74 High 29.03 Low 26.38 Last 26.89 Volume 5.4M Chg -1.76 (-6.14%) ▼

© StockCharts.com

You should always be selling into strength. This chart shows an example of if you start with 1000 shares you should be selling in 100 or 200 shares increments as the stock continues to run. Just ride the trend until it stops moving. You can watch daily movements for adding opportunities, but for fast moving stocks and trends like this you should always be cautious as they fall back as quick as they rise ! BE CAUTIOUS!

Exit point
Trend break

Sell into strength at different points
Do not add into this move
it is too fast too quick

Accelerated trend line

Entry Point

Early entry point
(if you are bottom fishing)

₁llll Volume 5,371,397

Alert: Danger
bearish vol
coming in

Great bullish vol pop
after vol declining

Increase in
bullish vol spike

245 Money Making Stock Chart Setups: Profiting from Swing Trading

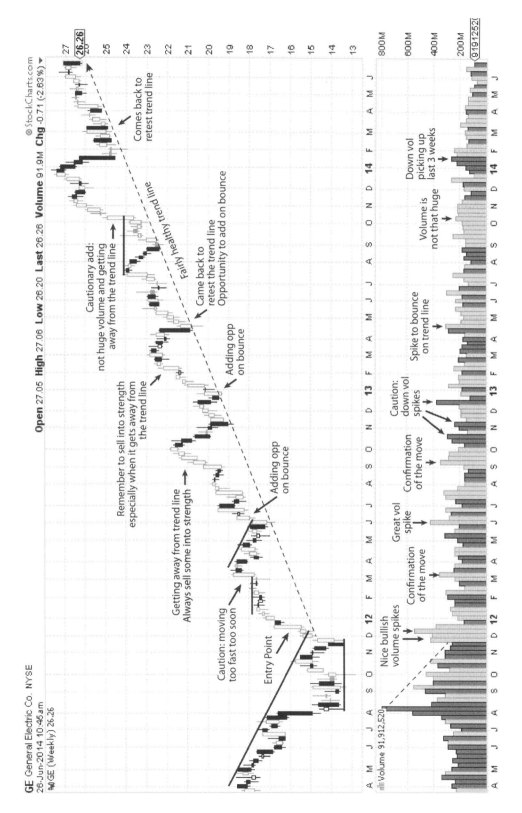

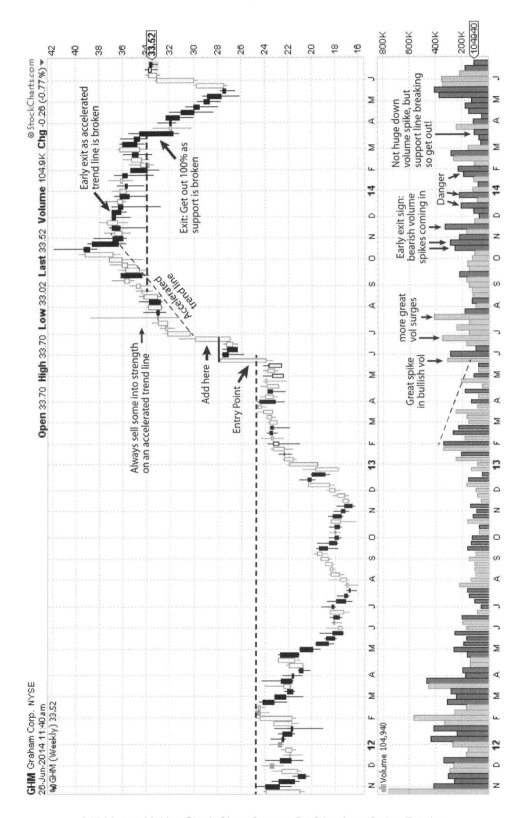

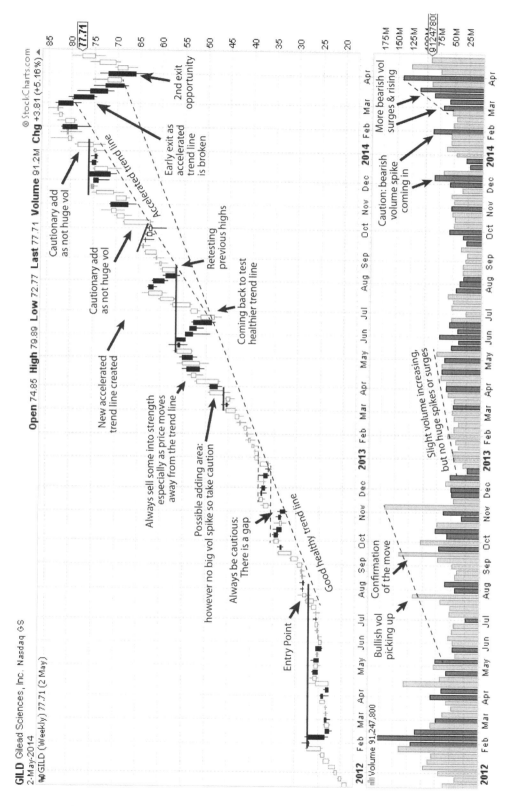

GILD Gilead Sciences, Inc. Nasdaq GS
2-May-2014
GILD (Weekly) 77.71 (2 May)

Open 74.85 High 79.89 Low 72.77 Last 77.71 Volume 91.2M Chg +3.81 (+5.16%)

StockCharts.com

2nd exit opportunity

Early exit as accelerated trend line is broken

Cautionary add as not huge vol

Cautionary add as not huge vol

New accelerated trend line created

Retesting previous highs

Coming back to test healthier trend line

Always sell some into strength especially as price moves away from the trend line

Possible adding area: however no big vol spike so take caution

Always be cautious: There is a gap

Entry Point

Good healthy trend line

Accelerated trend line

Volume 91,247,800

Bullish vol picking up

Confirmation of the move

Slight volume increasing, but no huge spikes or surges

Caution: bearish volume spike coming in

More bearish vol surges & rising

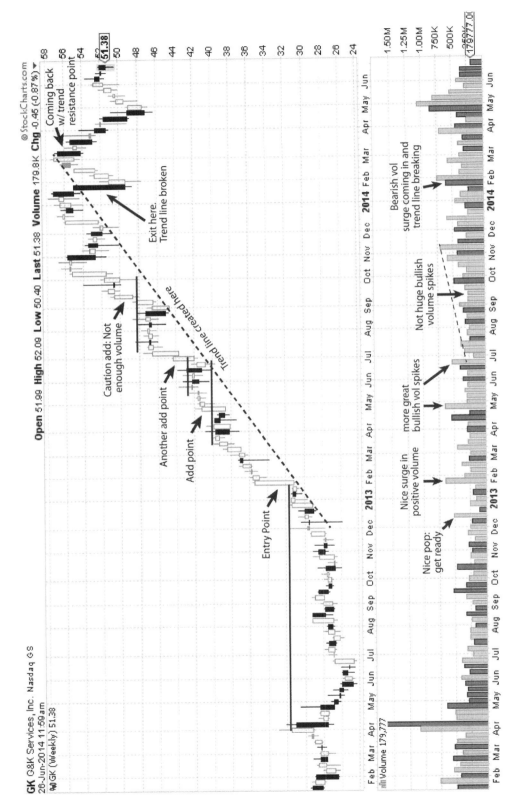

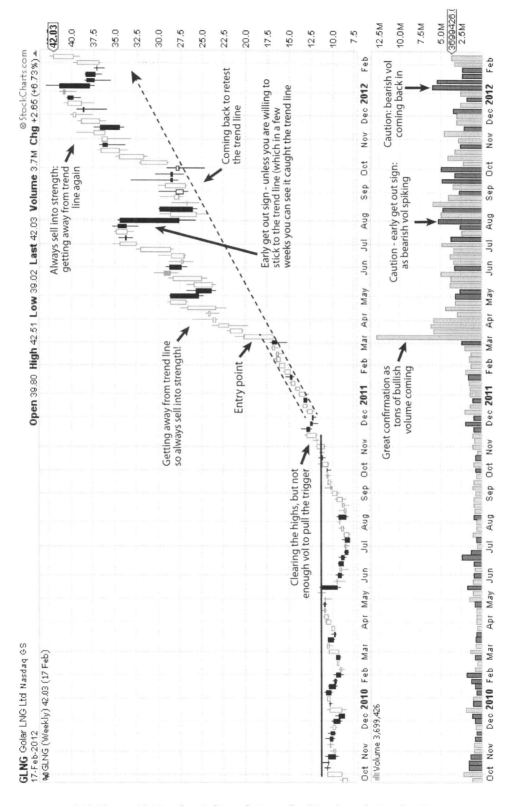

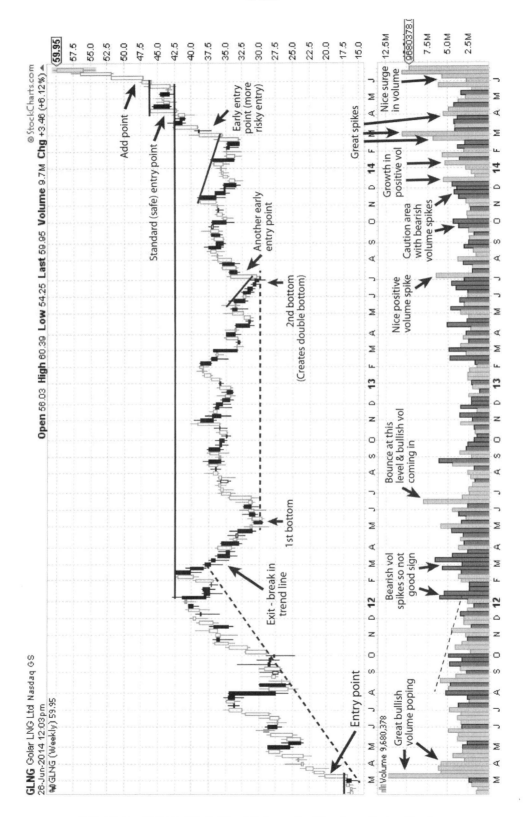

245 Money Making Stock Chart Setups: Profiting from Swing Trading

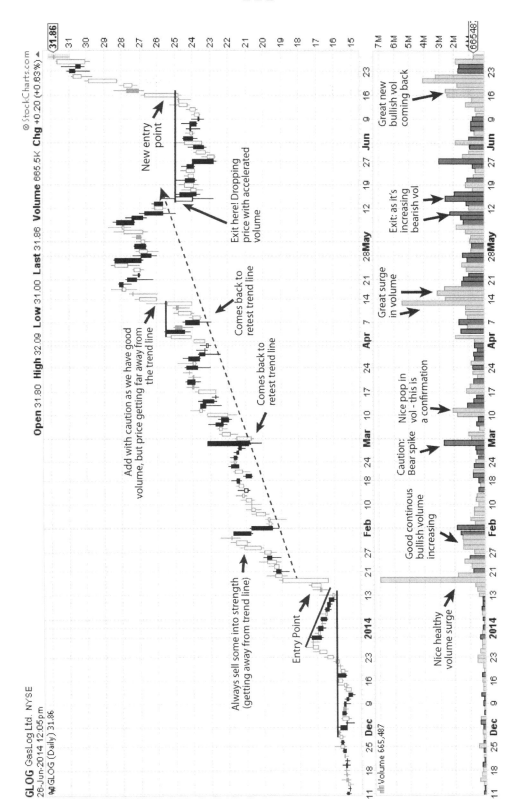

112

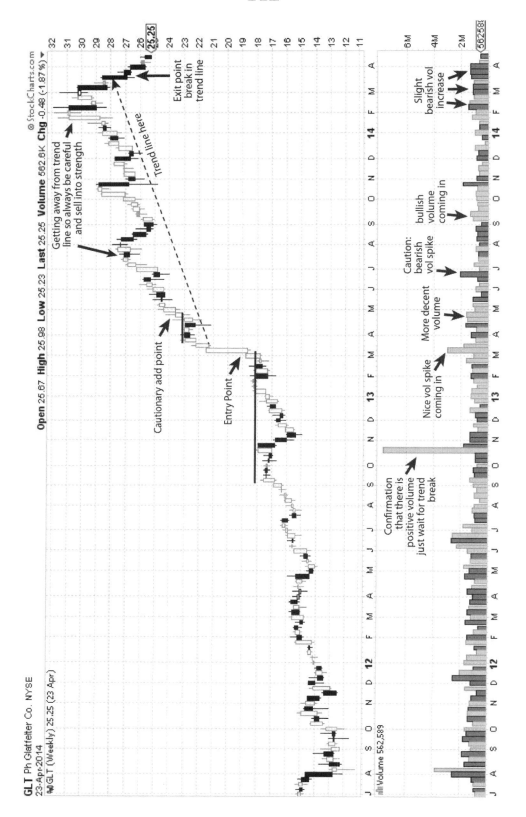

245 Money Making Stock Chart Setups: Profiting from Swing Trading

113

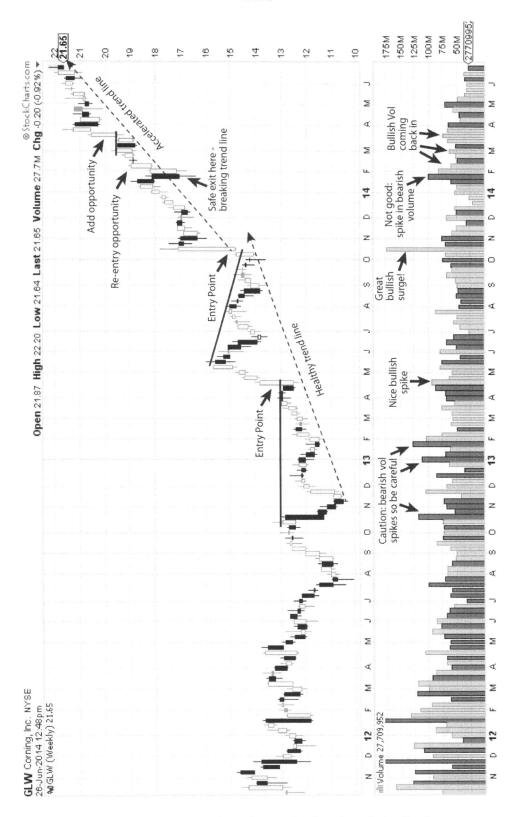

245 Money Making Stock Chart Setups: Profiting from Swing Trading

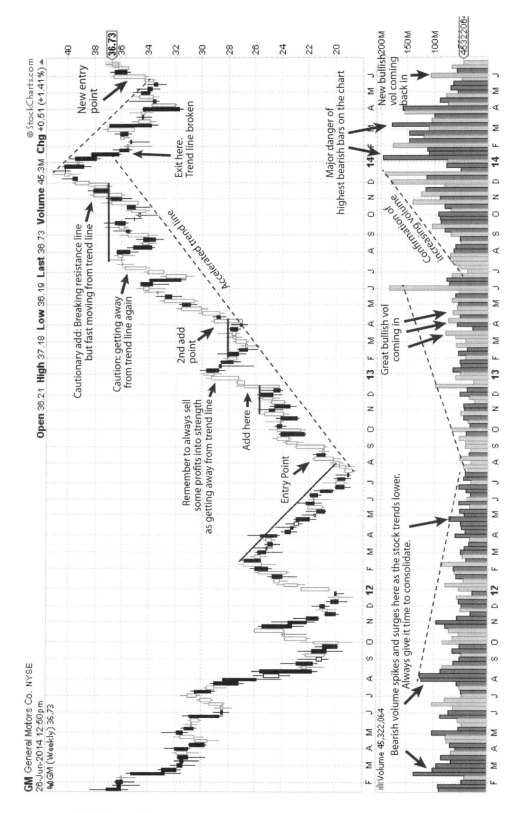

245 Money Making Stock Chart Setups: Profiting from Swing Trading

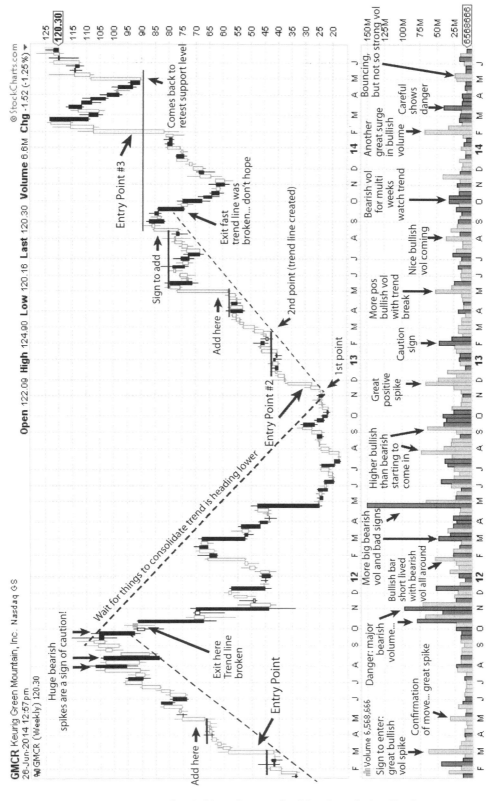

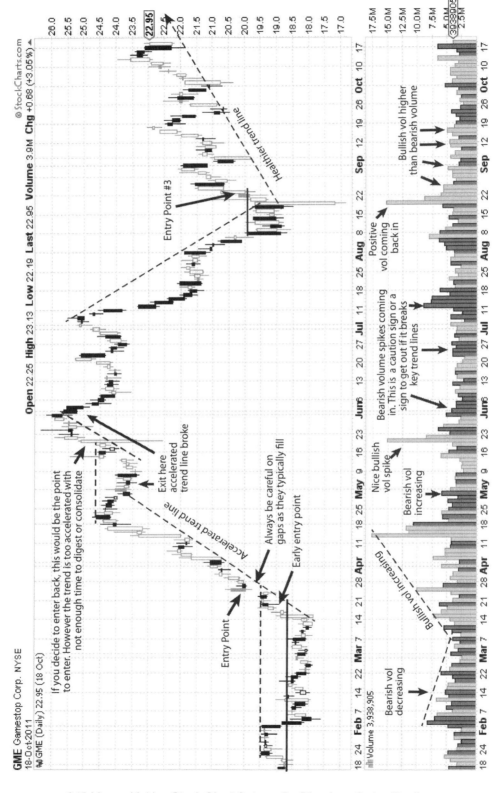

245 Money Making Stock Chart Setups: Profiting from Swing Trading

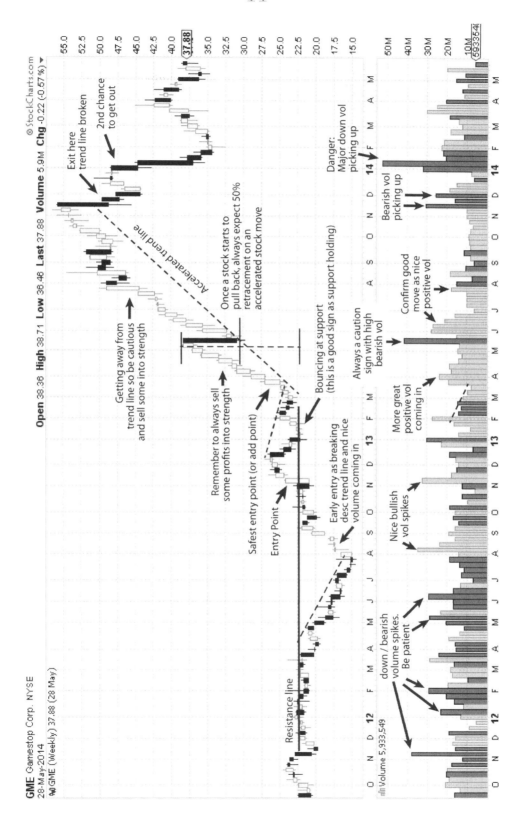

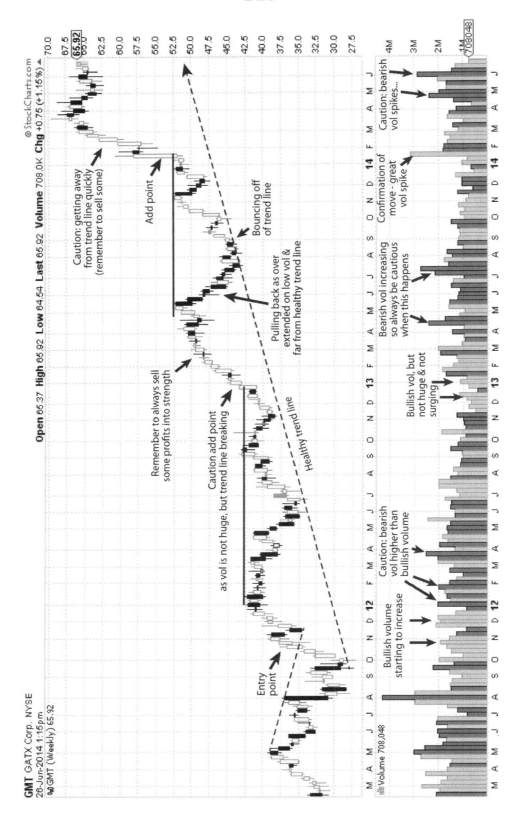

245 Money Making Stock Chart Setups: Profiting from Swing Trading

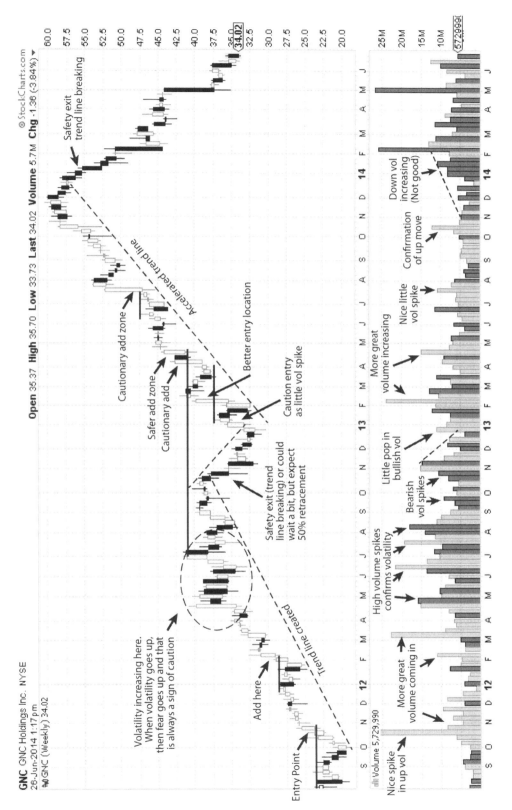

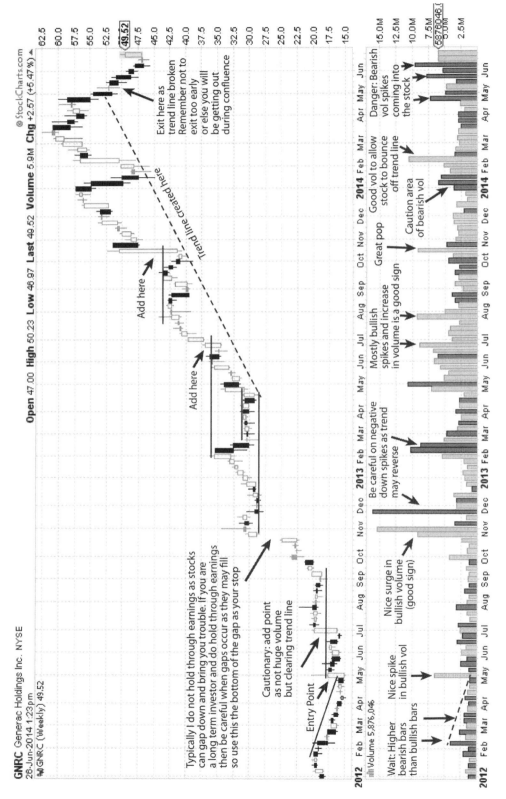

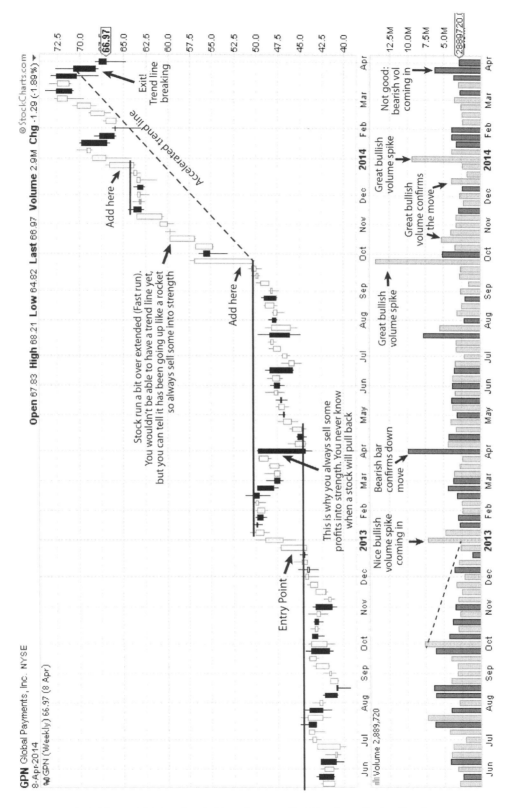

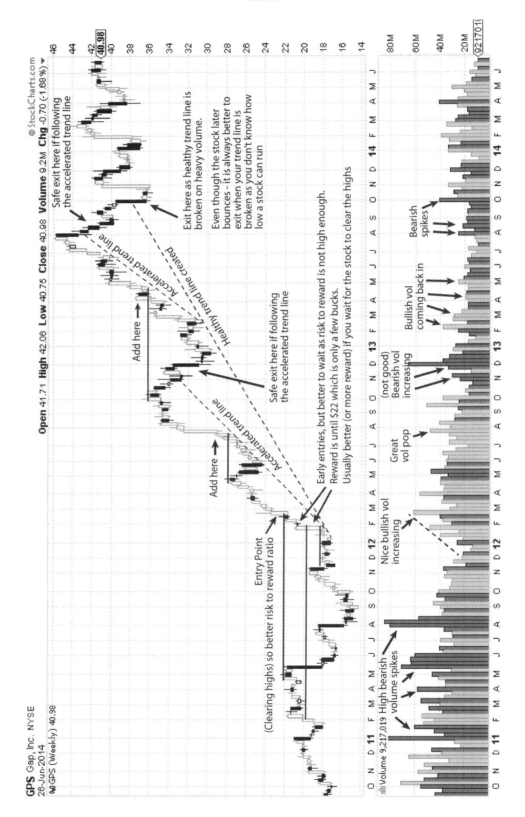

245 Money Making Stock Chart Setups: Profiting from Swing Trading

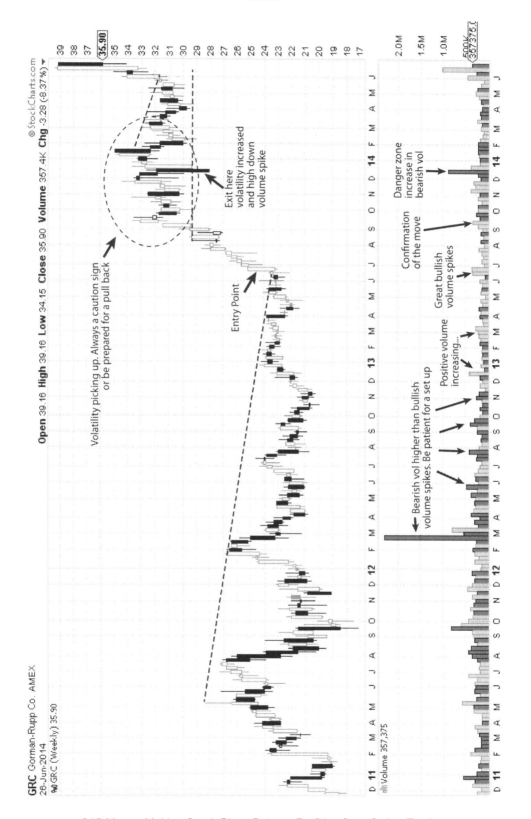

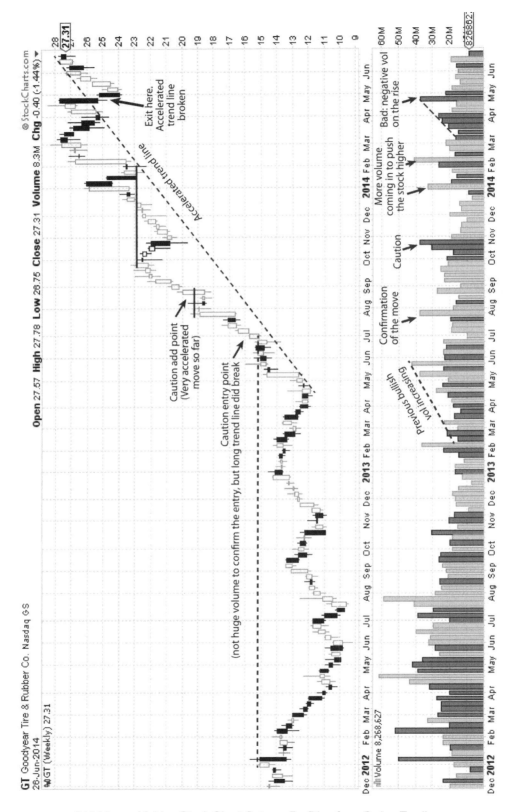

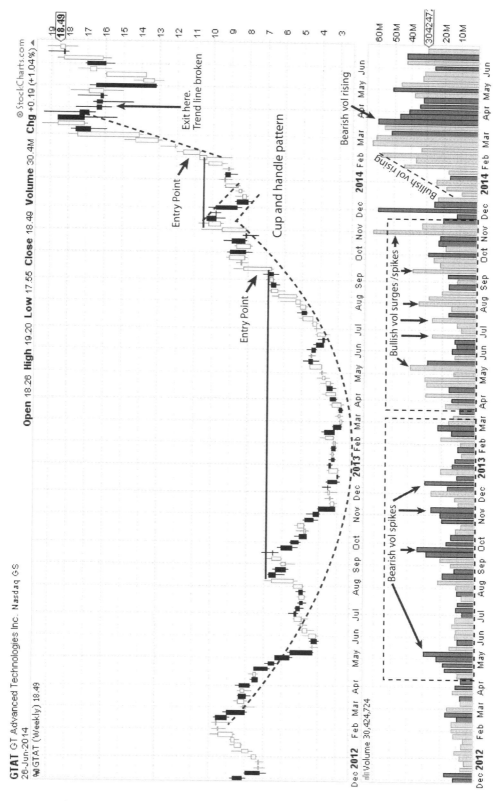

245 Money Making Stock Chart Setups: Profiting from Swing Trading

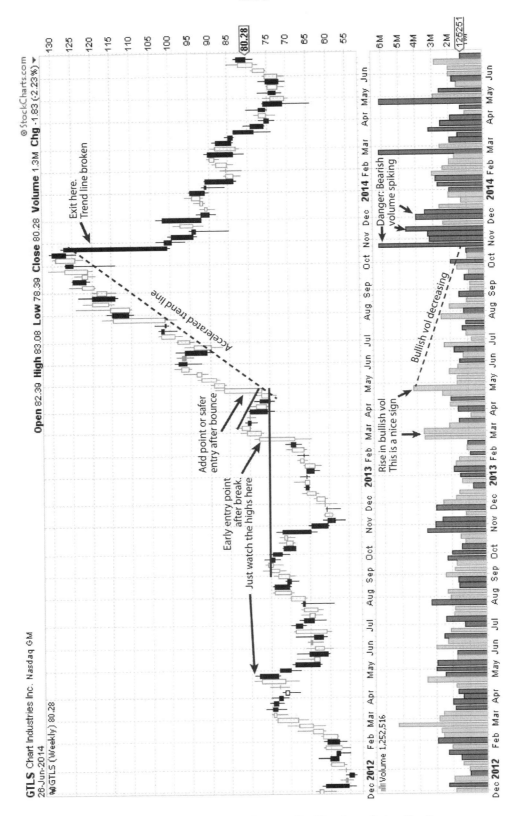

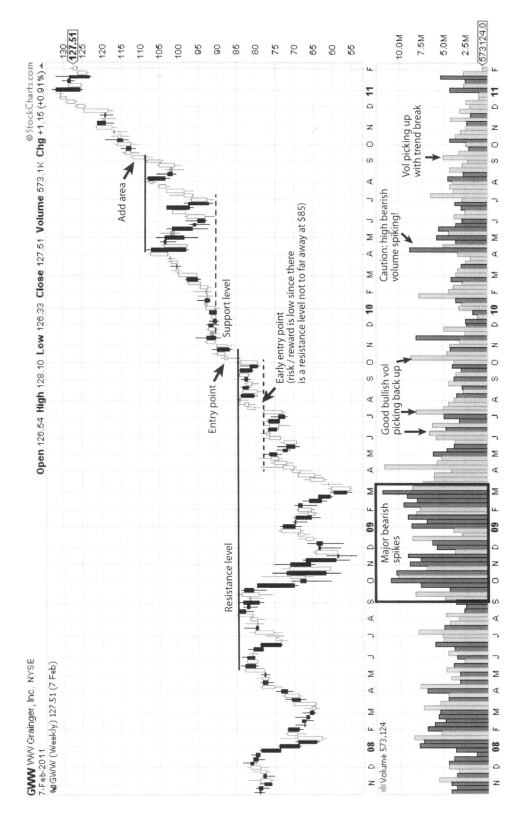

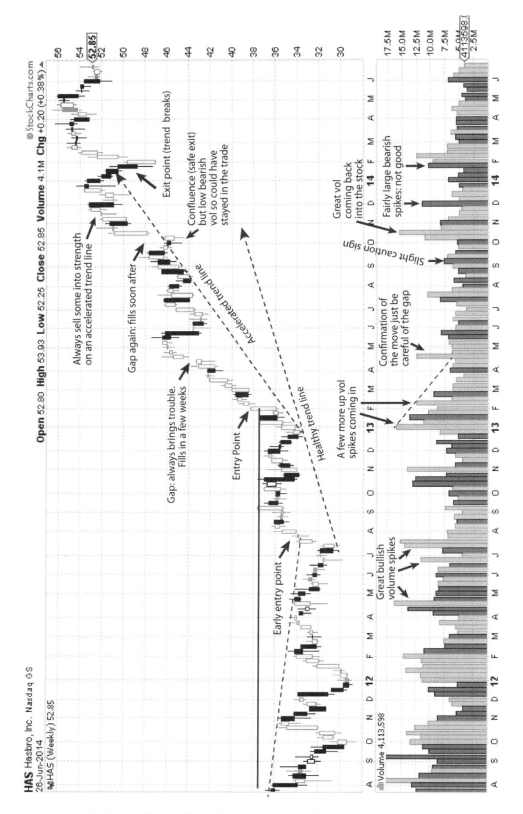

HAS Hasbro, Inc. Nasdaq GS
26-Jun-2014

Open 52.80 **High** 53.93 **Low** 52.25 **Close** 52.85 **Volume** 4.1M **Chg** +0.20 (+0.38%) ▲

© StockCharts.com

ⓦHAS (Weekly) 52.85

Always sell some into strength on an accelerated trend line

Gap again: fills soon after

Exit point (trend breaks)

Confluence (safe exit) but low bearish vol so could have stayed in the trade

Accelerated trend line

Gap: always brings trouble. Fills in a few weeks

Entry Point

Healthy trend line

Early entry point

Great vol coming back into the stock

Fairly large bearish spikes: not good

Slight caution sign

Confirmation of the move just be careful of the gap

A few more up vol spikes coming in

Great bullish volume spikes

ᴵᴸᴸ Volume 4,113,598

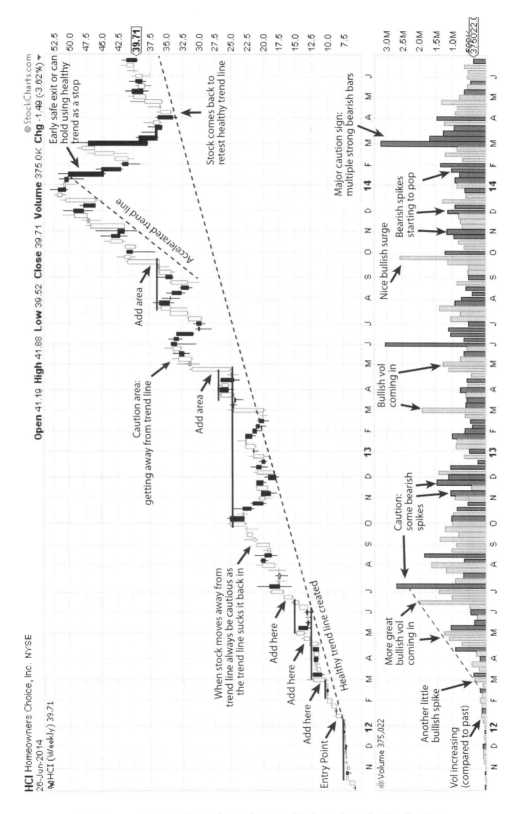

HCI Homeowners Choice, Inc. NYSE
28-Jun-2014
WHCI (Weekly) 39.71

Open 41.19 **High** 41.88 **Low** 39.52 **Close** 39.71 **Volume** 375.0K **Chg** -1.49 (-3.62%) ▼

© StockCharts.com

Early safe exit or can hold using healthy trend line as a stop

Accelerated trend line

Stock comes back to retest healthy trend line

Add area

Caution area: getting away from trend line

Add area

When stock moves away from trend line always be cautious as the trend line sucks it back in

Add here

Add here

Add here

Healthy trend line created

Entry Point

Major caution sign: multiple strong bearish bars

Bearish spikes starting to pop

Nice bullish surge

Bullish vol coming in

Caution: some bearish spikes

More great bullish vol coming in

Another little bullish spike

Vol increasing (compared to past)

Volume 375,022

245 Money Making Stock Chart Setups: Profiting from Swing Trading

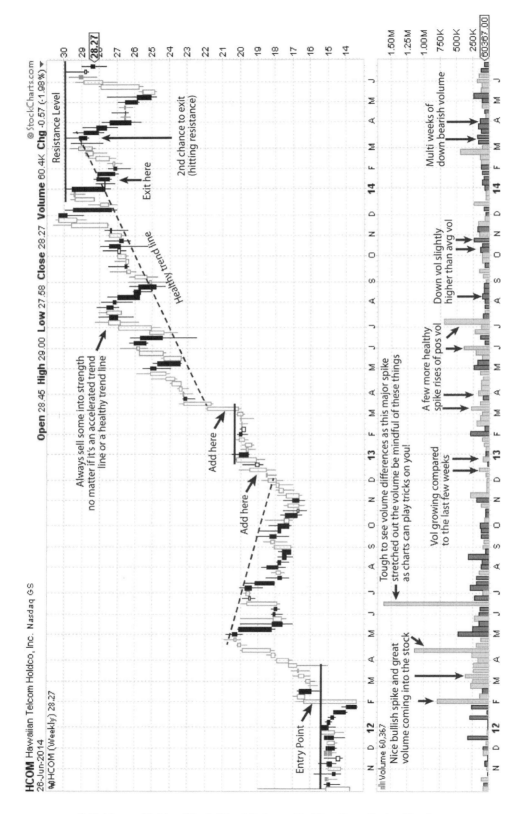

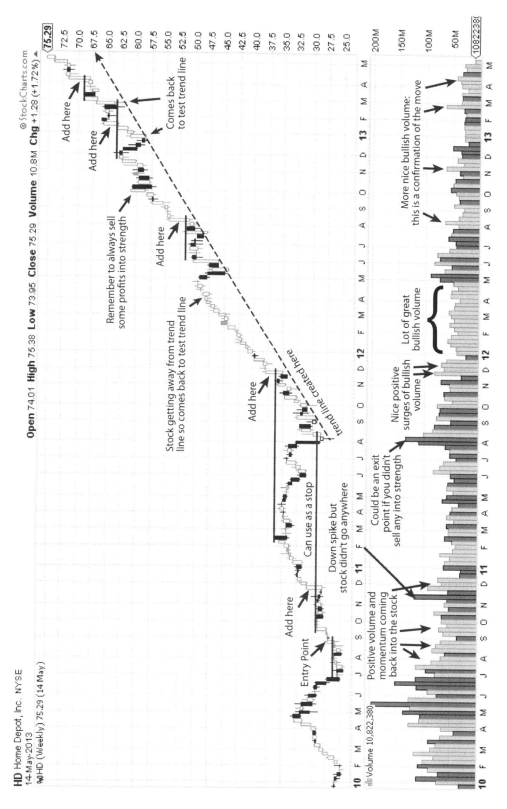

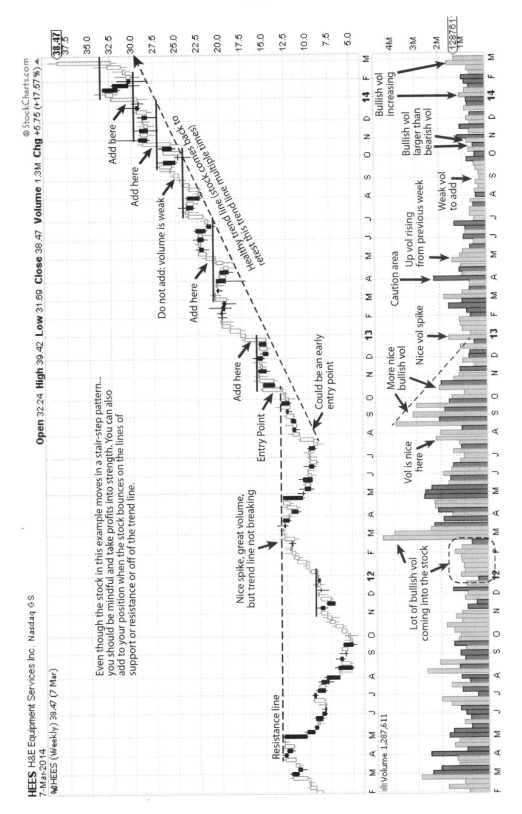

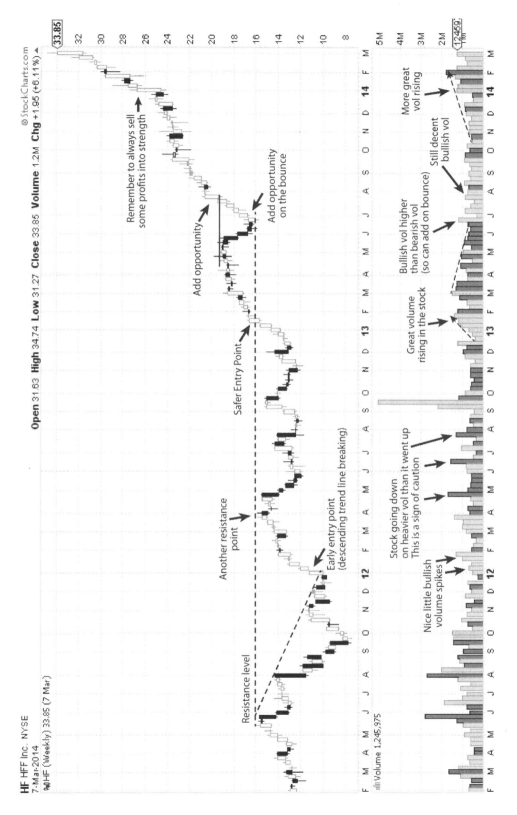

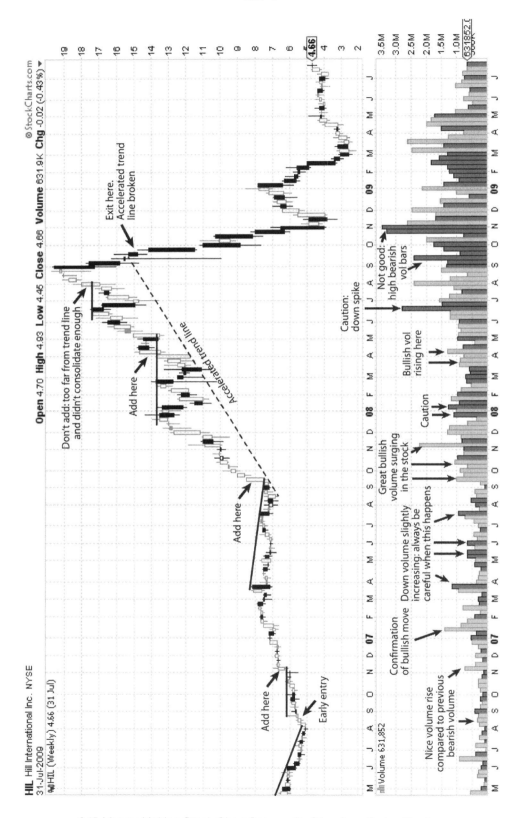

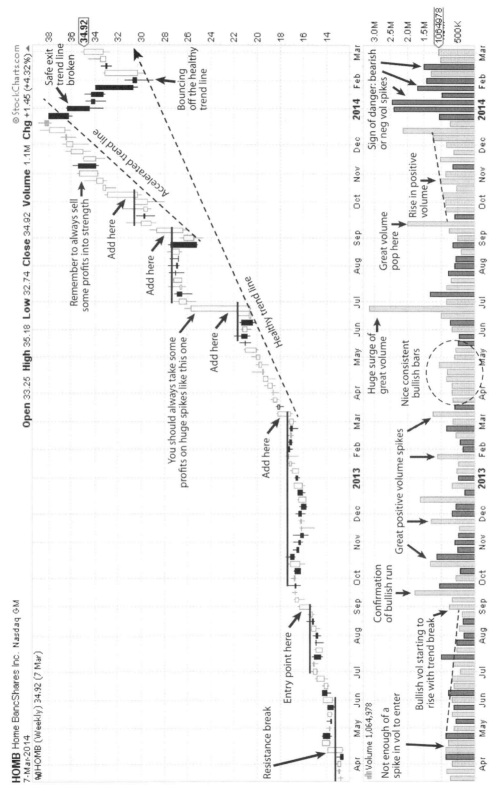

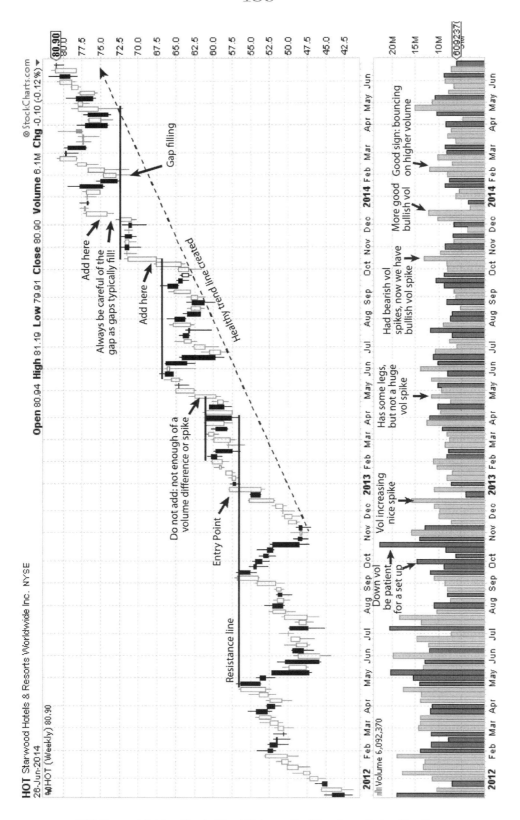

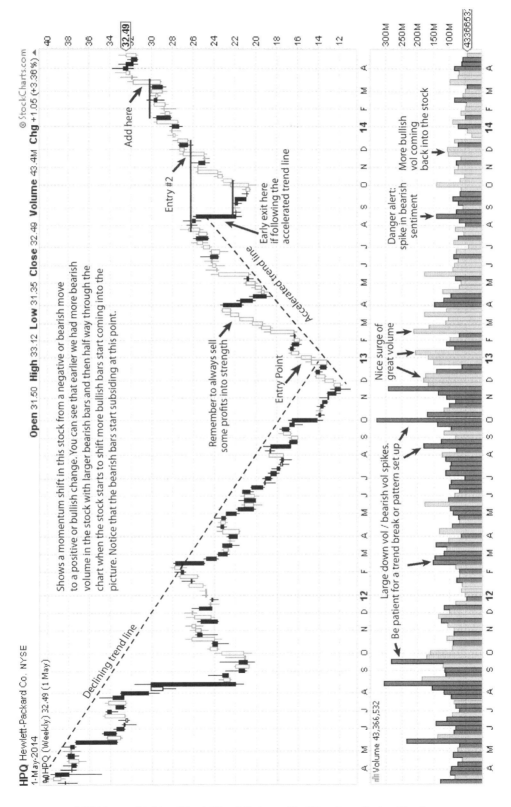

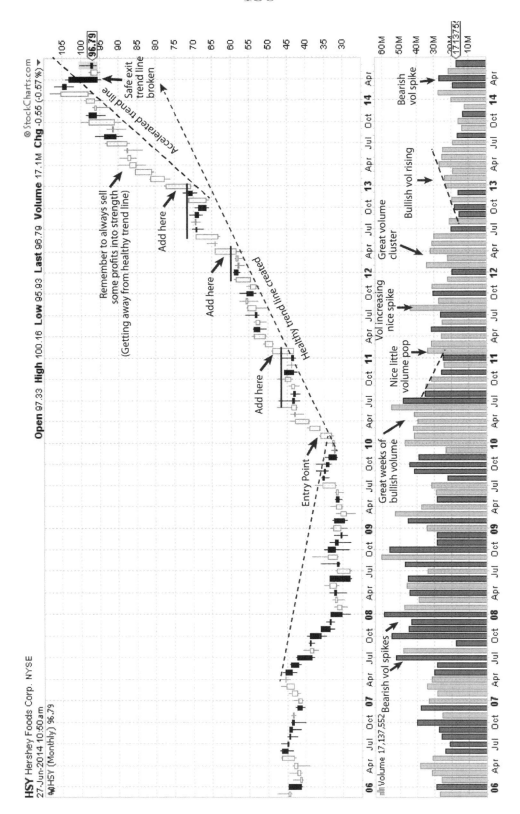

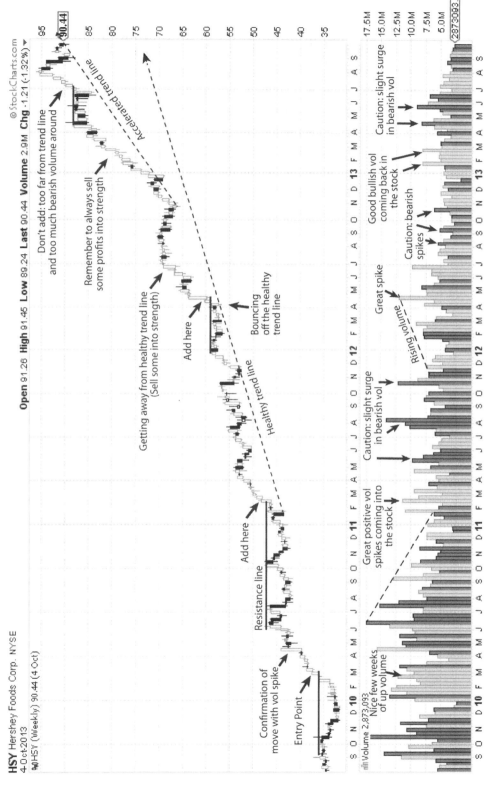

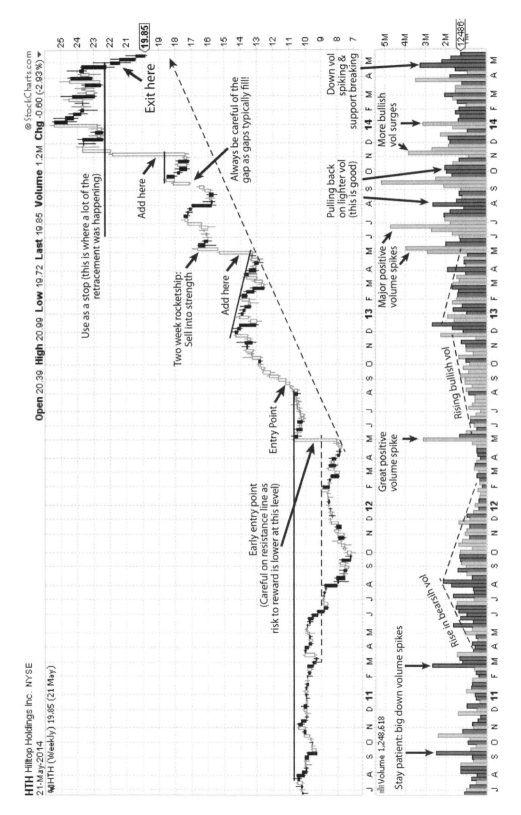

HTH Hilltop Holdings Inc. NYSE
21-May-2014
⚬ⓘHTH (Weekly) 19.85 (21 May)
© StockCharts.com
Open 20.39 **High** 20.99 **Low** 19.72 **Last** 19.85 **Volume** 1.2M **Chg** -0.60 (-2.93%) ▼

Use as a stop (this is where a lot of the retracement was happening)

Exit here

Add here

Always be careful of the gap as gaps typically fill!

Add here

Two week rocketship:
Sell into strength

Add here

Entry Point

Early entry point
(Careful on resistance line as risk to reward is lower at this level)

Down vol spiking & support breaking

More bullish vol surges

Pulling back on lighter vol (this is good)

Major positive volume spikes

Great positive volume spike

Rising bullish vol

Rise in bearish vol

ılıı Volume 1,248,618

Stay patient: big down volume spikes

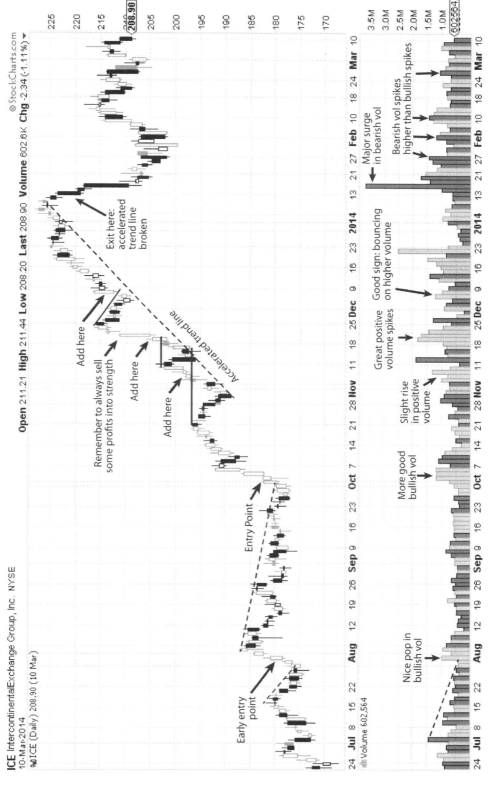

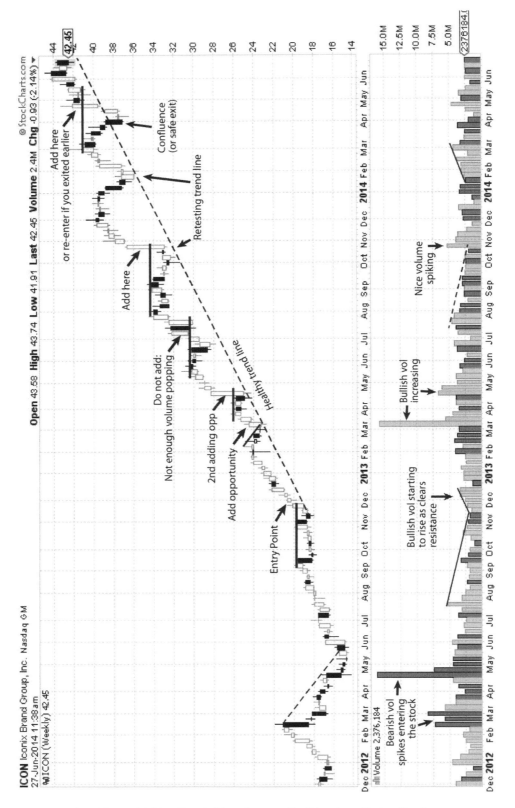

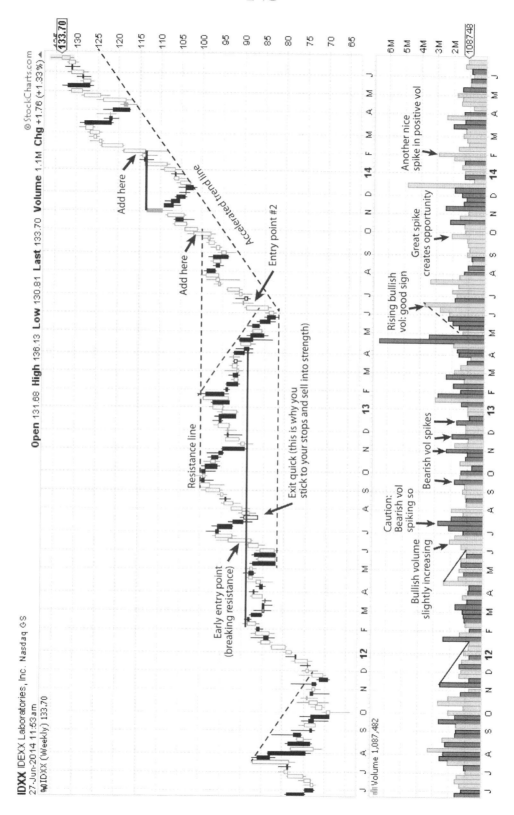

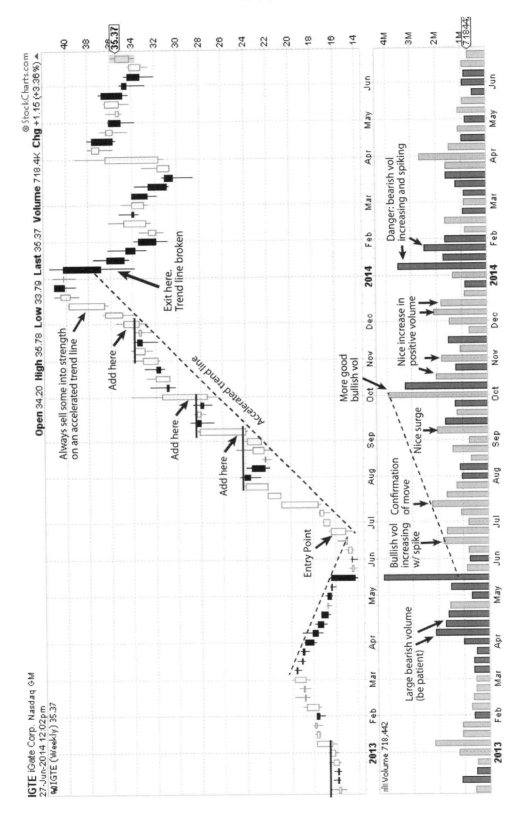

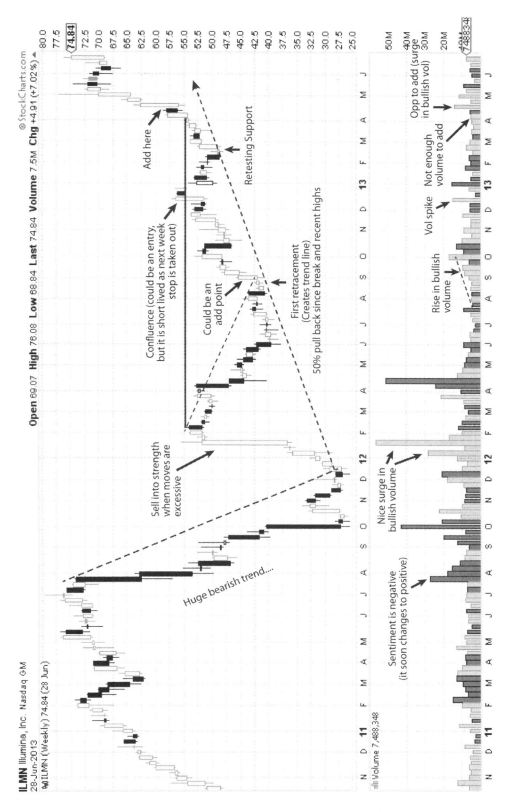

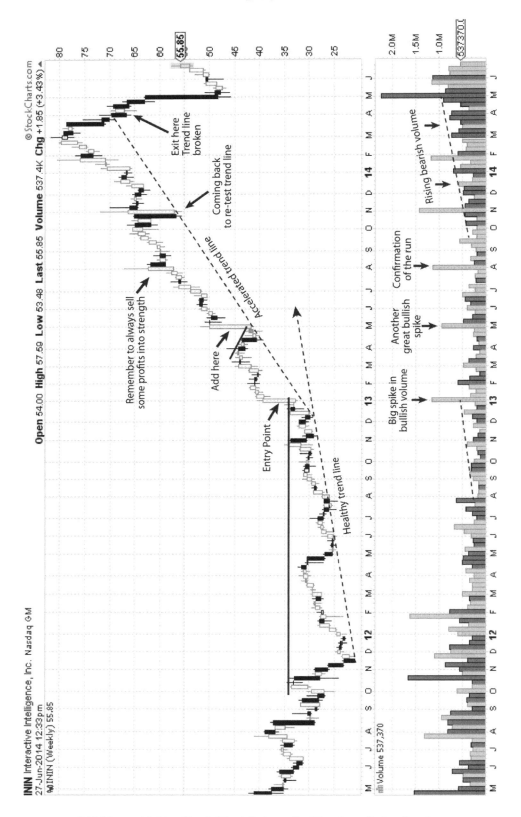

245 Money Making Stock Chart Setups: Profiting from Swing Trading

14⁷

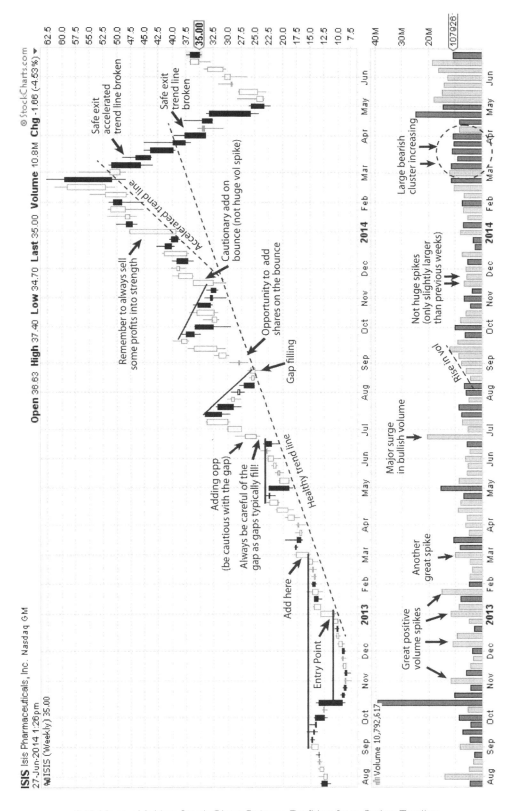

245 Money Making Stock Chart Setups: Profiting from Swing Trading

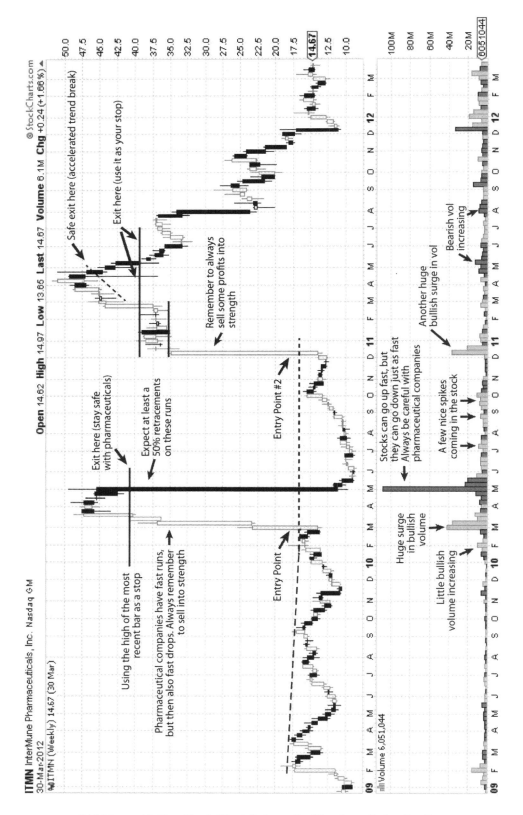

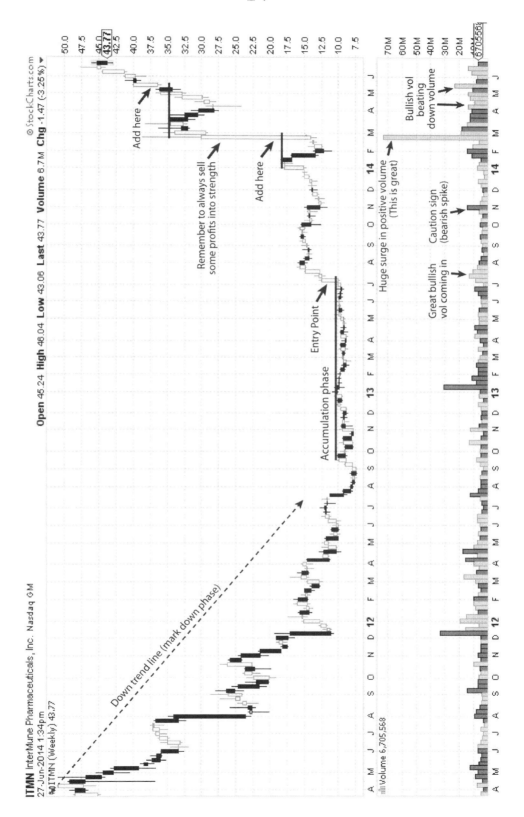

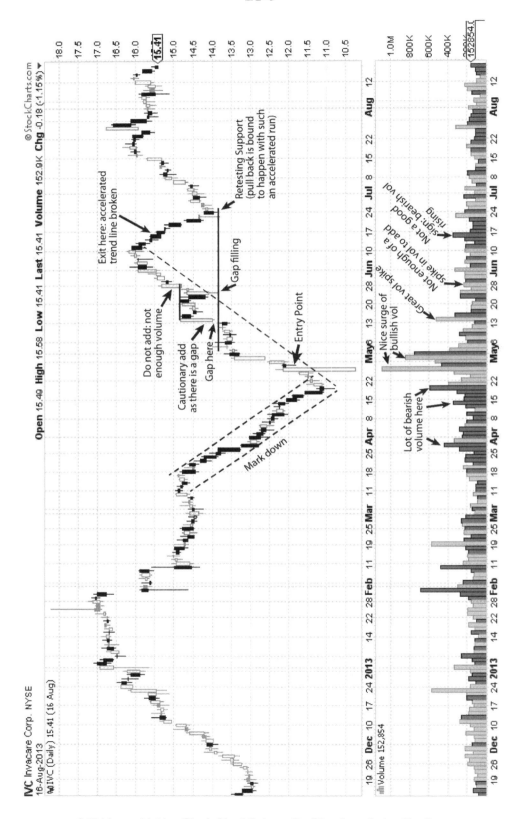

245 Money Making Stock Chart Setups: Profiting from Swing Trading

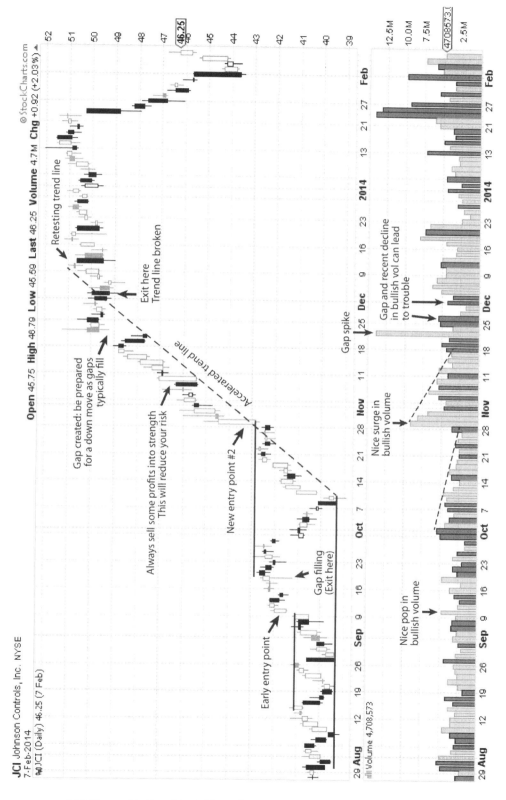

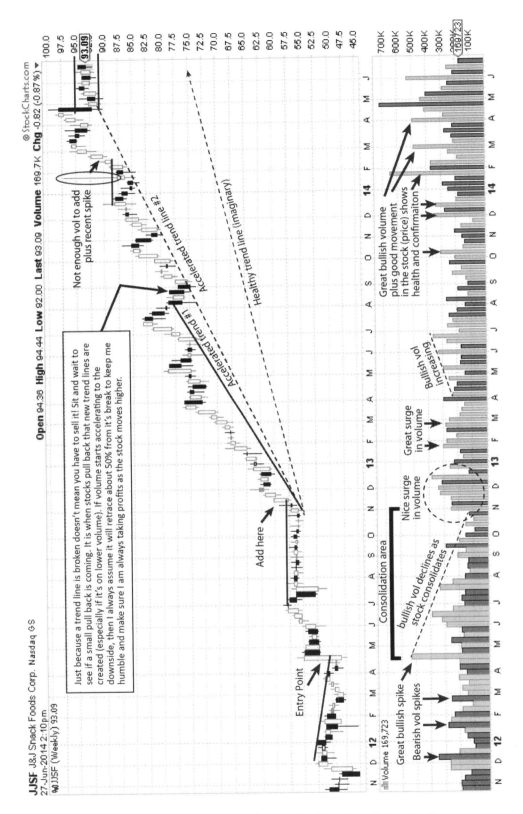

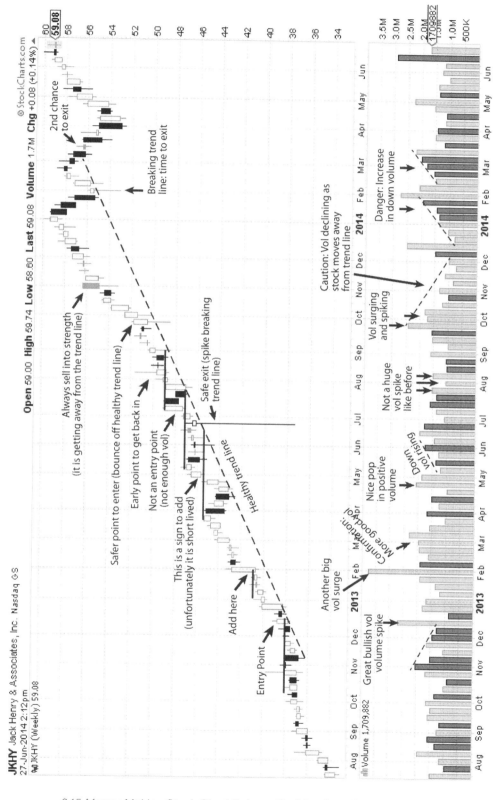

153

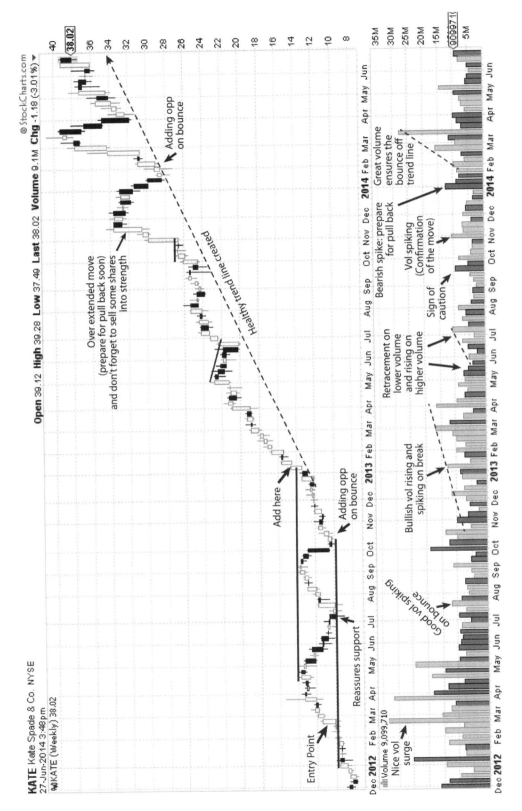

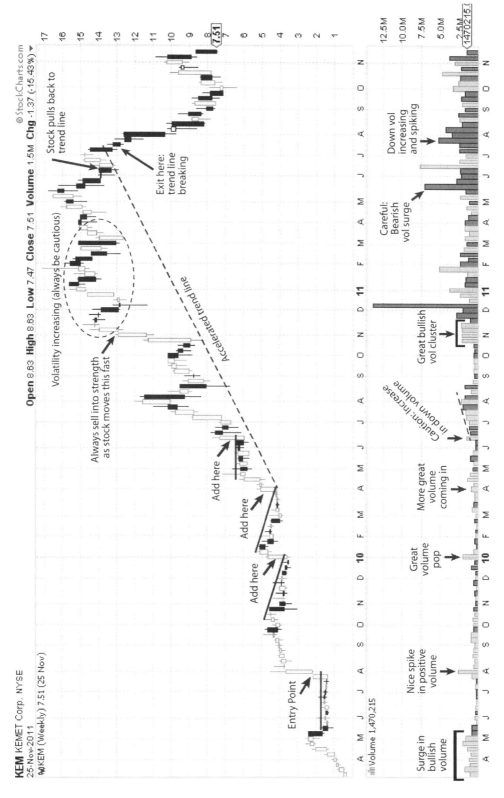

245 Money Making Stock Chart Setups: Profiting from Swing Trading

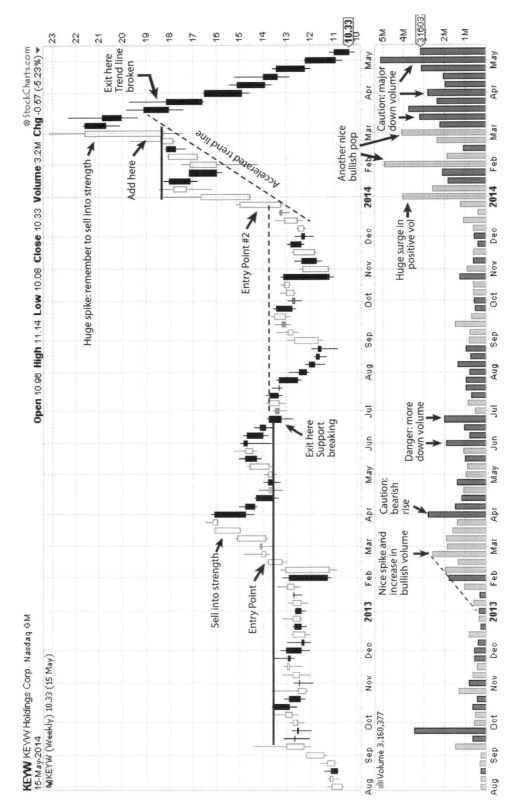

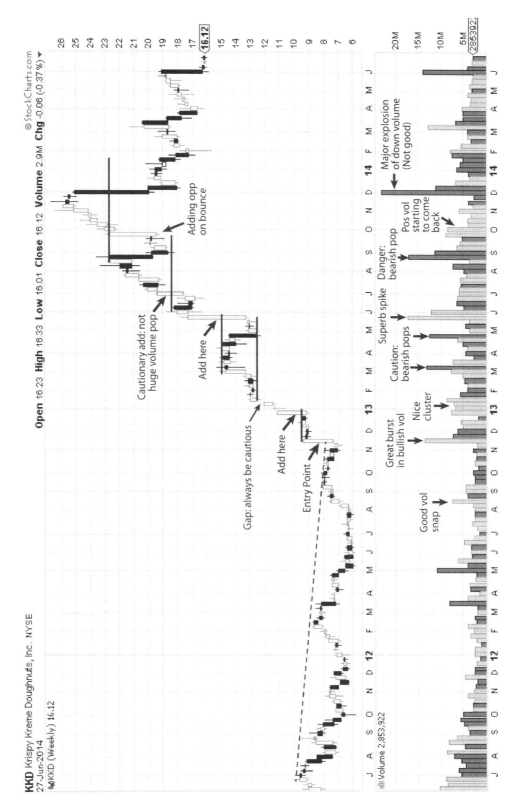

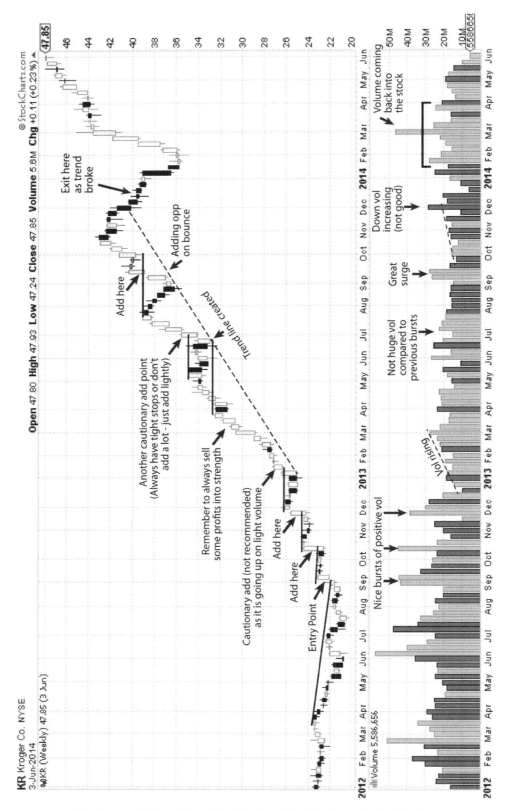

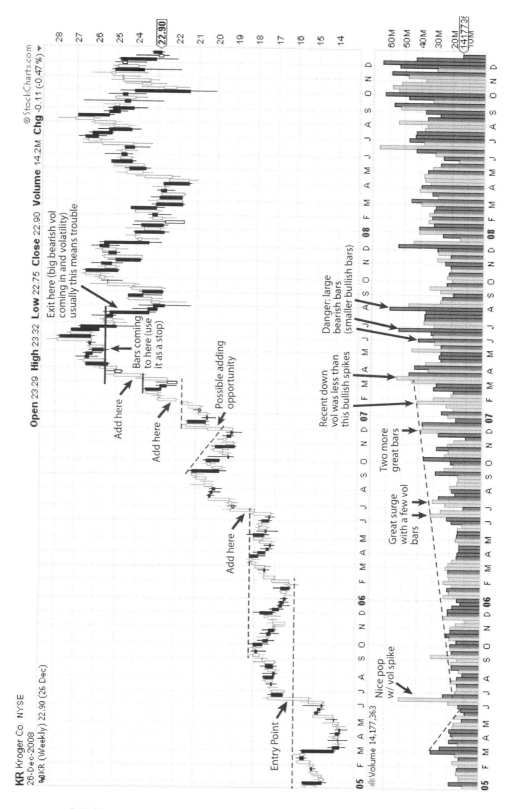

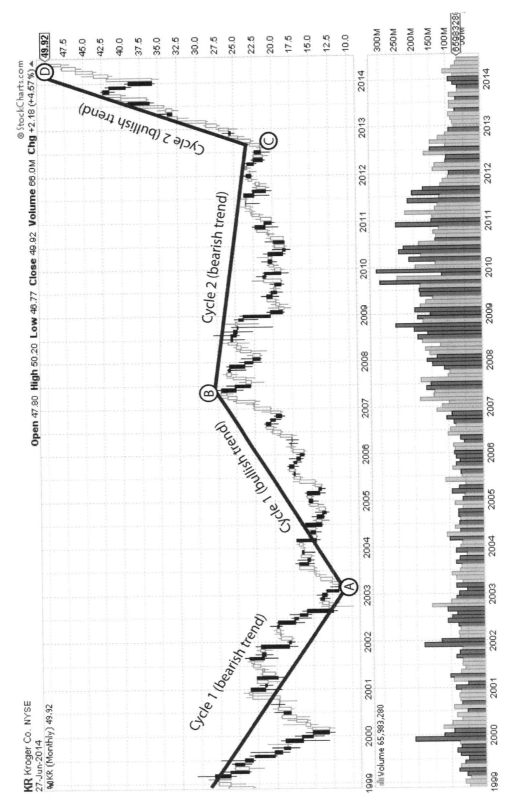

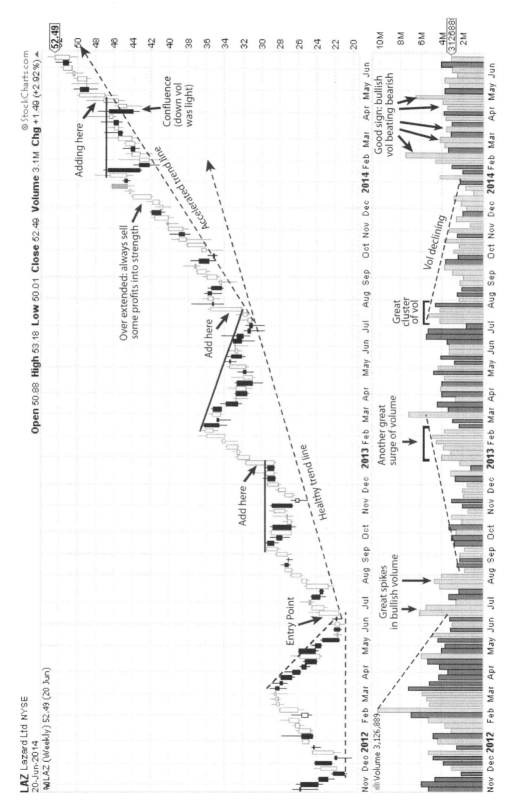

The chart is labeled as follows:

LAZ Lazard Ltd NYSE
20-Jun-2014
Open 50.88 High 53.18 Low 50.01 Close 52.49 Volume 3.1M Chg +1.49 (+2.92%)
© StockCharts.com
LAZ (Weekly) 52.49 (20 Jun)
Volume 3,126,889

Adding here

Confluence (down vol was light)

Over extended: always sell some profits into strength

Accelerated trend line

Add here

Add here

Healthy trend line

Entry Point

Good sign: bullish vol beating bearish

Great cluster of vol

Another great surge of volume

Vol declining

Great spikes in bullish volume

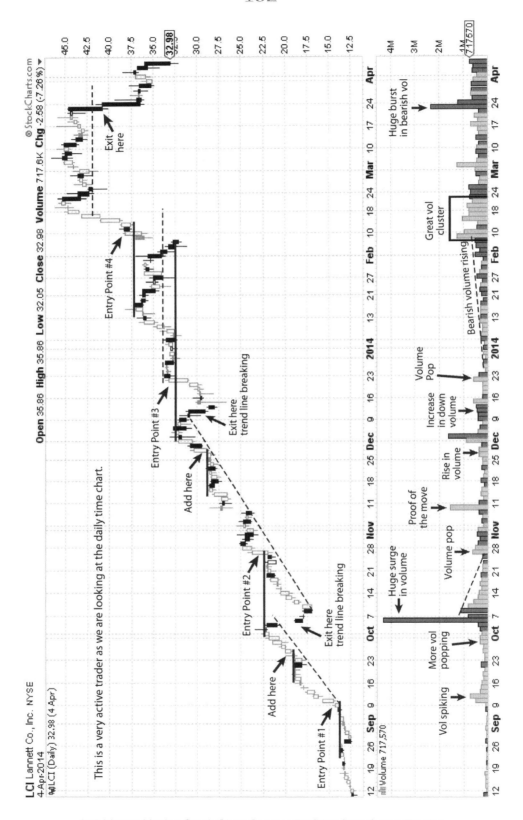

245 Money Making Stock Chart Setups: Profiting from Swing Trading

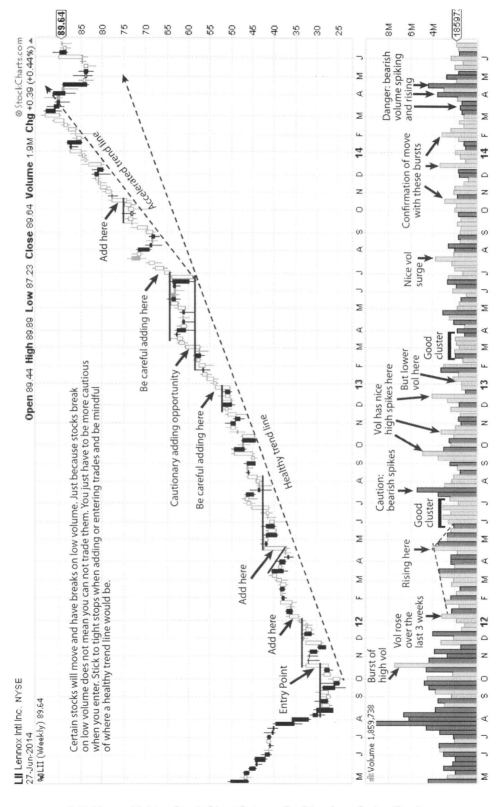

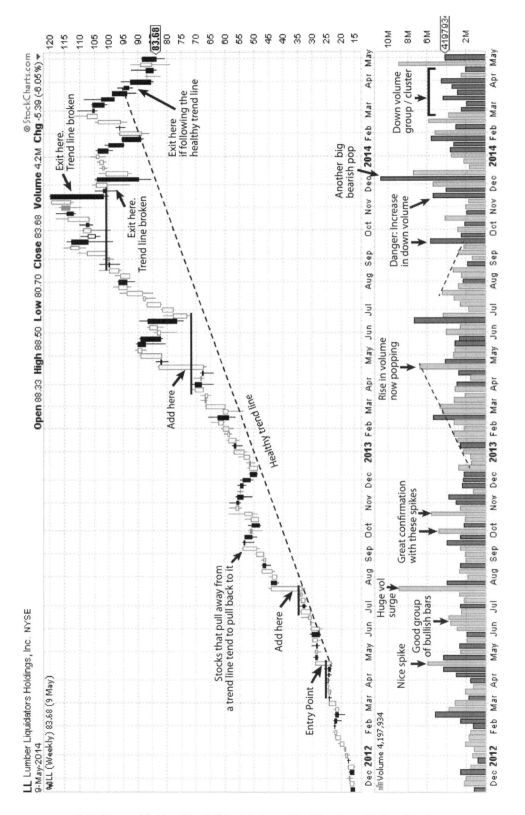

245 Money Making Stock Chart Setups: Profiting from Swing Trading

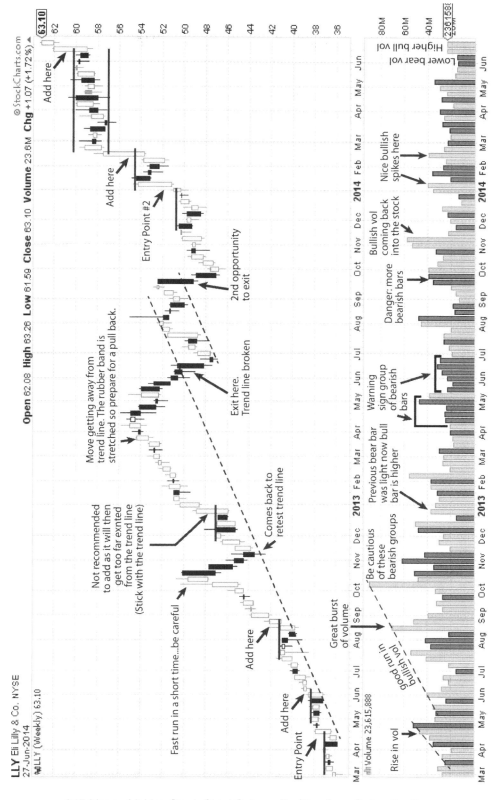

LLY Eli Lilly & Co. NYSE
27-Jun-2014
$LLY (Weekly) 63.10

Open 62.08 High 63.28 Low 61.59 Close 63.10 Volume 23.6M Chg +1.07 (+1.72%) ▲

© StockCharts.com

63.10

Add here

Add here

Entry Point #2

Move getting away from trend line. The rubber band is stretched so prepare for a pull back.

2nd opportunity to exit

Exit here. Trend line broken

Not recommended to add as it will then get too far exented from the trend line (Stick with the trend line)

Comes back to retest trend line

Fast run in a short time...be careful

Add here

Add here

Great burst of volume

Entry Point

Volume 23,615,888

Rise in vol

good run in bullish vol

Be cautious of these bearish groups

Previous bear bar was light now bull bar is higher

Warning sign group of bearish bars

Danger: more bearish bars

Bullish vol coming back into the stock

Nice bullish spikes here

Higher bull vol
Lower bear vol

236,158

245 Money Making Stock Chart Setups: Profiting from Swing Trading

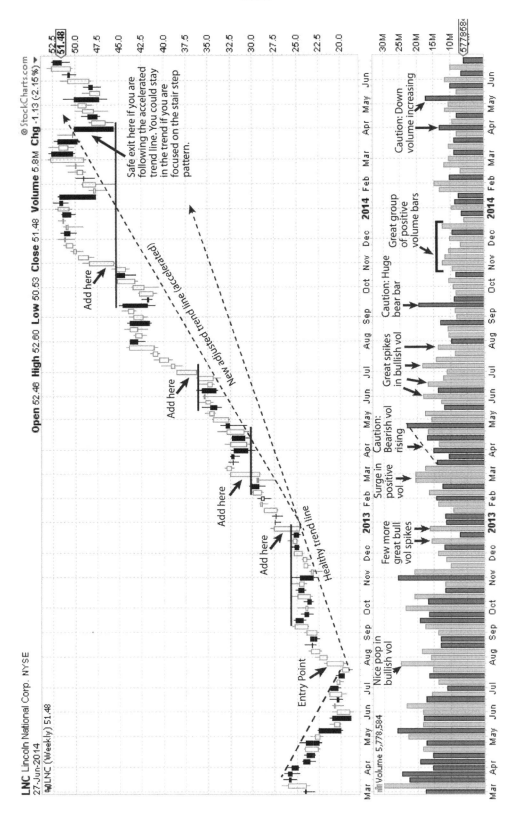

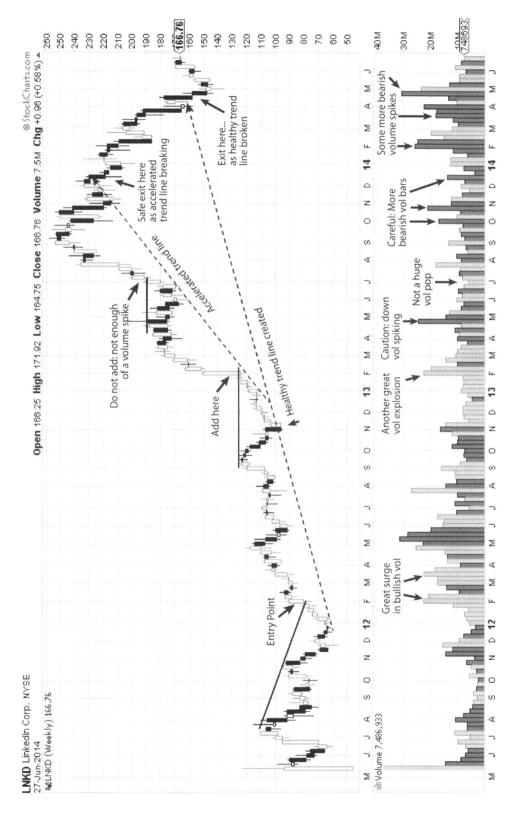

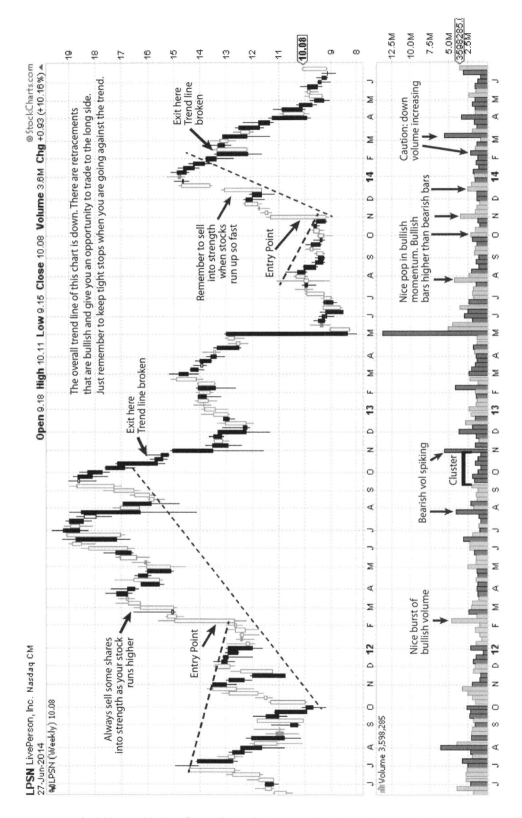

LPSN LivePerson, Inc. Nasdaq CM
27-Jun-2014
Open 9.18 **High** 10.11 **Low** 9.15 **Close** 10.08 **Volume** 3.8M **Chg** +0.93 (+10.16%) ▲
© StockCharts.com
ᵂ LPSN (Weekly) 10.08

The overall trend line of this chart is down. There are retracements that are bullish and give you an opportunity to trade to the long side. Just remember to keep tight stops when you are going against the trend.

Exit here Trend line broken

Remember to sell into strength when stocks run up so fast

Entry Point

Exit here Trend line broken

Always sell some shares into strength as your stock runs higher

Entry Point

Volume 3,598,285

Caution: down volume increasing

Nice pop in bullish momentum. Bullish bars higher than bearish bars

Bearish vol spiking

Cluster

Nice burst of bullish volume

245 Money Making Stock Chart Setups: Profiting from Swing Trading

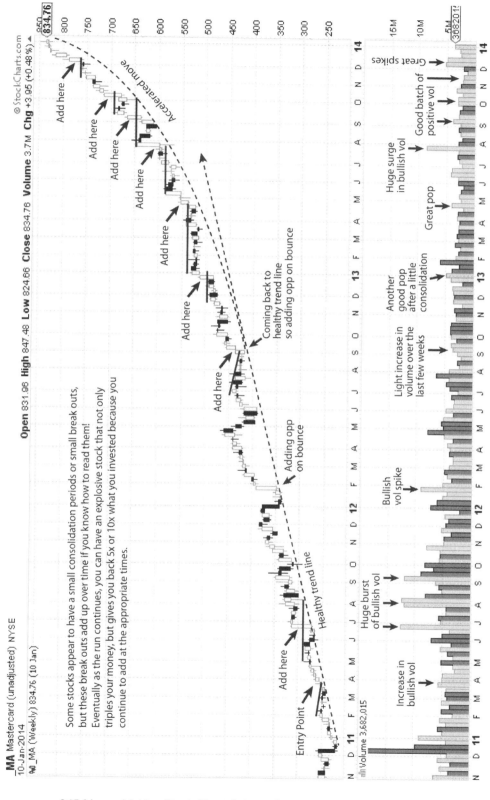

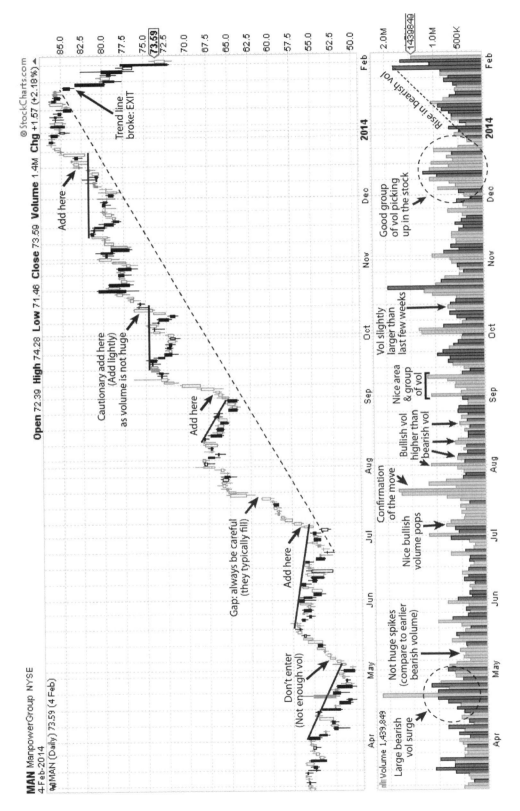

MAN ManpowerGroup NYSE
4-Feb-2014

Open 72.39 **High** 74.28 **Low** 71.46 **Close** 73.59 **Volume** 1.4M **Chg** +1.57 (+2.18%) ▲

MAN (Daily) 73.59 (4 Feb)

© StockCharts.com

73.59

Trend line broke: EXIT

Add here

Cautionary add here (Add lightly) as volume is not huge

Add here

Gap: always be careful (they typically fill)

Add here

Don't enter (Not enough vol)

Volume 1,439,849

Large bearish vol surge

Not huge spikes (compare to earlier bearish volume)

Nice bullish volume pops

Confirmation of the move

Bullish vol higher than bearish vol

Nice area & group of vol

Vol slightly larger than last few weeks

Good group of vol picking up in the stock

Rise in bearish vol

1439849

245 Money Making Stock Chart Setups: Profiting from Swing Trading

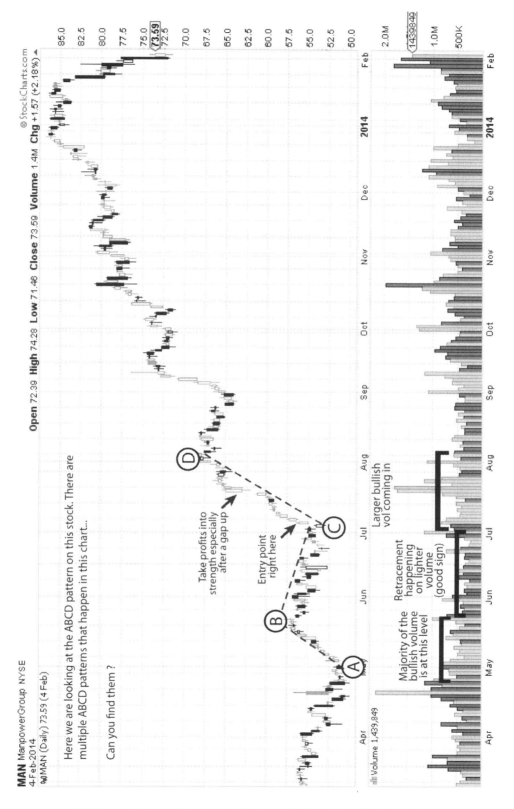

MAN ManpowerGroup NYSE
4-Feb-2014
MAN (Daily) 73.59 (4 Feb)

Open 72.39 **High** 74.28 **Low** 71.46 **Close** 73.59 **Volume** 1.4M **Chg** +1.57 (+2.18%) ▲

© StockCharts.com

Here we are looking at the ABCD pattern on this stock. There are multiple ABCD patterns that happen in this chart...

Can you find them?

Take profits into strength especially after a gap up

Entry point right here

Larger bullish vol coming in

Retracement happening on lighter volume (good sign)

Majority of the bullish volume is at this level

Volume 1,439,849

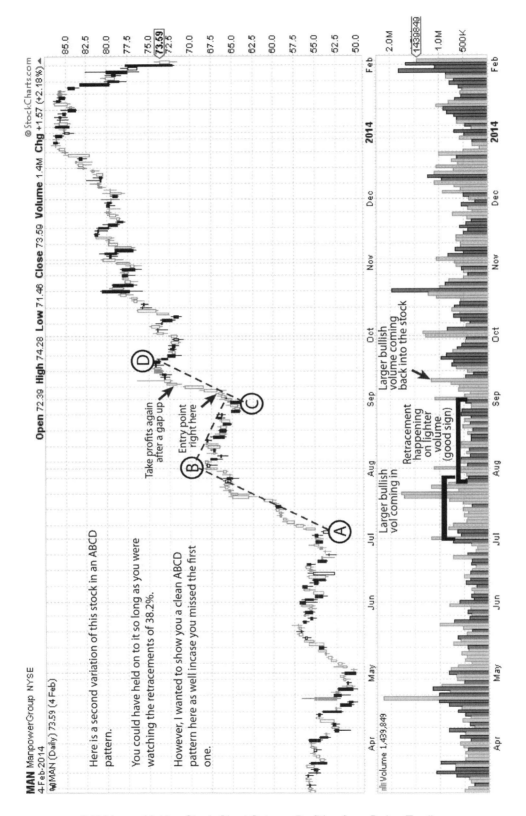

MAN ManpowerGroup NYSE
4-Feb-2014
Open 72.39 **High** 74.28 **Low** 71.46 **Close** 73.59 **Volume** 1.4M **Chg** +1.57 (+2.18%) ▲
© StockCharts.com

W MAN (Daily) 73.59 (4 Feb)

Here is a second variation of this stock in an ABCD pattern.

You could have held on to it so long as you were watching the retracements of 38.2%.

However, I wanted to show you a clean ABCD pattern here as well incase you missed the first one.

Take profits again after a gap up.

Entry point right here

Larger bullish vol coming in

Retracement happening on lighter volume (good sign)

Larger bullish volume coming back into the stock

Volume 1,439,849

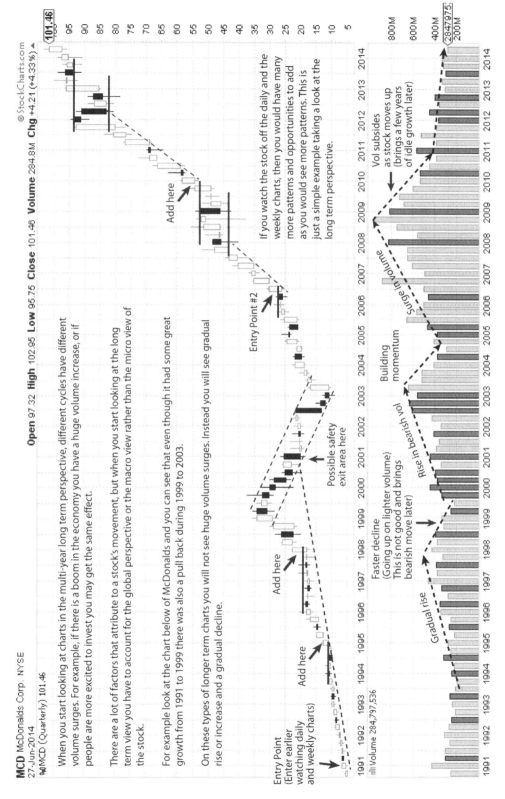

The chart and its annotations (rotated):

MCD McDonalds Corp. NYSE
27-Jun-2014

Open 97.32 **High** 102.95 **Low** 95.75 **Close** 101.46 **Volume** 284.8M **Chg** +4.21 (+4.33%) ▲

© StockCharts.com

MCD (Quarterly) 101.46

When you start looking at charts in the multi-year long term perspective, different cycles have different volume surges. For example, if there is a boom in the economy you have a huge volume increase, or if people are more excited to invest you may get the same effect.

There are a lot of factors that attribute to a stock's movement, but when you start looking at the long term view you have to account for the global perspective or the macro view rather than the micro view of the stock.

For example look at the chart below of McDonalds and you can see that even though it had some great growth from 1991 to 1999 there was also a pull back during 1999 to 2003.

On these types of longer term charts you will not see huge volume surges. Instead you will see gradual rise or increase and a gradual decline.

If you watch the stock off the daily and the weekly charts, then you would have many more patterns and opportunities to add as you would see more patterns. This is just a simple example taking a look at the long term perspective.

Add here

Entry Point #2

Add here

Possible safety exit area here

Entry Point
(Enter earlier watching daily and weekly charts)

Add here

Volume 284,797,536

Vol subsides as stock moves up (brings a few years of idle growth later)

Building momentum

Surge in volume

Rise in bearish vol

Faster decline (Going up on lighter volume) This is not good and brings bearish move later)

Gradual rise

800M
600M
400M
284797975
200M

245 Money Making Stock Chart Setups: Profiting from Swing Trading

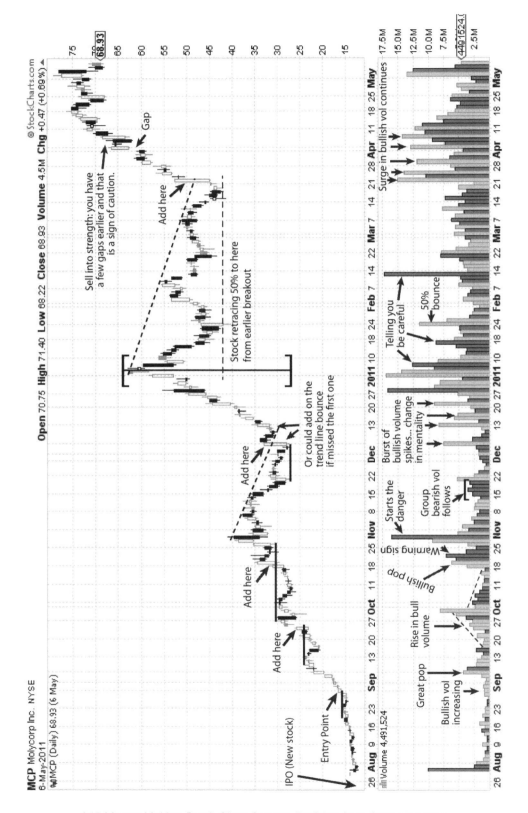

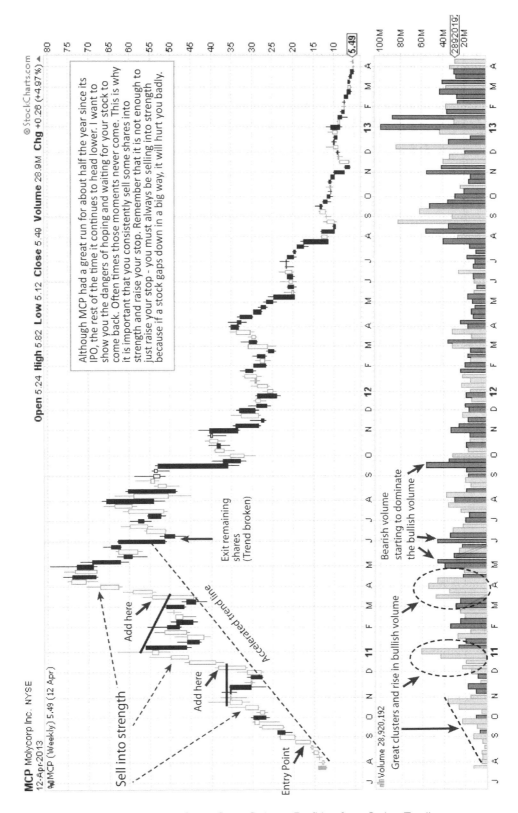

245 Money Making Stock Chart Setups: Profiting from Swing Trading

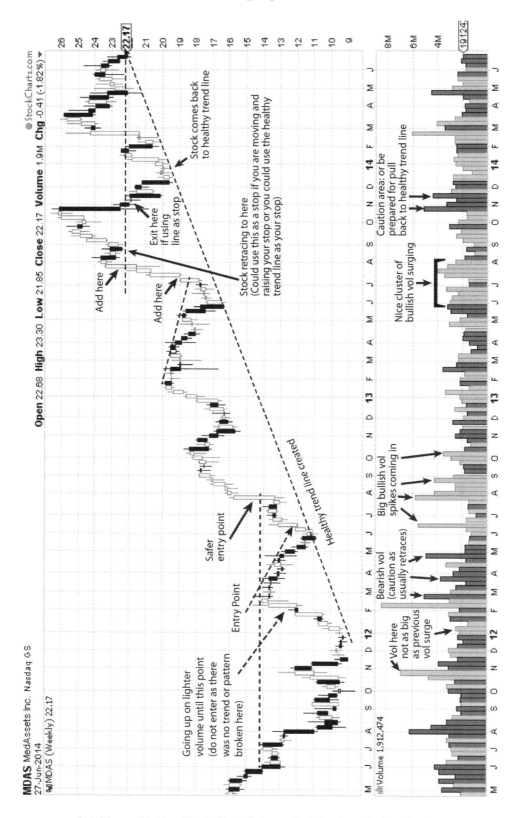

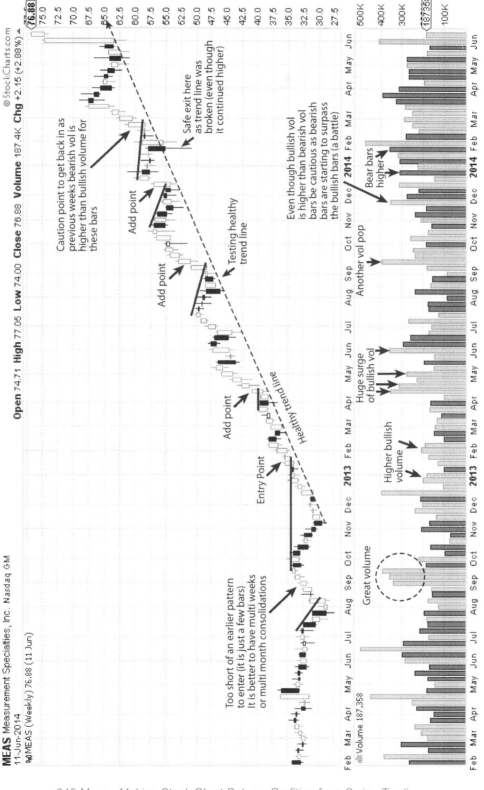

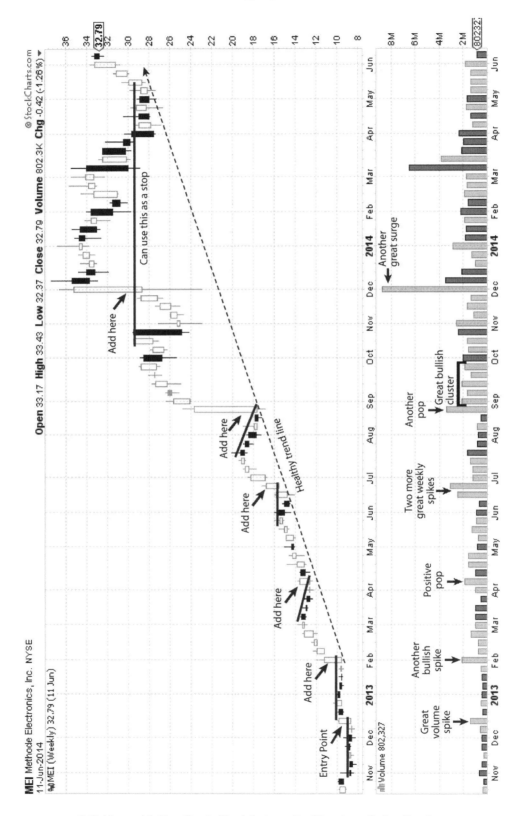

179

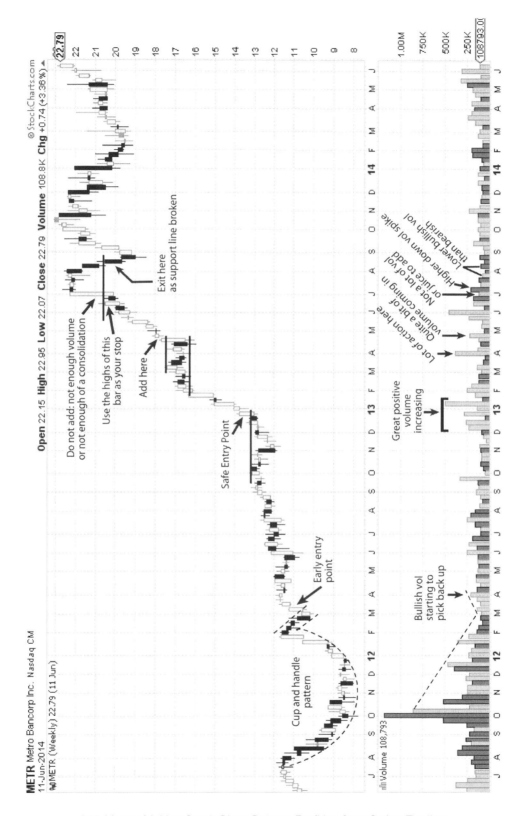

245 Money Making Stock Chart Setups: Profiting from Swing Trading

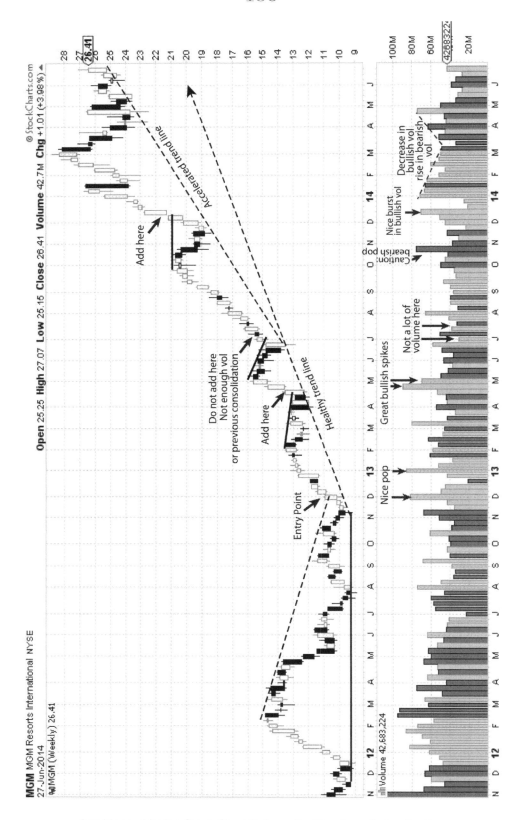

245 Money Making Stock Chart Setups: Profiting from Swing Trading

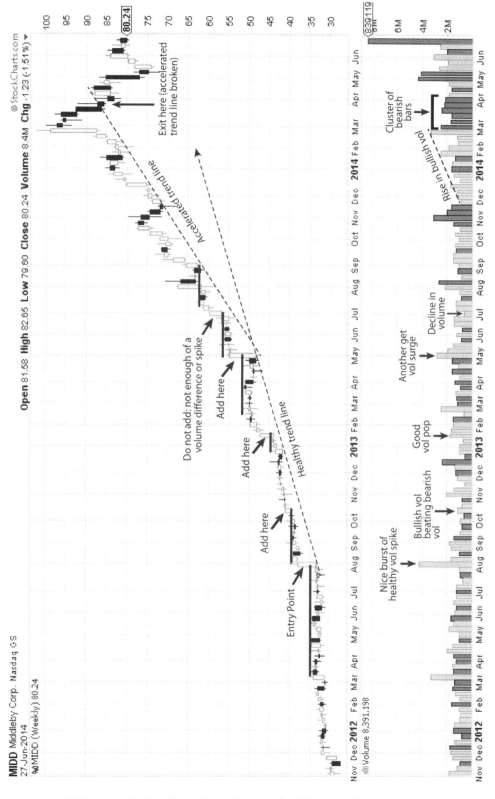

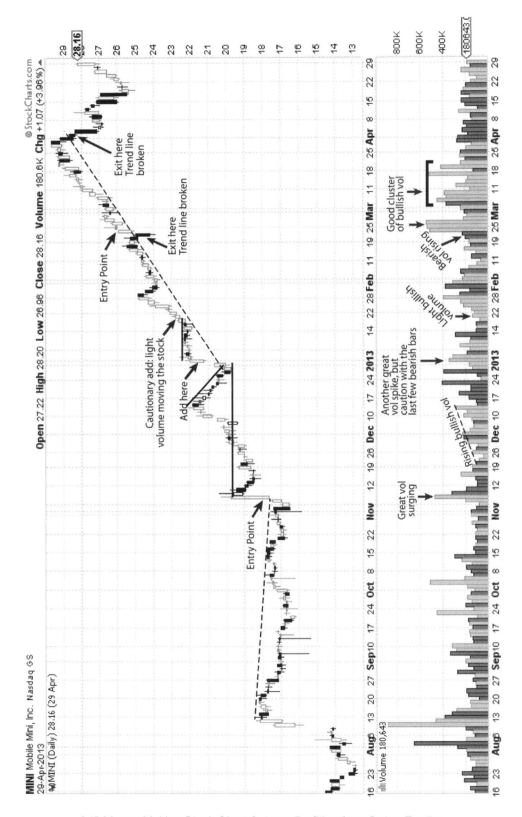

MINI Mobile Mini, Inc. Nasdaq GS
29-Apr-2013
Open 27.22 **High** 28.20 **Low** 26.96 **Close** 28.16 **Volume** 180.6K **Chg** +1.07 (+3.96%) ▲
© StockCharts.com

Exit here
Trend line
broken

Exit here
Trend line broken

Entry Point

Cautionary add: light
volume moving the stock

Add here

Entry Point

Good cluster
of bullish vol

Bearish
vol rising

Light bullish
volume

Another great
vol spike, but
caution with the
last few bearish bars

Rising bullish vol

Great vol
surging

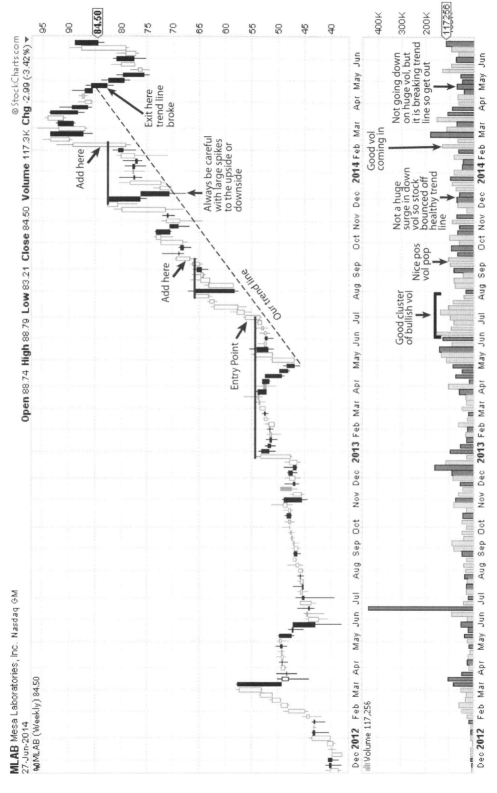

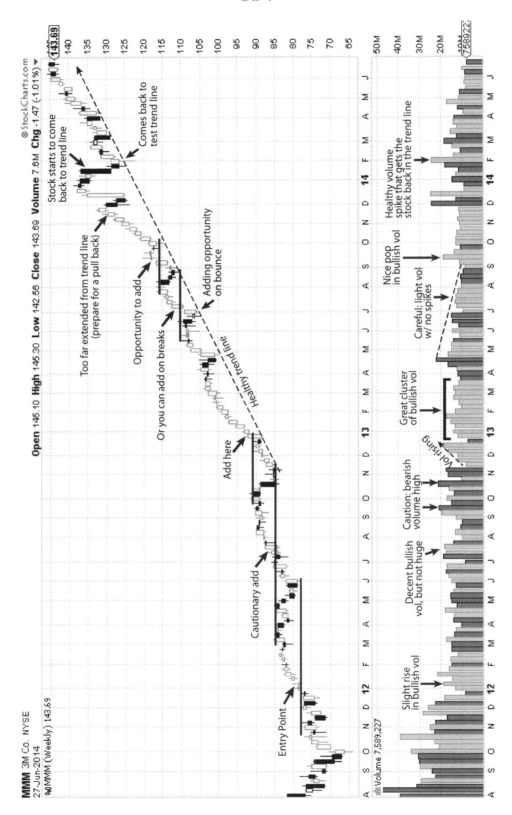

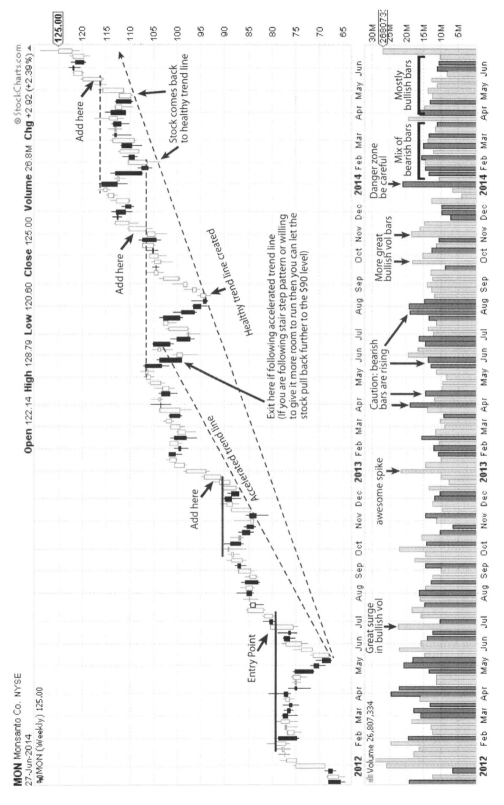

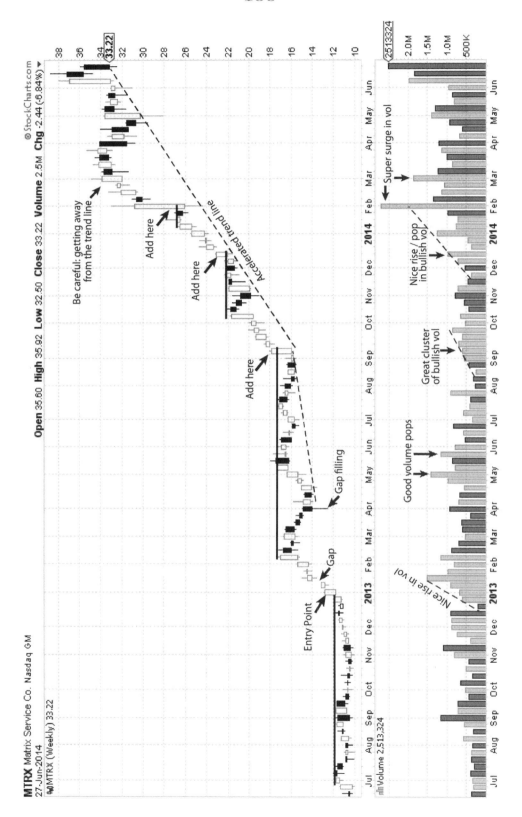

187

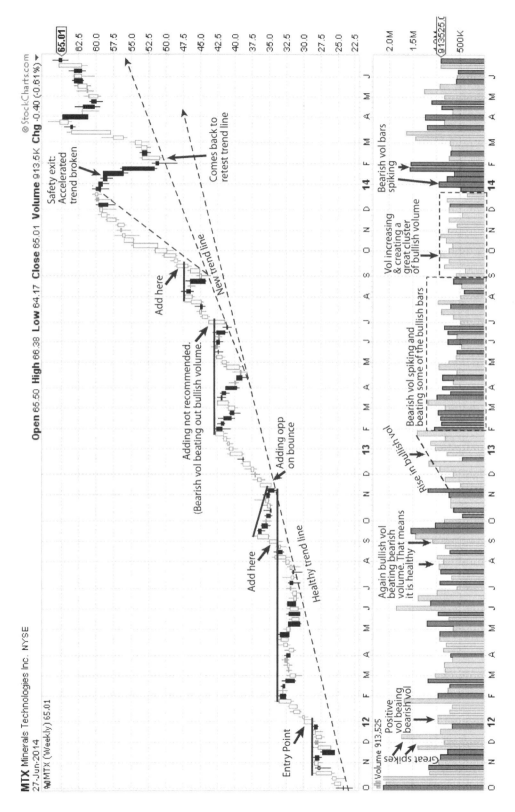

245 Money Making Stock Chart Setups: Profiting from Swing Trading

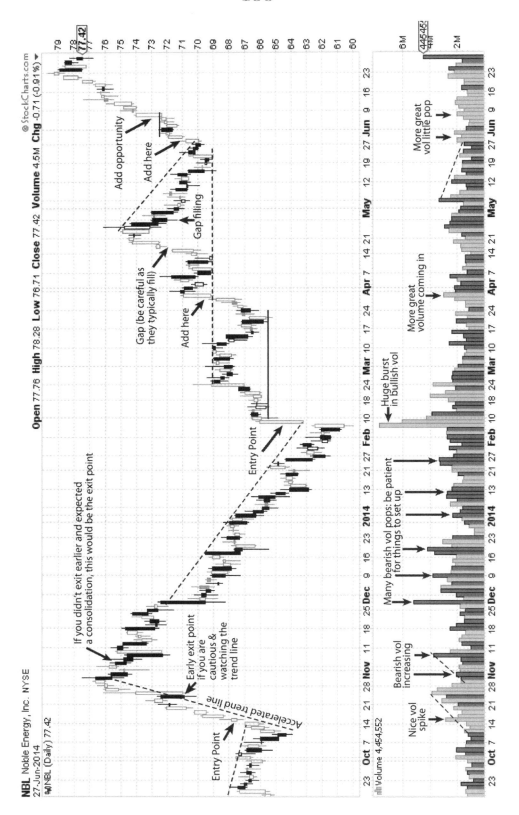

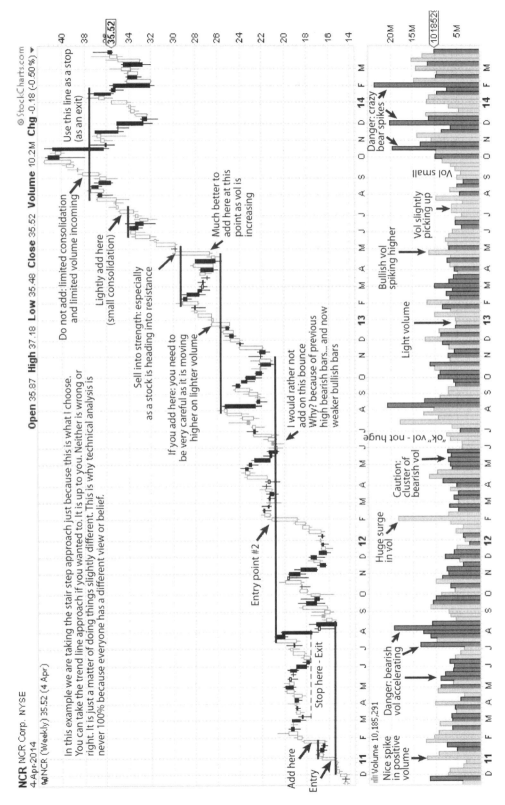

NCR NCR Corp. NYSE
4-Apr-2014
NCR (Weekly) 35.52 (4 Apr)

Open 35.87 High 37.18 Low 35.48 Close 35.52 Volume 10.2M Chg -0.18 (-0.50%) ▼

@ StockCharts.com

In this example we are taking the stair step approach just because this is what I choose. You can take the trend line approach if you wanted to. It is up to you. Neither is wrong or right. It is just a matter of doing things slightly different. This is why technical analysis is never 100% because everyone has a different view or belief.

Do not add: limited consolidation and limited volume incoming

Use this line as a stop (as an exit)

Lightly add here (small consolidation)

Sell into strength: especially as a stock is heading into resistance

Much better to add here at this point as vol is increasing

If you add here; you need to be very careful as it is moving higher on lighter volume

I would rather not add on this bounce Why? because of previous high bearish bars... and now weaker bullish bars

Entry point #2

Stop here - Exit

Add here

Entry

Volume 10,185,291

Nice spike in positive volume

Danger: bearish vol accelerating

Huge surge in vol

Caution: cluster of bearish vol

"ok" vol - not huge

Light volume

Bullish vol spiking higher

Vol slightly picking up

Vol small

Danger: crazy bear spikes

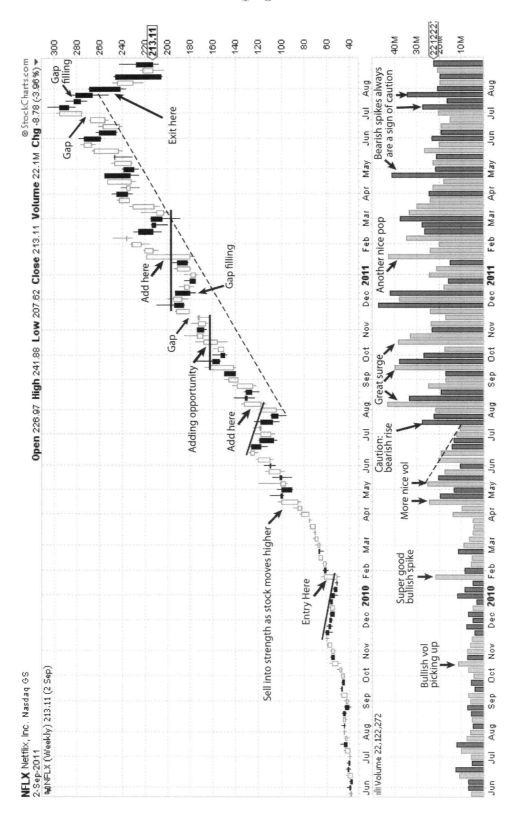

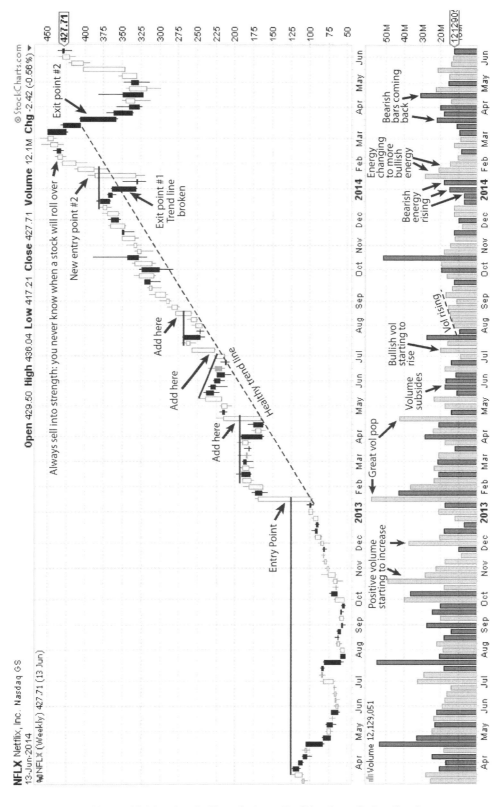

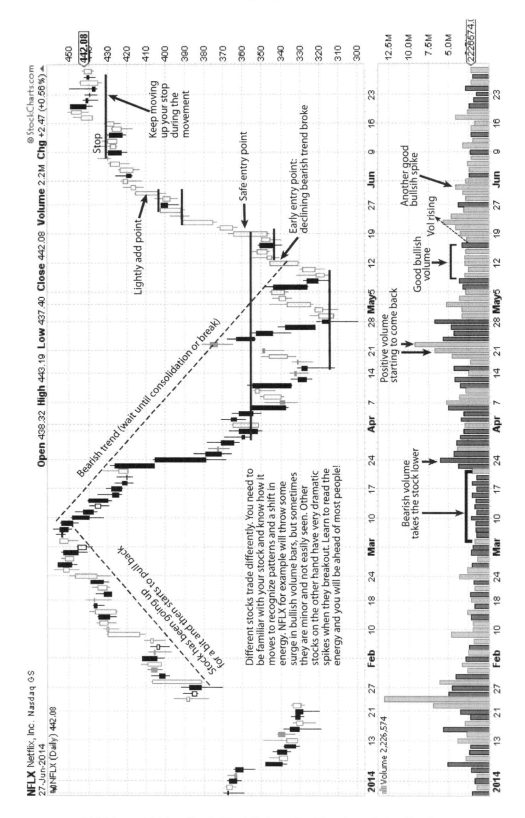

245 Money Making Stock Chart Setups: Profiting from Swing Trading

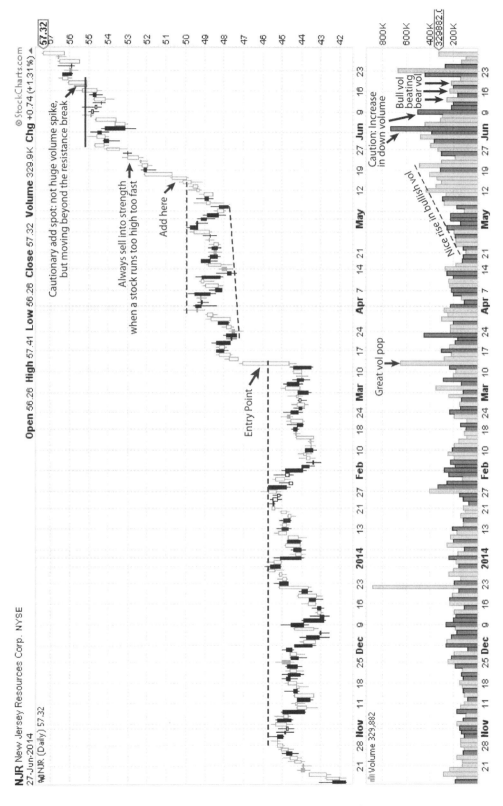

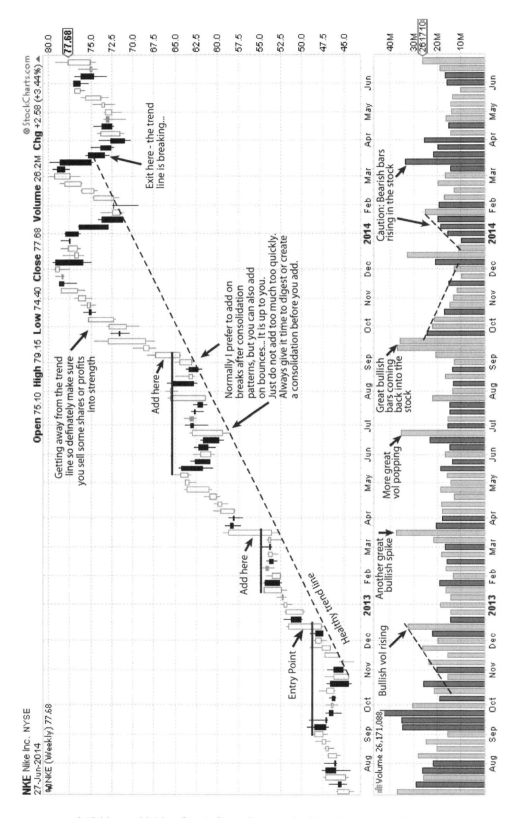

The chart is labeled as follows:

NKE Nike Inc. NYSE
27-Jun-2014
Open 75.10 **High** 79.15 **Low** 74.40 **Close** 77.68 **Volume** 28.2M **Chg** +2.58 (+3.44%)
@StockCharts.com
w NKE (Weekly) 77.68

Annotations on the price chart:
- Getting away from the trend line so definately make sure you sell some shares or profits into strength
- Exit here - the trend line is breaking...
- Add here
- Normally I prefer to add on breaks after consolidation patterns, but you can also add on bounces... It is up to you. Just do not add too much too quickly. Always give it time to digest or create a consolidation before you add.
- Add here
- Entry Point
- Healthy trend line

Volume chart annotations:
- Volume 26,171,088
- Bullish vol rising
- Another great bullish spike
- More great vol popping
- Great bullish bars coming back into the stock
- Caution: Bearish bars rising in the stock

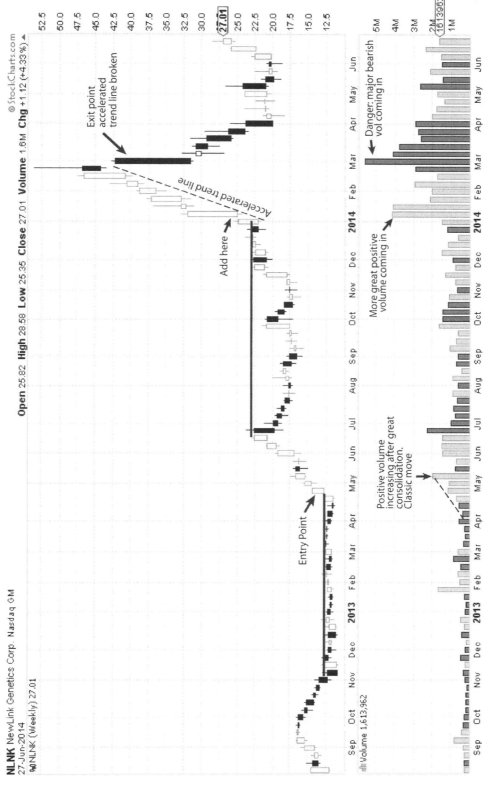

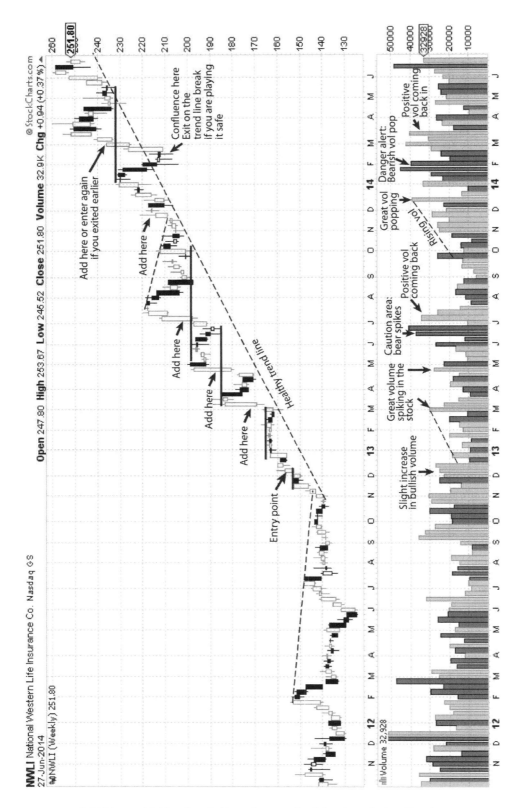

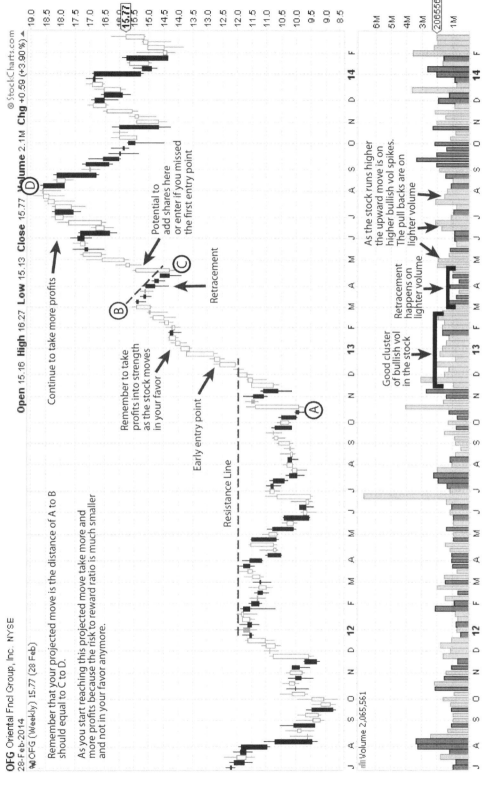

198

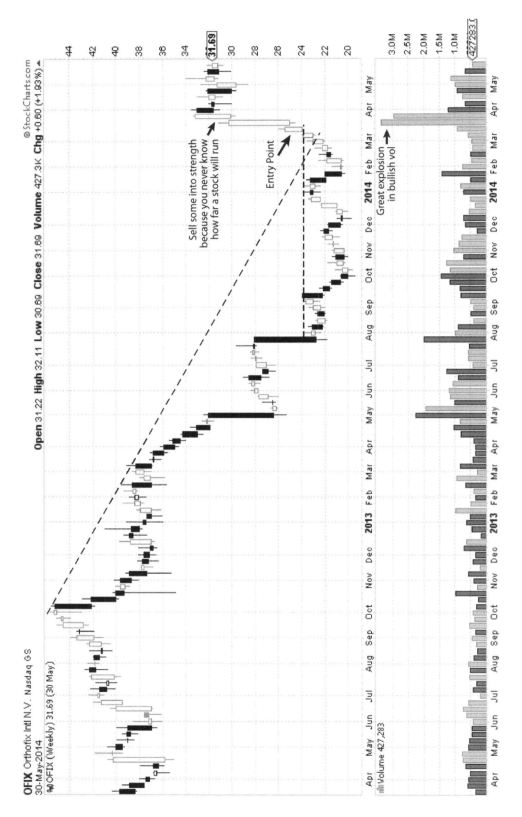

245 Money Making Stock Chart Setups: Profiting from Swing Trading

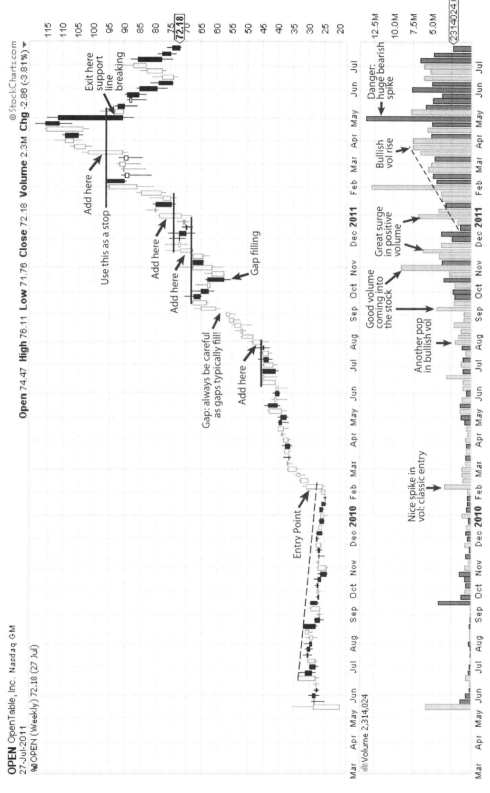

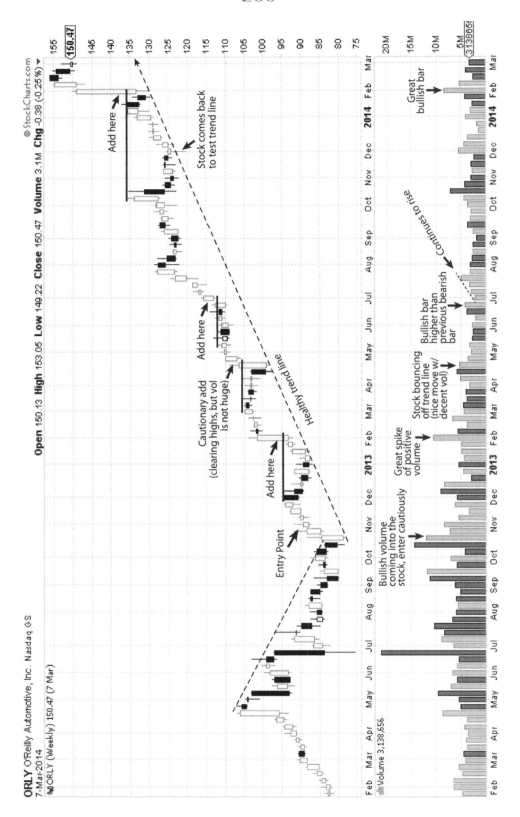

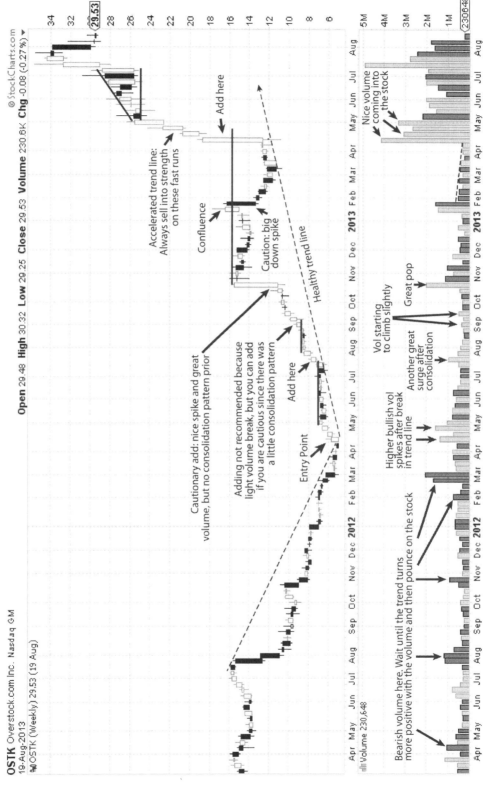

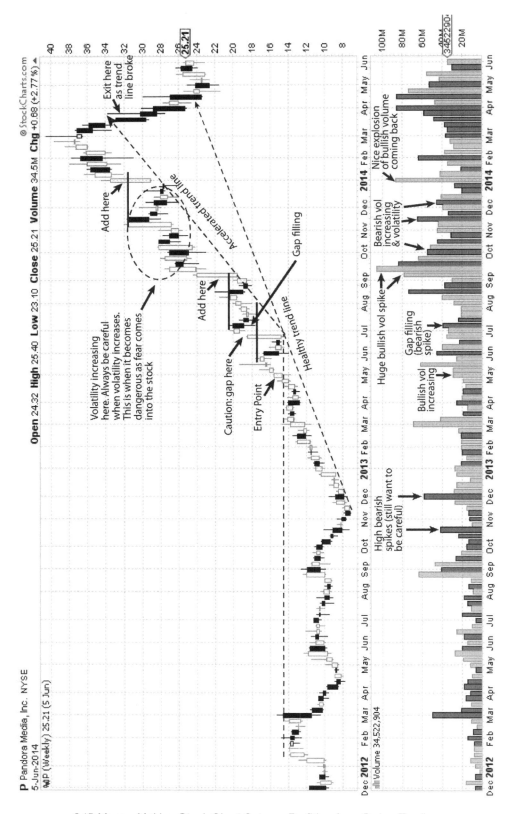

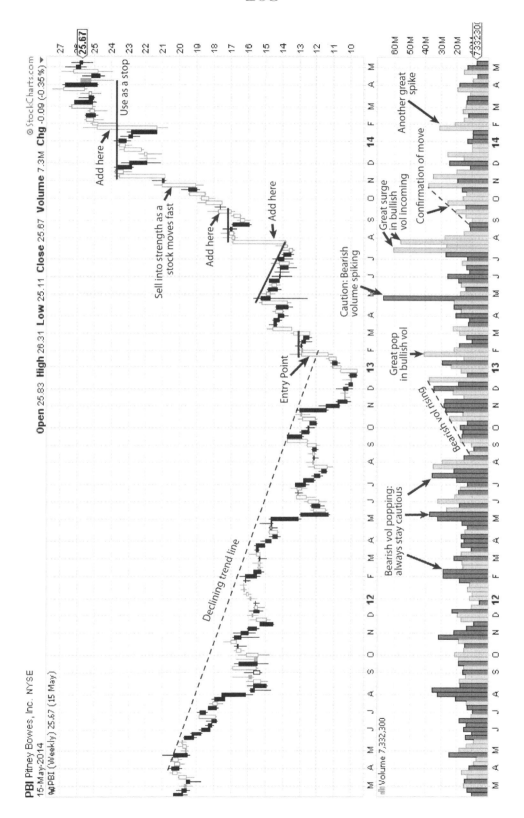

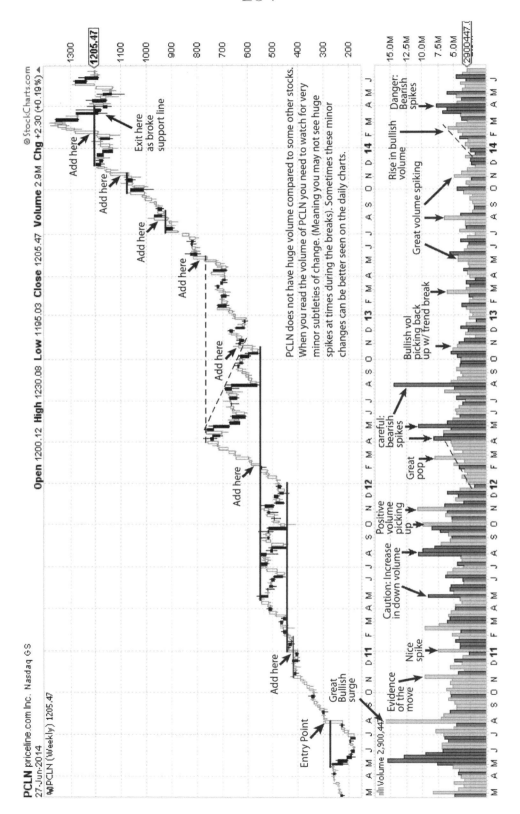

PCLN priceline.com Inc. Nasdaq GS
27-Jun-2014

Open 1200.12 **High** 1230.08 **Low** 1195.03 **Close** 1205.47 **Volume** 2.9M **Chg** +2.30 (+0.19%) ▲

© StockCharts.com

◾ⓦ PCLN (Weekly) 1205.47

1205.47

Add here

Exit here as broke support line

Add here

Add here

Add here

Add here

Add here

Add here

Add here

Entry Point

Great Bullish surge

PCLN does not have huge volume compared to some other stocks. When you read the volume of PCLN you need to watch for very minor subtleties of change. (Meaning you may not see huge spikes at times during the breaks). Sometimes these minor changes can be better seen on the daily charts.

Danger: Bearish spikes

Rise in bullish volume

Great volume spiking

Bullish vol picking back up w/ trend break

careful: bearish spikes

Great pop!

Positive volume picking up

Caution: Increase in down volume

Nice spike

Evidence of the move

◾ⓜ PCLN Volume 2,900,447

2900447.0

245 Money Making Stock Chart Setups: Profiting from Swing Trading

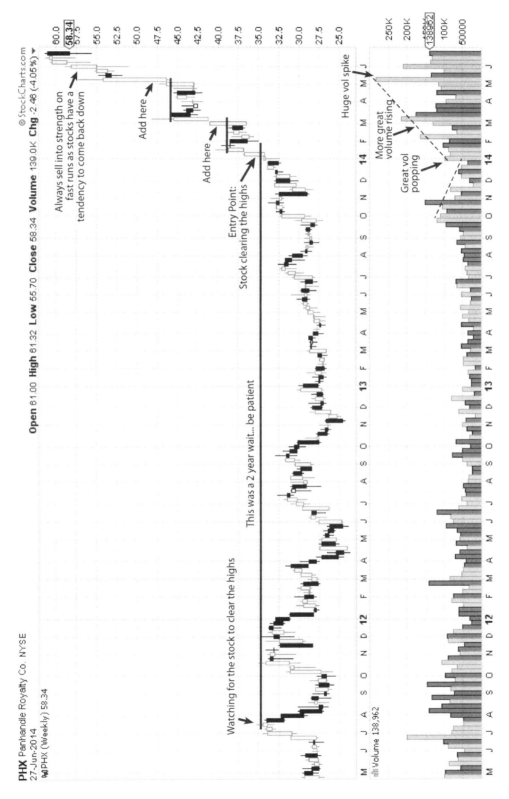

PHX Panhandle Royalty Co. NYSE
27-Jun-2014   © StockCharts.com
Open 61.00 High 61.32 Low 55.70 Close 58.34 Volume 139.0K Chg -2.46 (-4.05%) ▼

Always sell into strength on
fast runs as stocks have a
tendency to come back down

Add here

Add here

Entry Point:
Stock clearing the highs

This was a 2 year wait... be patient

Watching for the stock to clear the highs

Huge vol spike

More great
volume rising

Great vol
popping

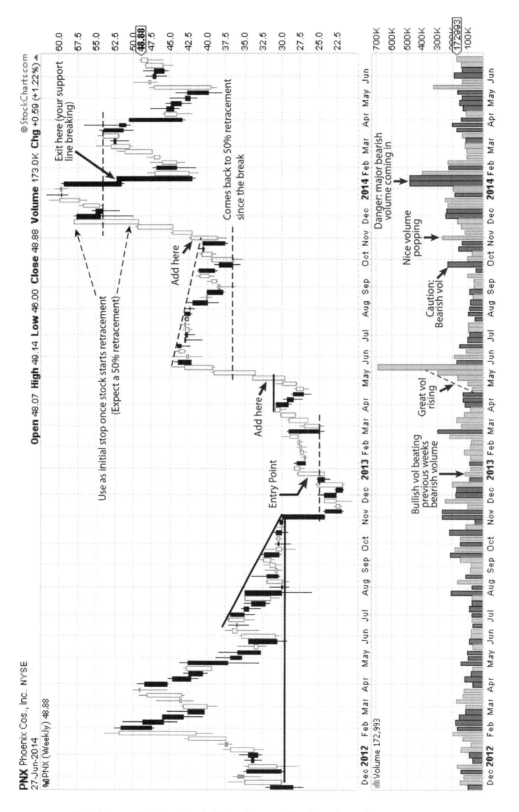

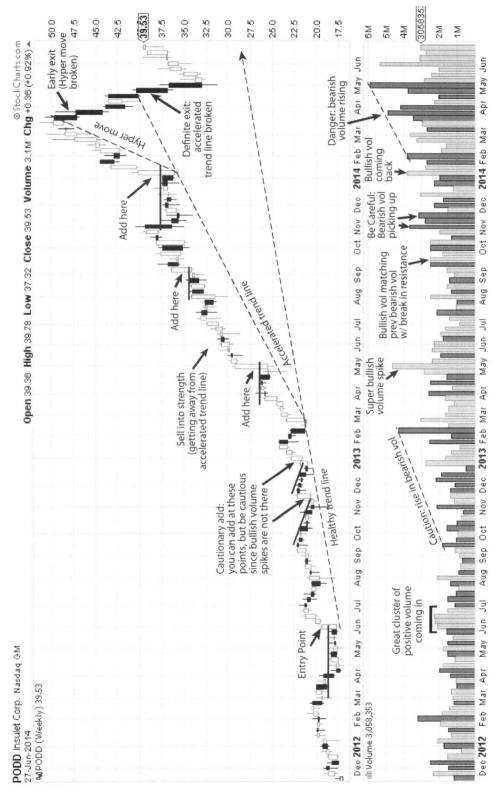

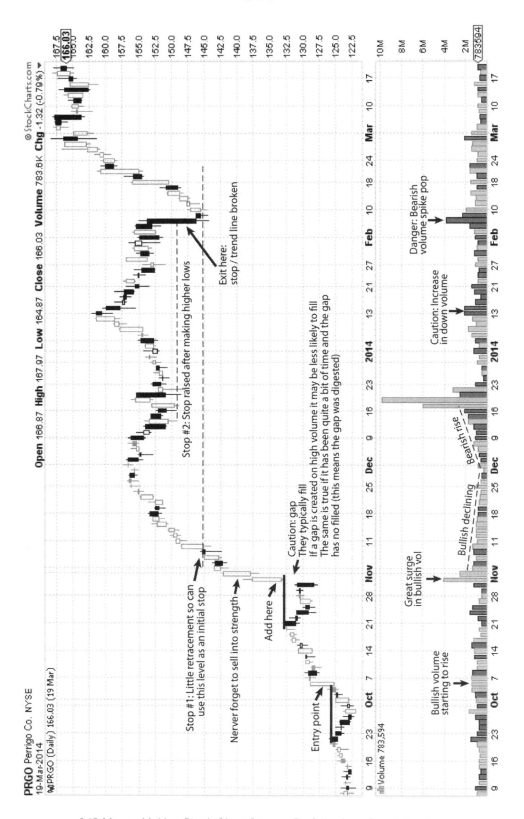

PRGO Perrigo Co. NYSE

19-Mar-2014

Open 166.87 **High** 167.97 **Low** 164.87 **Close** 166.03 **Volume** 783.6K **Chg** -1.32 (-0.79%) ▼

© StockCharts.com

�ūPRGO (Daily) 166.03 (19 Mar)

166.03

Exit here:
stop / trend line broken

Stop #2: Stop raised after making higher lows

Stop #1: Little retracement so can
use this level as an initial stop

Nerver forget to sell into strength

Add here

Caution: gap
They typically fill
If a gap is created on high volume it may be less likely to fill
The same is true if it has been quite a bit of time and the gap
has no filled (this means the gap was digested)

Entry point

ᴇᴛᴘ Volume 783,594

Danger: Bearish
volume spike pop

Caution: Increase
in down volume

Bearish rise

Bullish declining

Great surge
in bullish vol

Bullish volume
starting to rise

783594

245 Money Making Stock Chart Setups: Profiting from Swing Trading

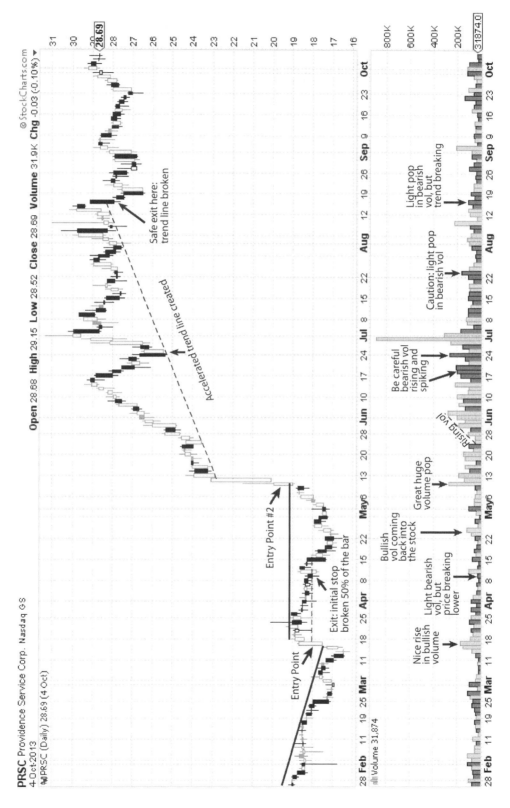

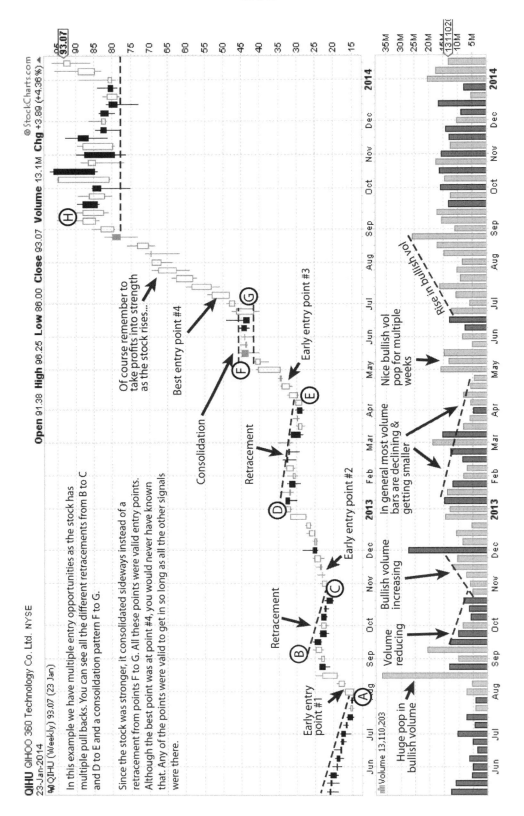

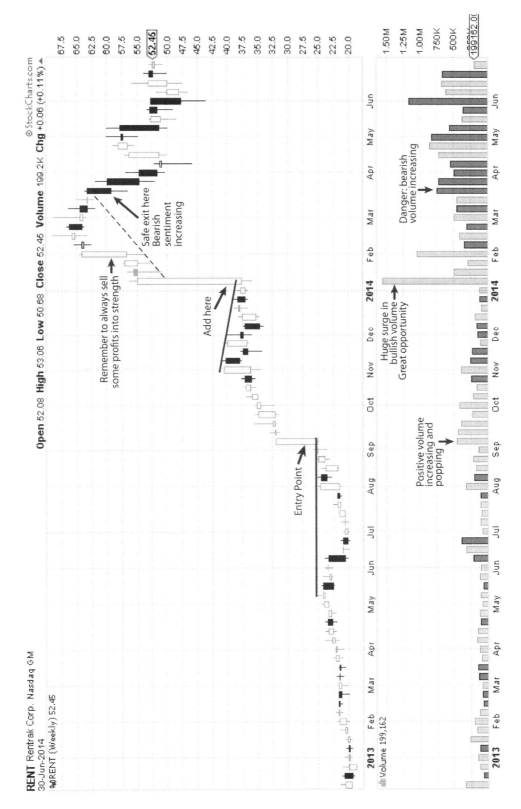

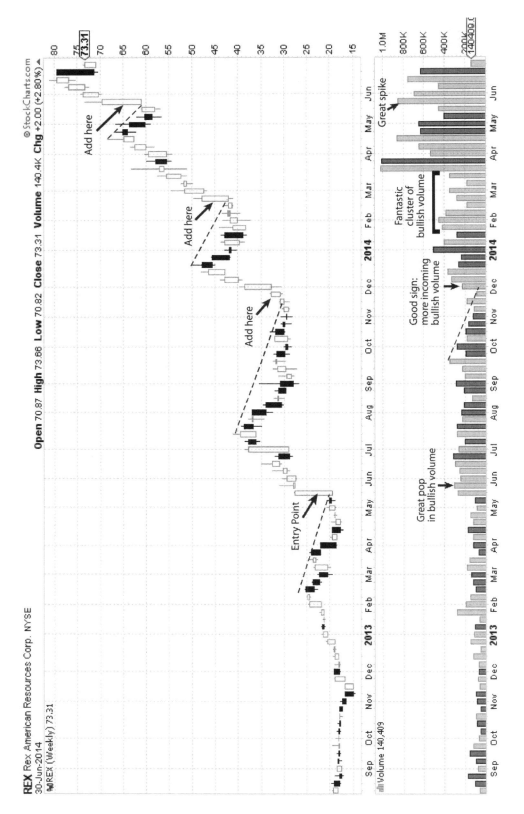

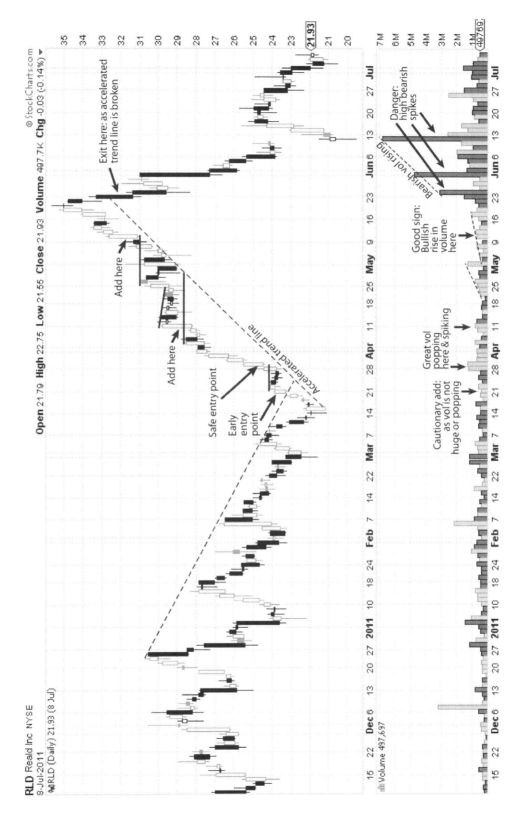

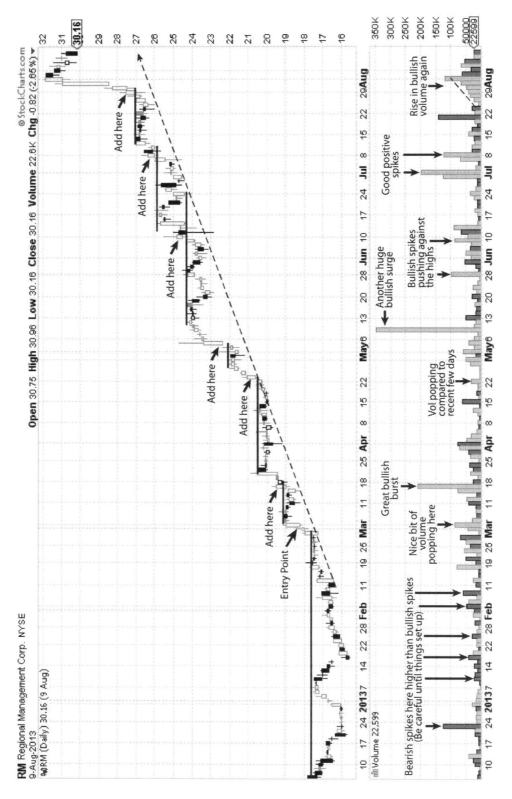

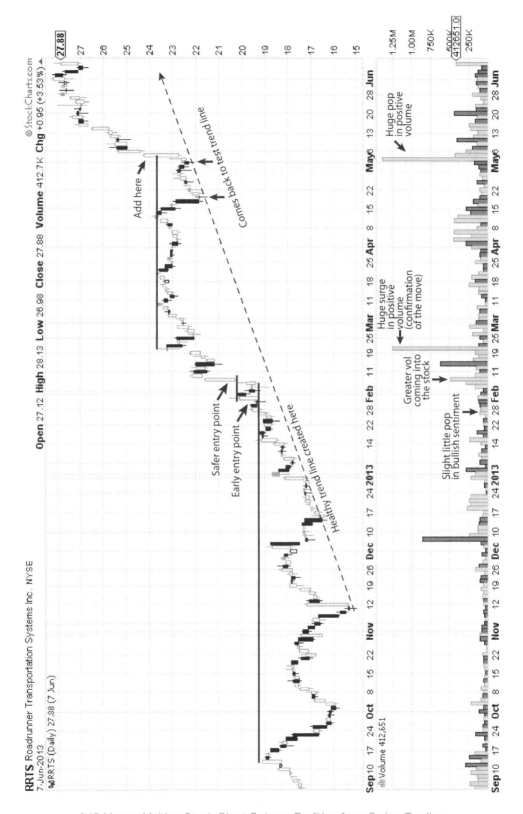

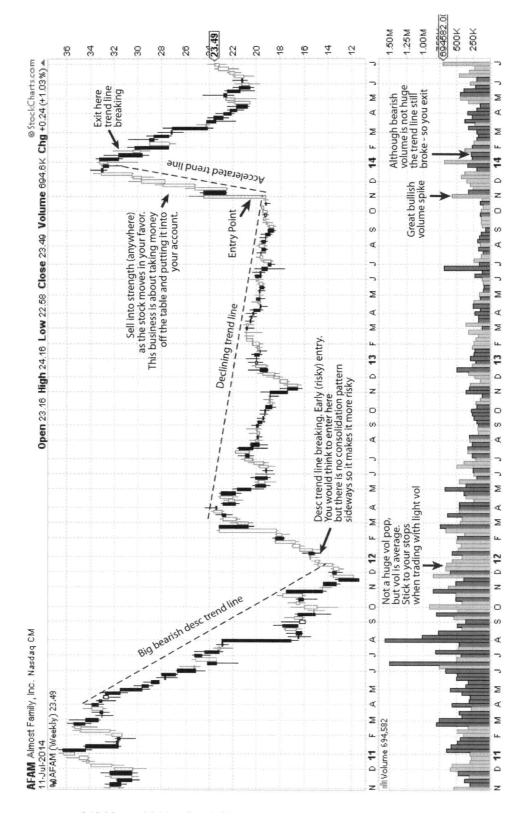

AFAM Almost Family, Inc. Nasdaq CM
11-Jul-2014

Open 23.16 **High** 24.16 **Low** 22.58 **Close** 23.49 **Volume** 894.8K **Chg** +0.24 (+1.03%) ▲

@ StockCharts.com

W AFAM (Weekly) 23.49

Exit here
trend line
breaking

Sell into strength (anywhere)
as the stock moves in your favor.
This business is about taking money
off the table and putting it into
your account.

Accelerated trend line

Entry Point

Declining trend line

Desc trend line breaking. Early (risky) entry.
You would think to enter here
but there is no consolidation pattern
sideways so it makes it more risky

Big bearish desc trend line

ılıı Volume 694,582

Although bearish
volume is not huge
the trend line still
broke - so you exit

Great bullish
volume spike

Not a huge vol pop,
but vol is average.
Stick to your stops
when trading with light vol

245 Money Making Stock Chart Setups: Profiting from Swing Trading

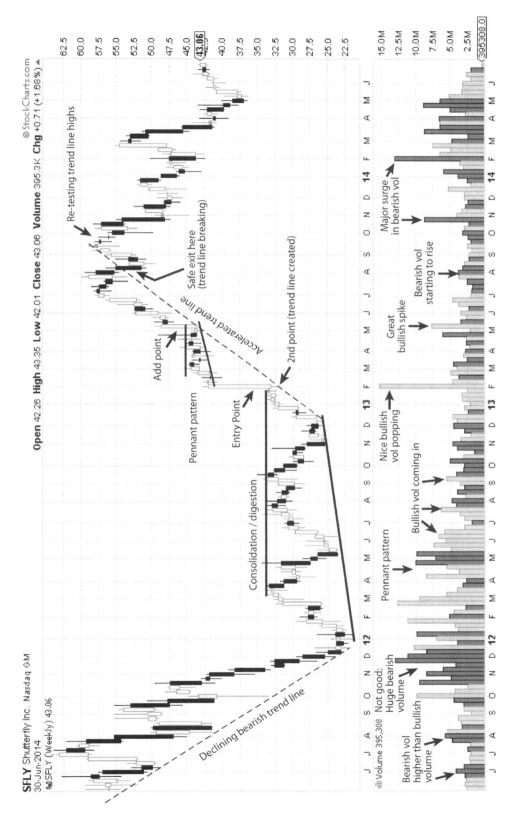

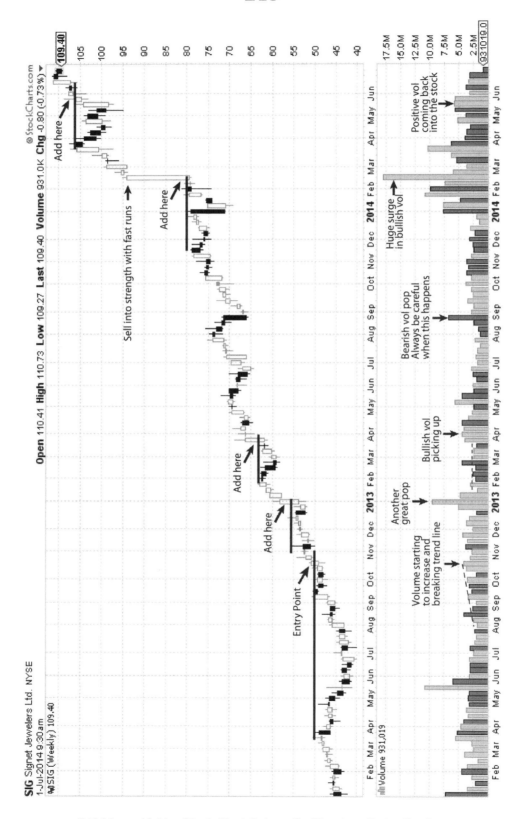

245 Money Making Stock Chart Setups: Profiting from Swing Trading

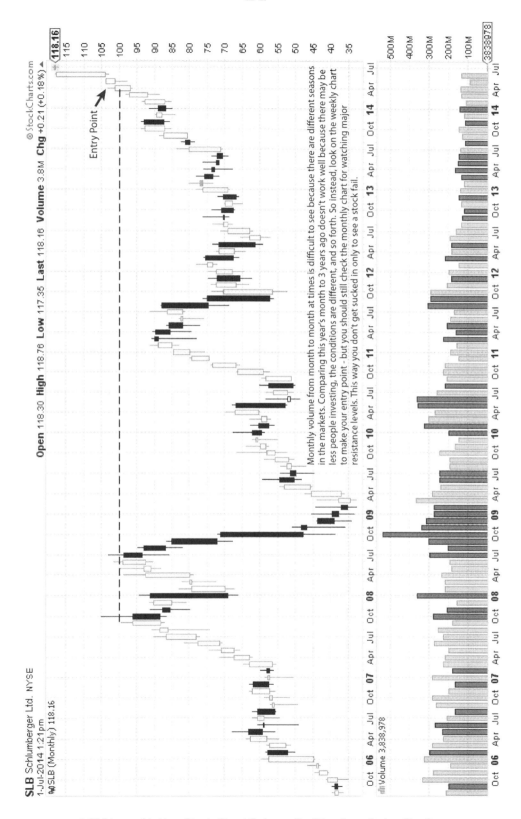

SLB Schlumberger Ltd. NYSE
1-Jul-2014 1:21pm
◎ StockCharts.com
Open 118.30 High 118.78 Low 117.35 Last 118.18 Volume 3.8M Chg +0.21 (+0.18%) ▲

SLB (Monthly) 118.16

Entry Point

118.16

Monthly volume from month to month at times is difficult to see because there are different seasons in the markets. Comparing this year's month to 3 years ago doesn't work well because there may be less people investing, the conditions are different, and so forth. So instead, look on the weekly chart to make your entry point - but you should still check the monthly chart for watching major resistance levels. This way you don't get sucked in only to see a stock fail.

Volume 3,838,978

3838978

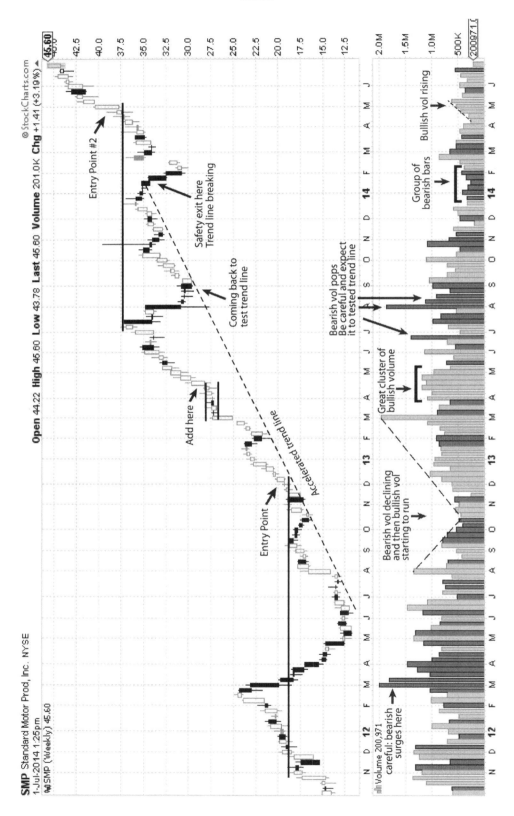

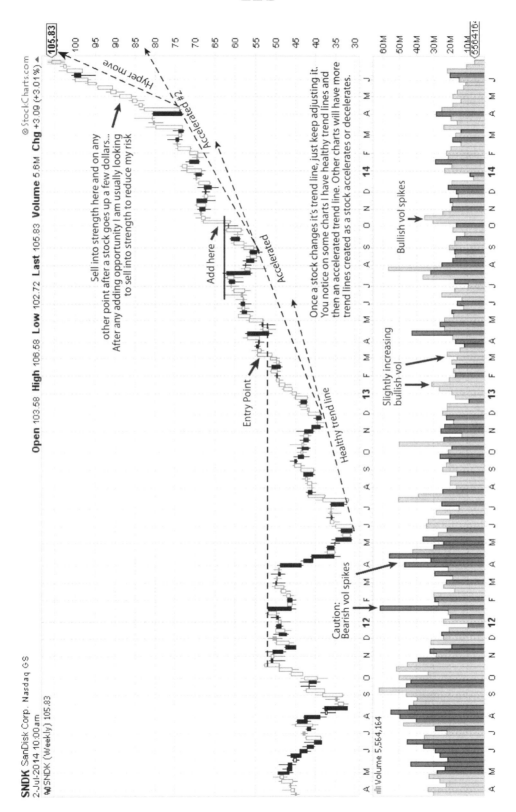

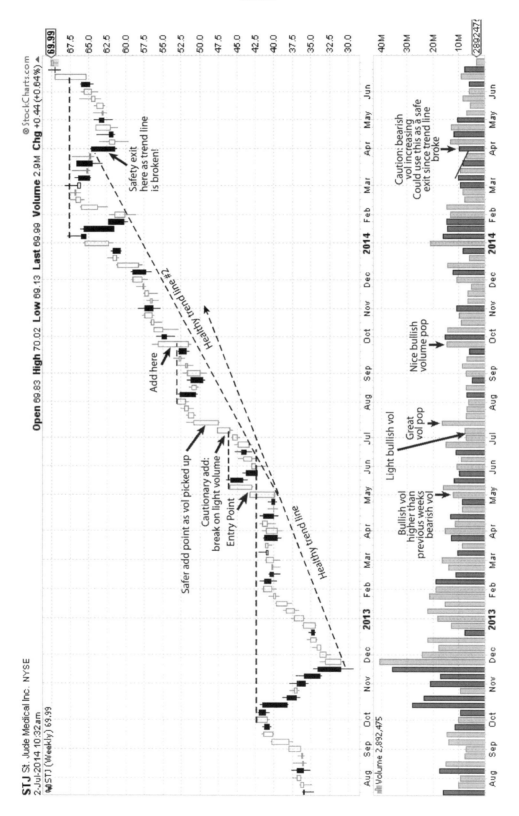

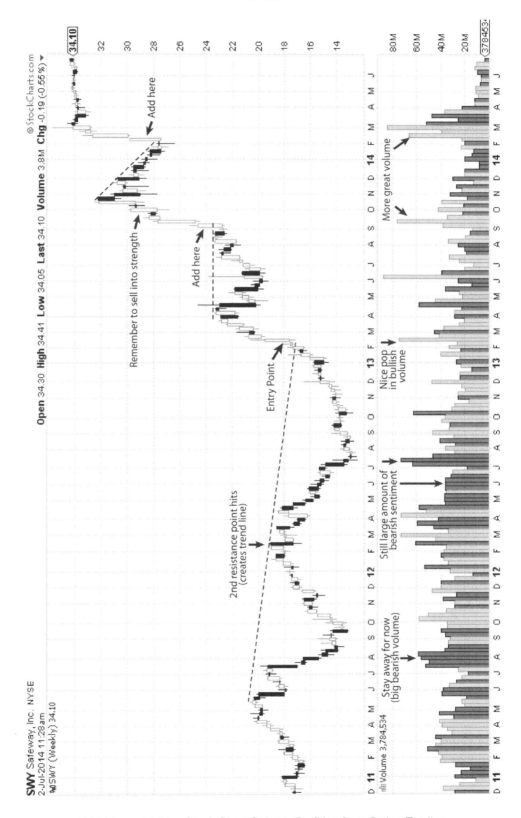

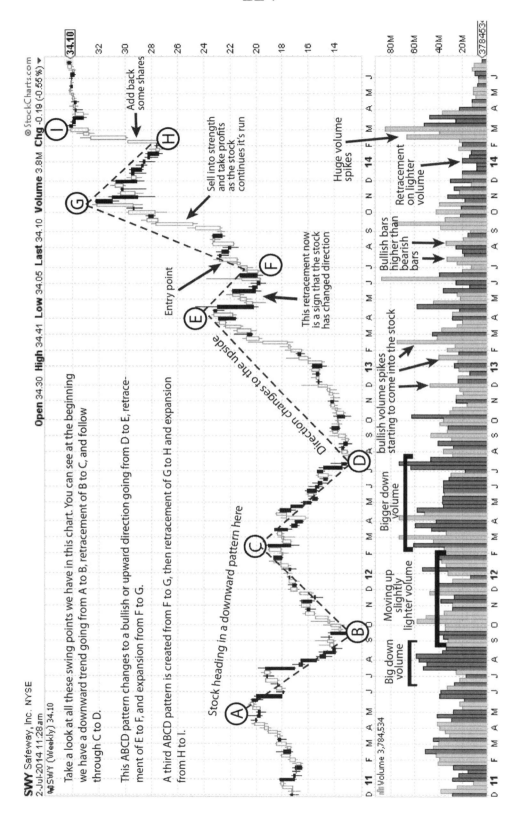

SWY Safeway, Inc. NYSE
2-Jul-2014 11:28am
ⓦ SWY (Weekly) 34.10
Open 34.30 High 34.41 Low 34.05 Last 34.10 Volume 3.8M Chg -0.19 (-0.55%) ▼
© StockCharts.com
34.10

Take a look at all these swing points we have in this chart. You can see at the beginning we have a downward trend going from A to B, retracement of B to C, and follow through C to D.

This ABCD pattern changes to a bullish or upward direction going from D to E, retracement of E to F, and expansion from F to G.

A third ABCD pattern is created from F to G, then retracement of G to H and expansion from H to I.

Add back some shares

Sell into strength and take profits as the stock continues it's run

Entry point

This retracement now is a sign that the stock has changed direction

Direction changes to the upside

Stock heading in a downward pattern here

Huge volume spikes

Retracement on lighter volume

Bullish bars higher than bearish bars

bullish volume spikes starting to come into the stock

Bigger down volume

Moving up slightly lighter volume

Big down volume

Volume 3,784,534

3784534

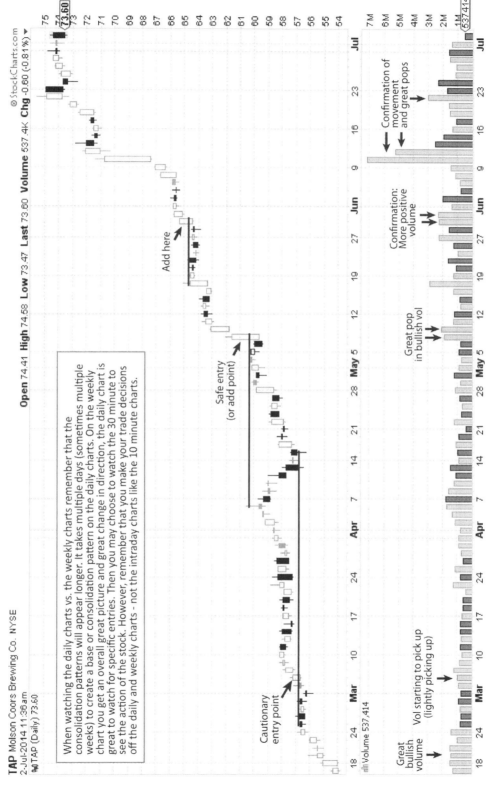

TAP Molson Coors Brewing Co. NYSE
2-Jul-2014 11:38am
Open 74.41 High 74.58 Low 73.73 Last 73.60 Volume 537.4K Chg -0.60 (-0.81%) ▼
TAP (Daily) 73.60
© StockCharts.com
73.60

When watching the daily charts vs. the weekly charts remember that the consolidation patterns will appear longer. It takes multiple days (sometimes multiple weeks) to create a base or consolidation pattern on the daily charts. On the weekly chart you get an overall great picture and great change in direction, the daily chart is great to watch for specific entries. Then you may choose to watch the 30 minute to see the action of the stock. However, remember that you make your trade decisions off the daily and weekly charts - not the intraday charts like the 10 minute charts.

Add here

Safe entry
(or add point)

Cautionary
entry point

Great
bullish
volume

Vol starting to pick up
(lightly picking up)

Great pop
in bullish vol

Confirmation:
More positive
volume

Confiration of
movement
and great pops

Volume 537,414

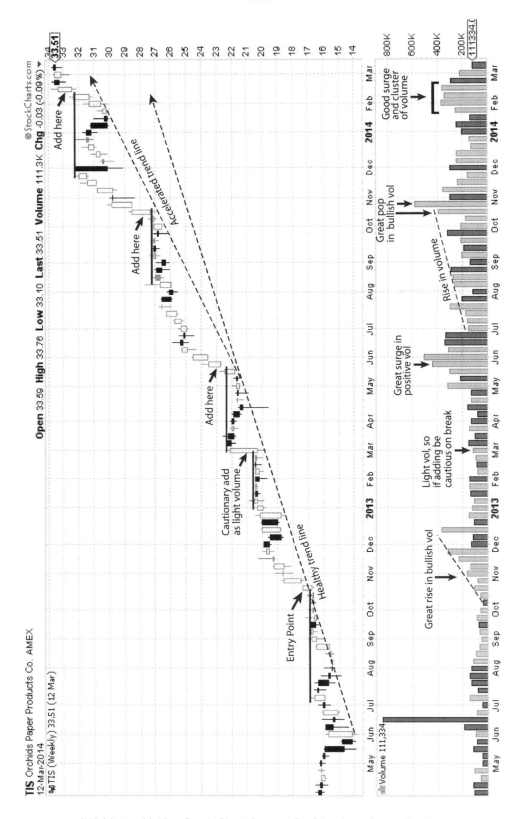

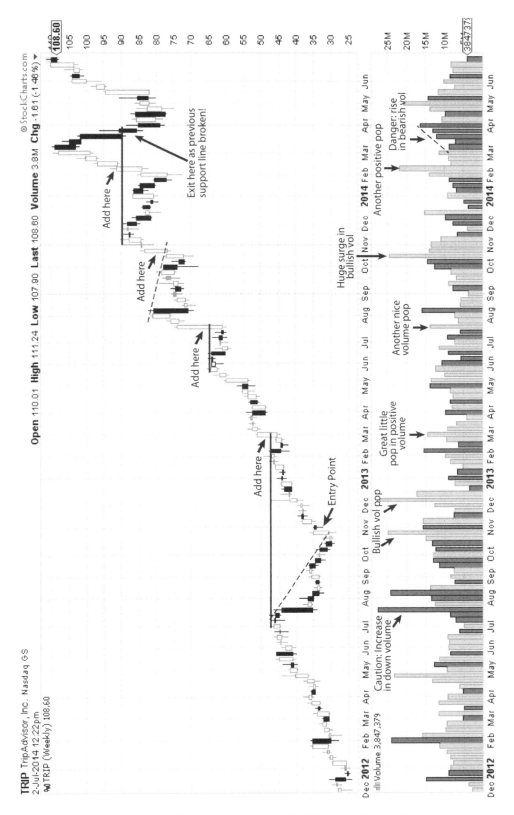

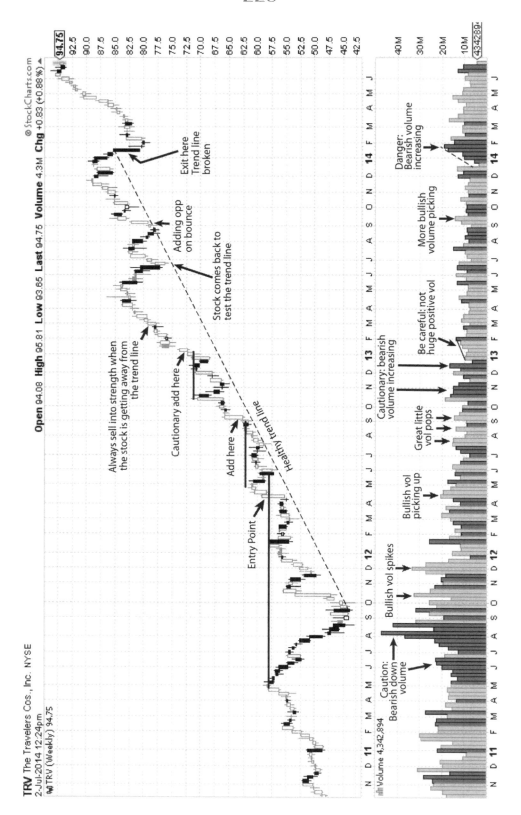

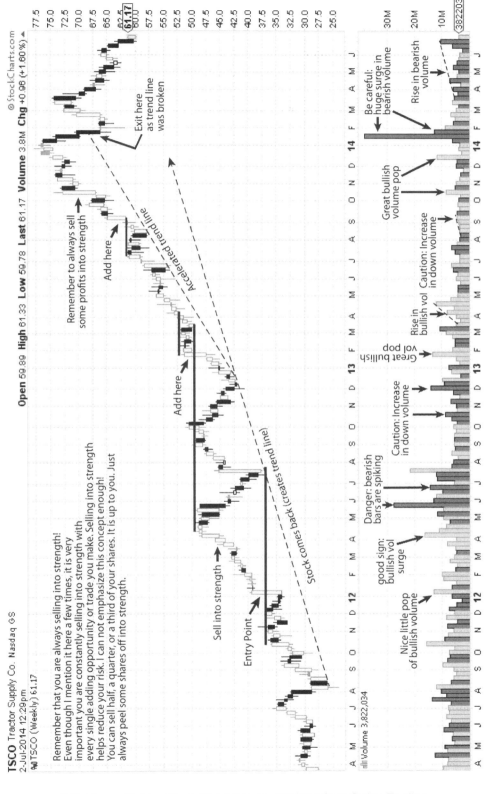

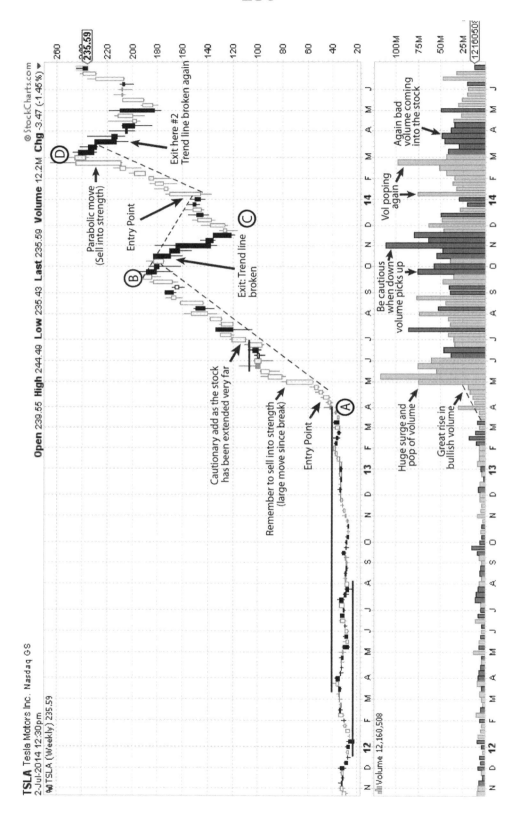

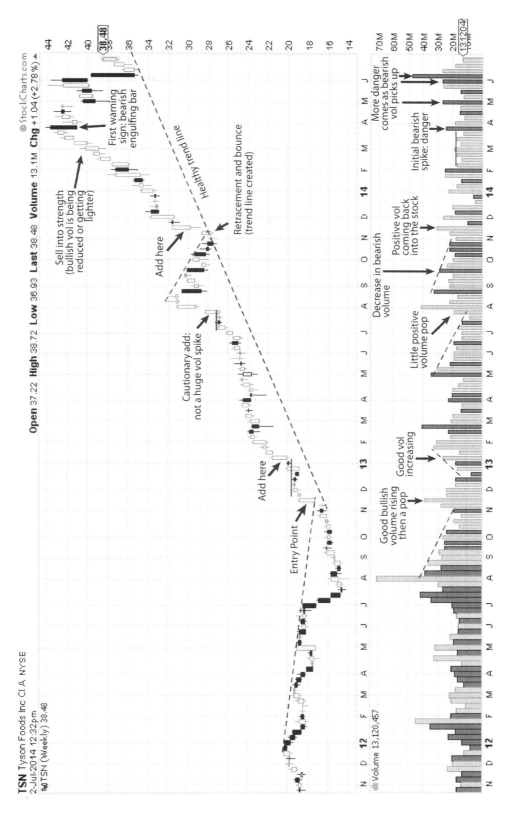

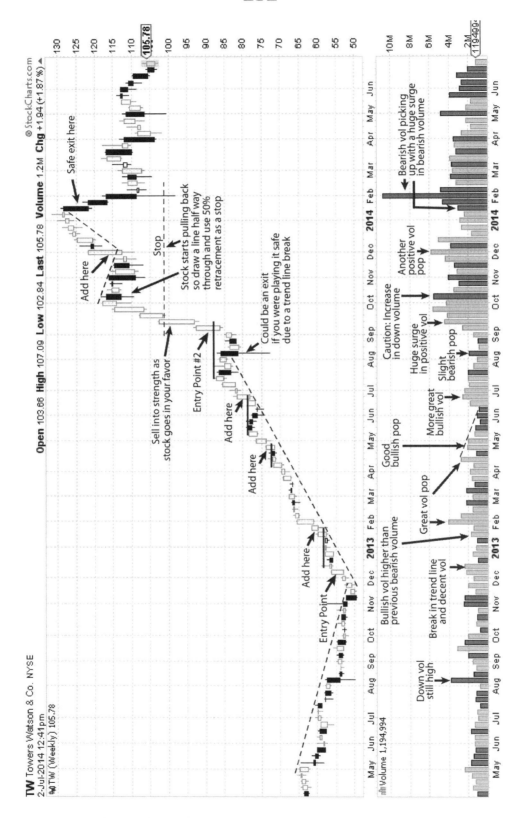

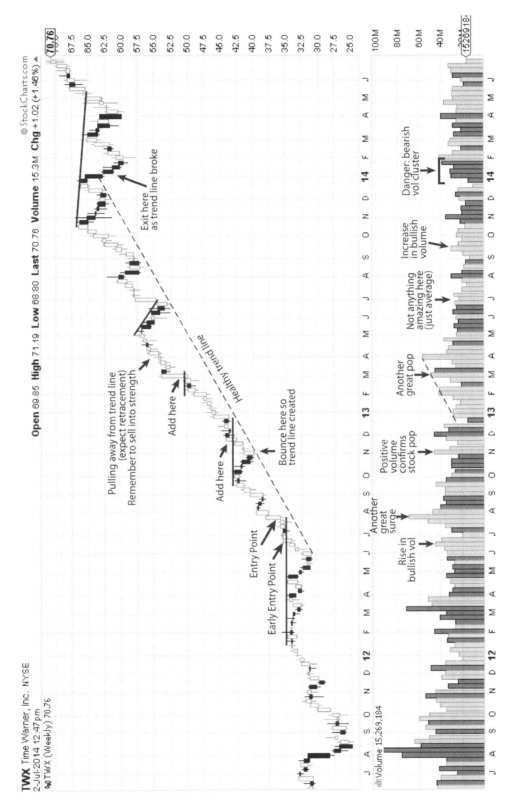

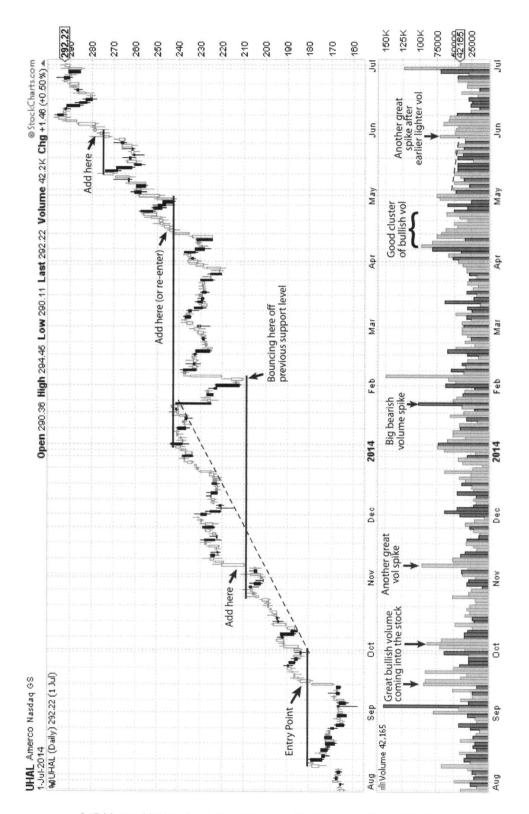

245 Money Making Stock Chart Setups: Profiting from Swing Trading

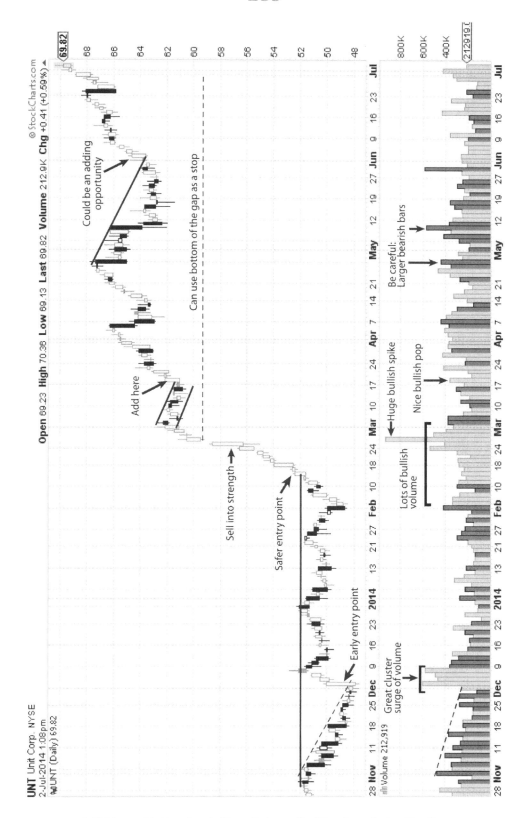

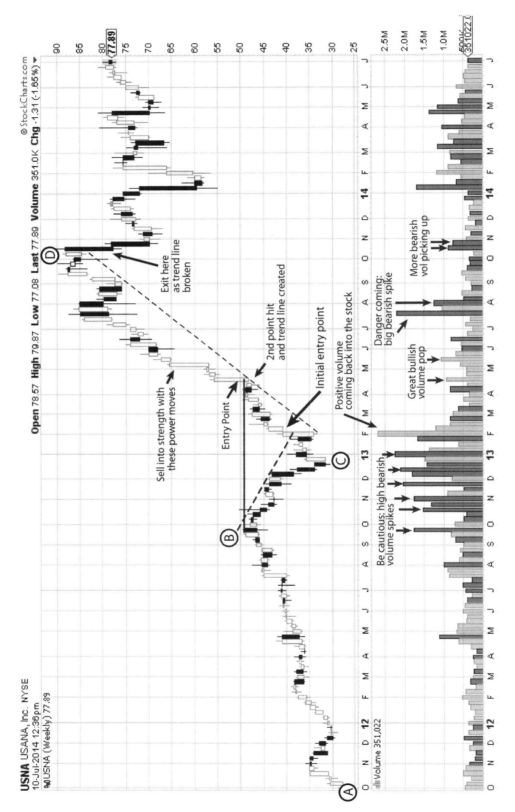

245 Money Making Stock Chart Setups: Profiting from Swing Trading

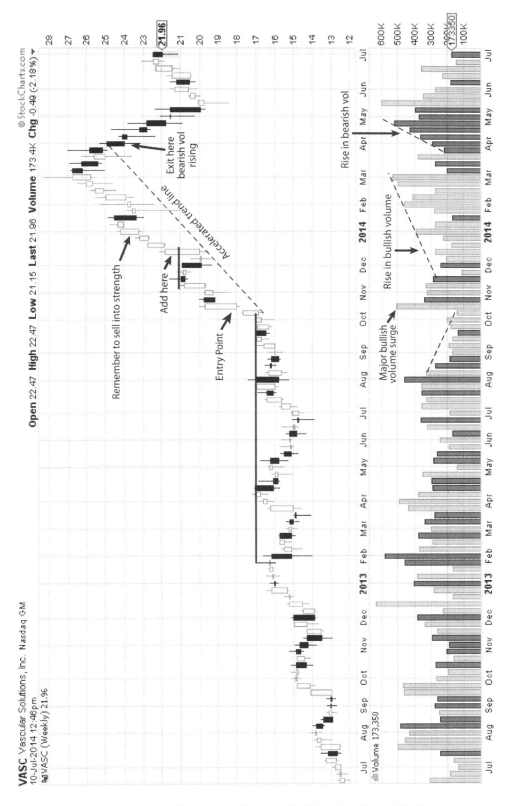

245 Money Making Stock Chart Setups: Profiting from Swing Trading

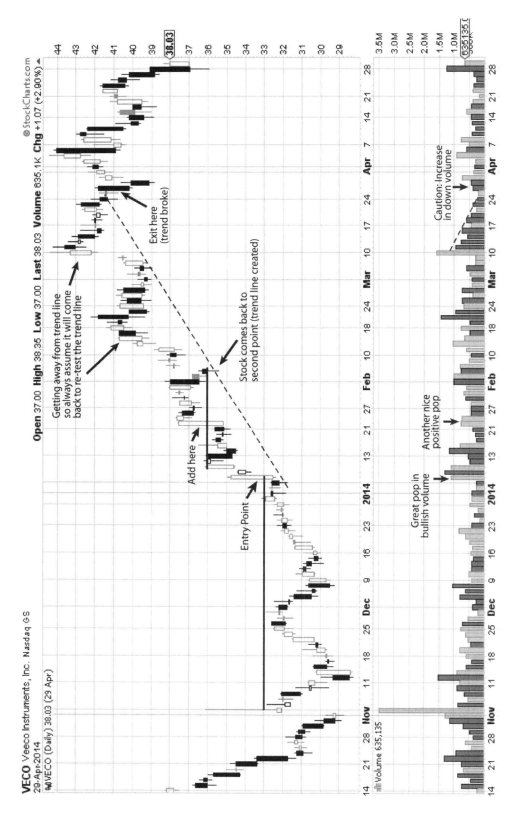

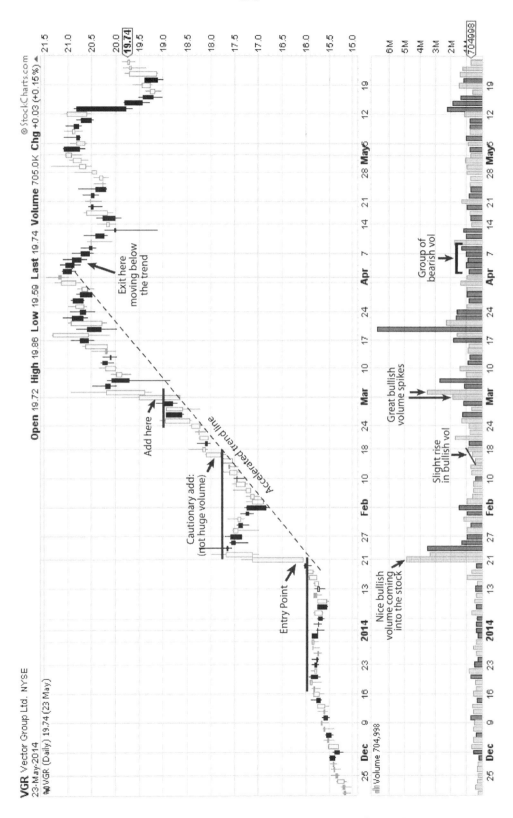

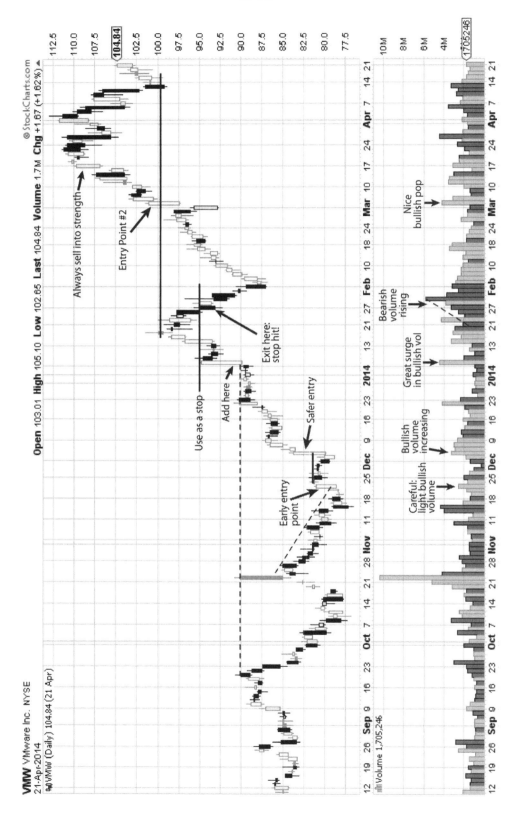

245 Money Making Stock Chart Setups: Profiting from Swing Trading

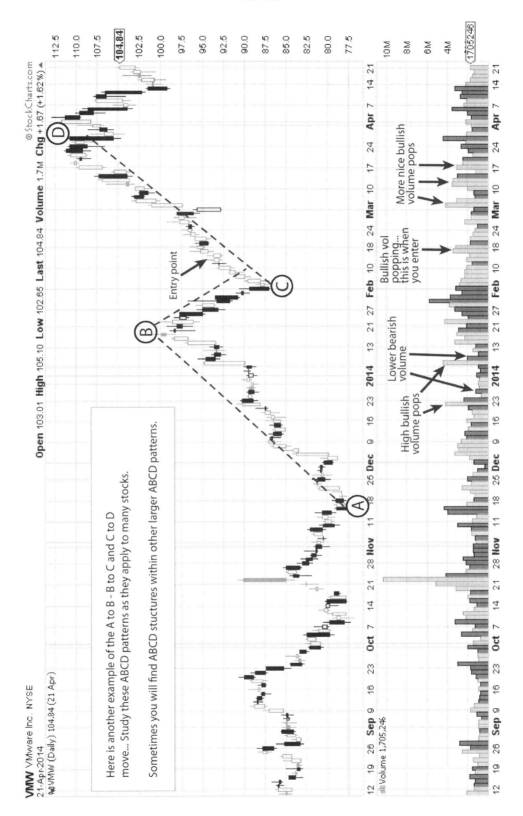

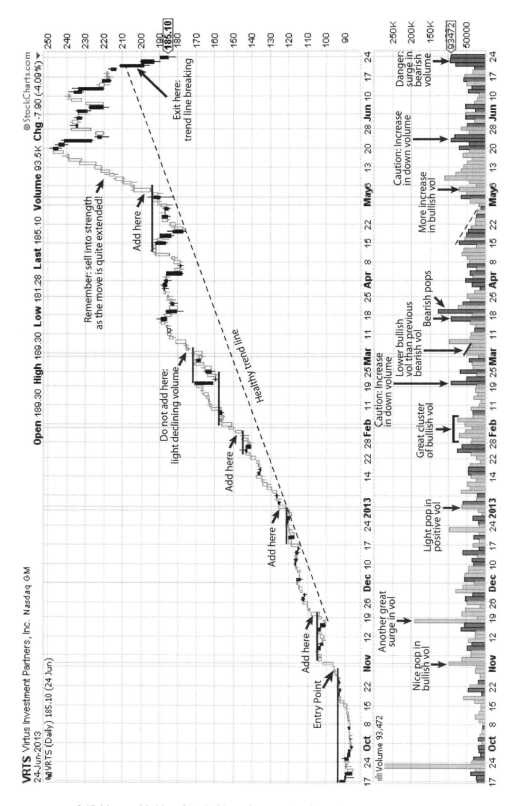

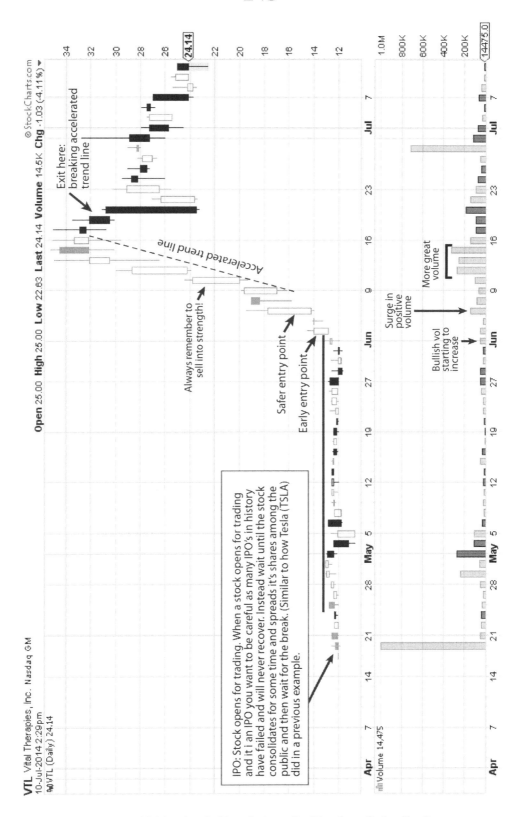

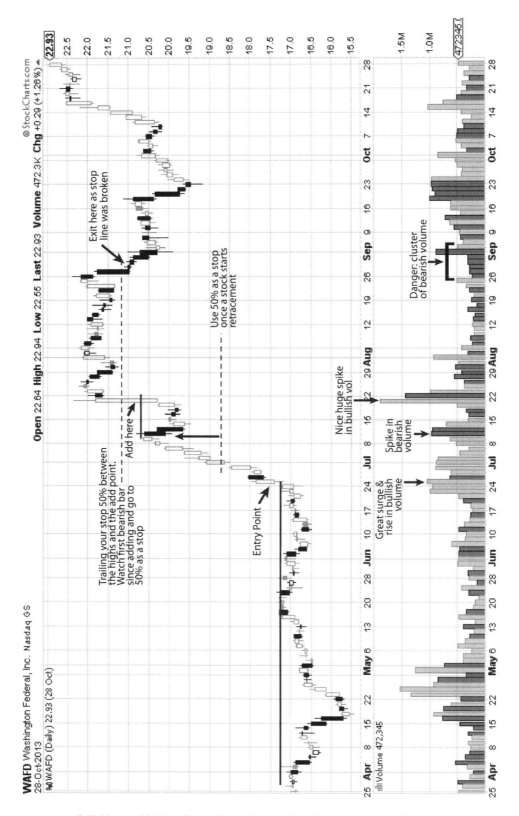

WAFD Washington Federal, Inc. Nasdaq GS
28-Oct-2013

Open 22.84 **High** 22.94 **Low** 22.55 **Last** 22.93 **Volume** 472.3K **Chg** +0.29 (+1.28%) ▲

22.93

© StockCharts.com

WAFD (Daily) 22.93 (28 Oct)

Volume 472,345

472,345

Exit here as stop
line was broken

Use 50% as a stop
once a stock starts
retracement

Trailing your stop 50% between
the highs and the add point.
Watch first bearish bar
since adding and go to
50% as a stop

Add here

Entry Point

Nice huge spike
in bullish vol

Spike in bearish
volume

Danger: cluster
of bearish volume

Great surge &
rise in bullish
volume

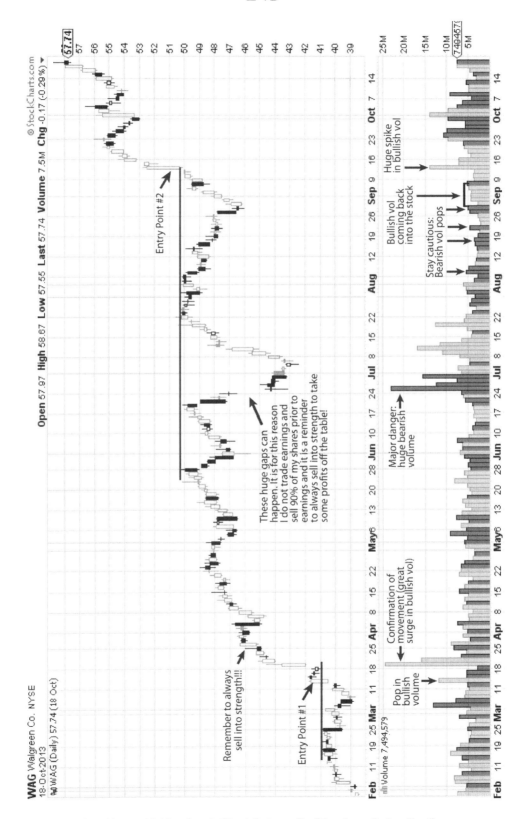

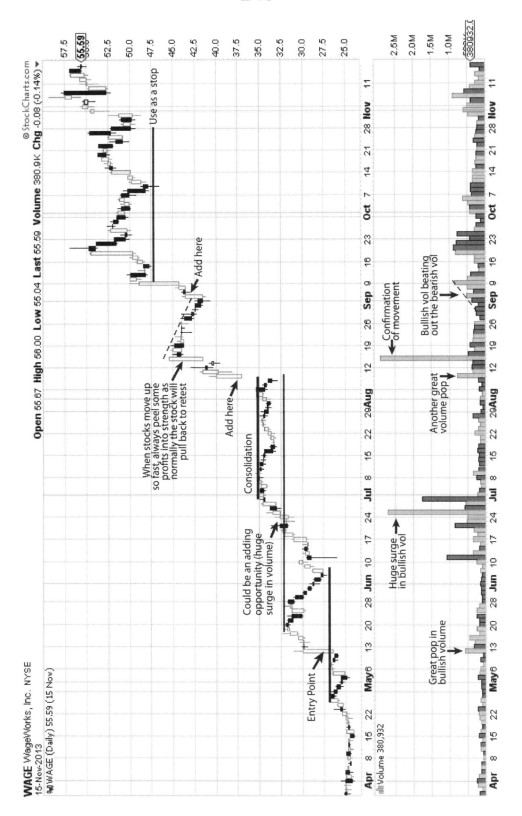

245 Money Making Stock Chart Setups: Profiting from Swing Trading

2↲7

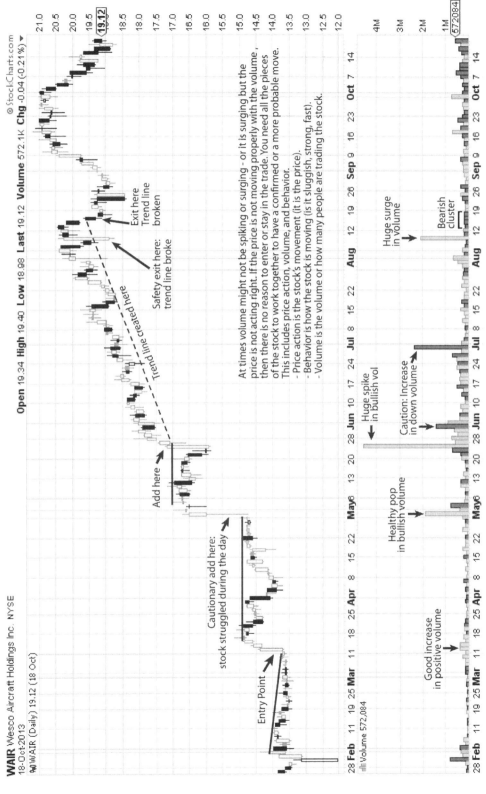

At times volume might not be spiking or surging - or it is surging but the price is not acting right. If the price is not moving properly with the volume, then there is no reason to enter or stay in the trade. You need all the pieces of the stock to work together to have a confirmed or a more probable move. This includes price action, volume, and behavior.
- Price action is the stock's movement (it is the price).
- Behavior is how the stock is moving (is it sluggish, strong, fast).
- Volume is the volume or how many people are trading the stock.

2-8

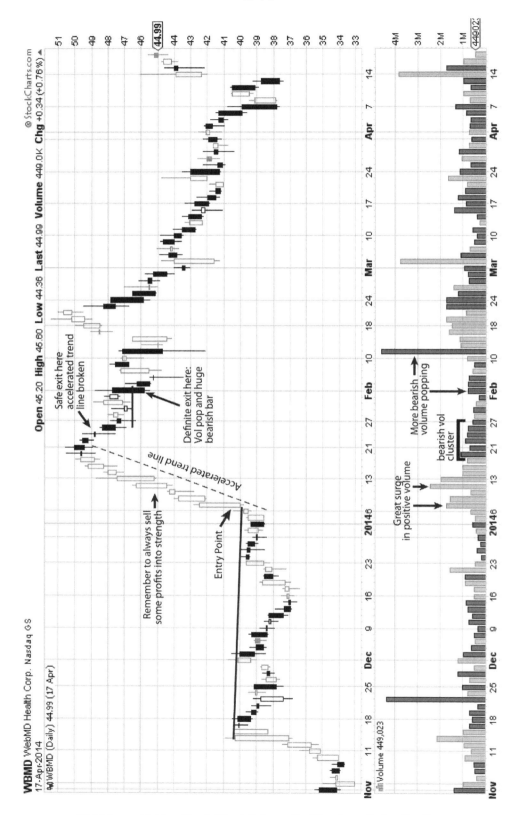

245 Money Making Stock Chart Setups: Profiting from Swing Trading

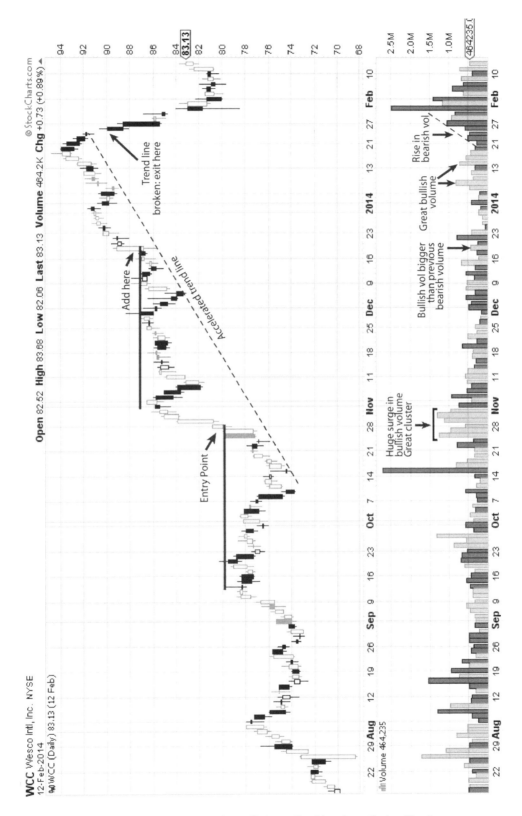

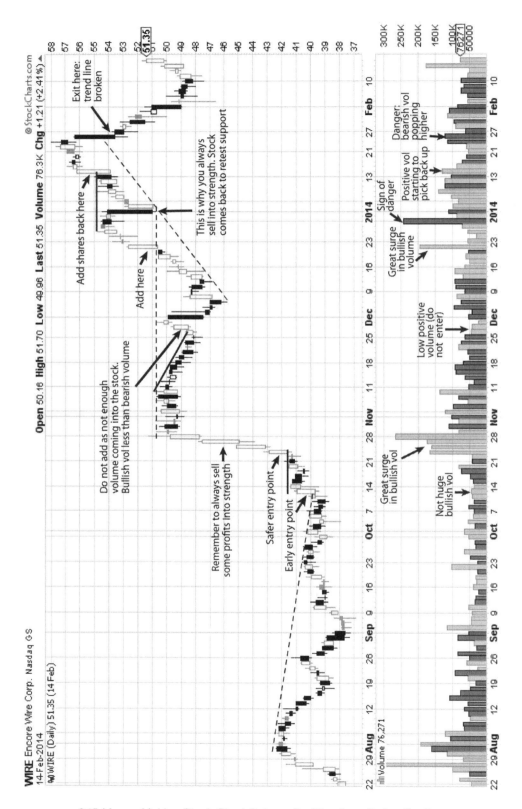

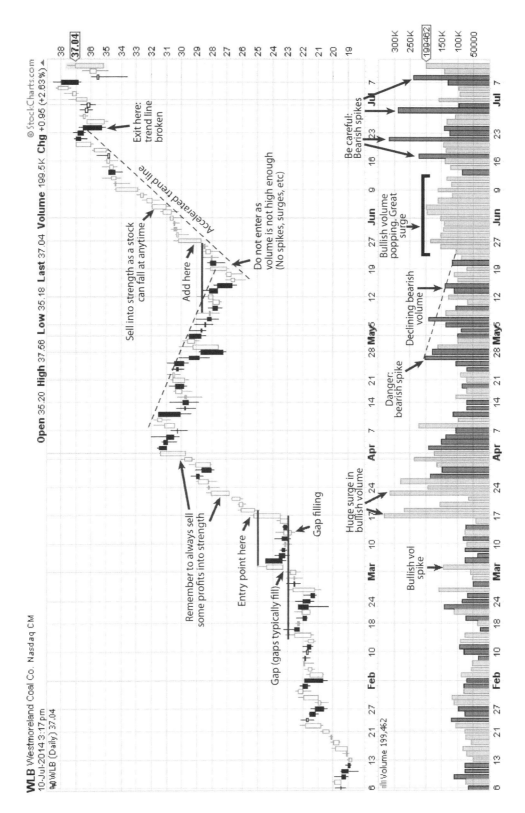

245 Money Making Stock Chart Setups: Profiting from Swing Trading

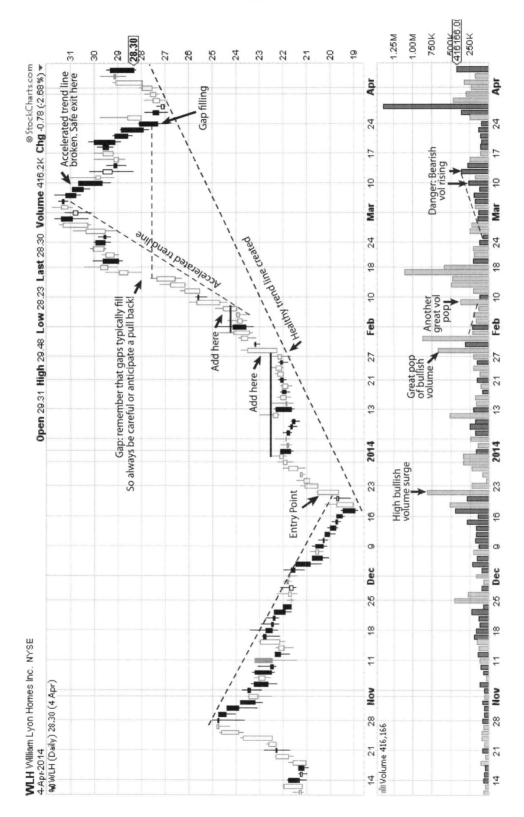

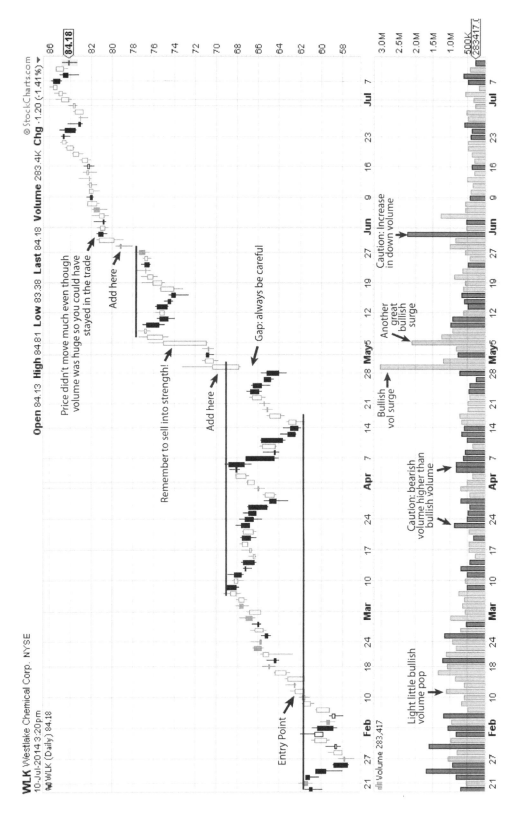

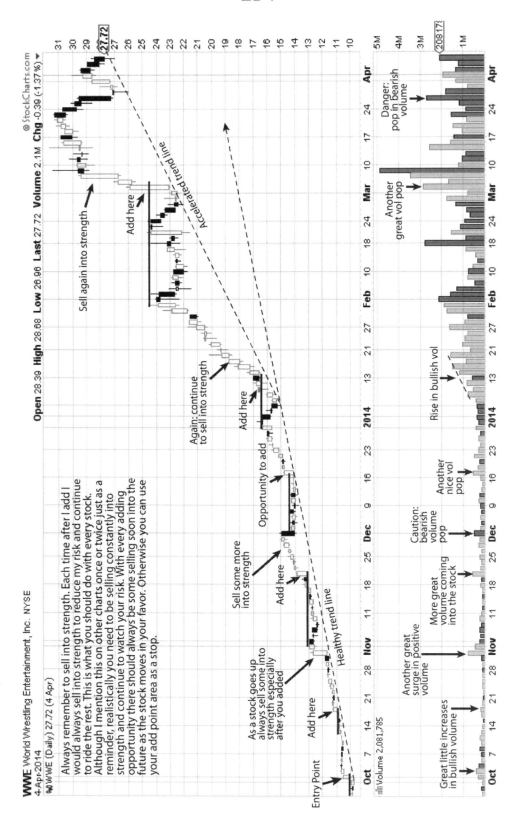

WWE World Wrestling Entertainment, Inc. NYSE
4-Apr-2014

Open 28.39 High 28.68 Low 26.98 Last 27.72 Volume 2.1M Chg -0.39 (-1.37%) ▼

WWE (Daily) 27.72 (4 Apr)

Always remember to sell into strength. Each time after I add I would always sell into strength to reduce my risk and continue to ride the rest. This is what you should do with every stock. Although I mention this on other charts once or twice just as a reminder, realistically you need to be selling constantly into strength and continue to watch your risk. With every adding opportunity there should always be some selling soon into the future as the stock moves in your favor. Otherwise you can use your add point area as a stop.

Sell again into strength

Add here

Accelerated trend line

Again; continue to sell into strength

Add here

Opportunity to add

Sell some more into strength

Add here

Healthy trend line

As a stock goes up always sell some into strength especially after you added

Add here

Entry Point

Volume 2,081,785

27.72

208173

Danger: pop in bearish volume

Another great vol pop

Rise in bullish vol

Caution: bearish volume pop

Another nice vol pop

More great volume coming into the stock

Another great surge in positive volume

Great little increases in bullish volume

@StockCharts.com

245 Money Making Stock Chart Setups: Profiting from Swing Trading

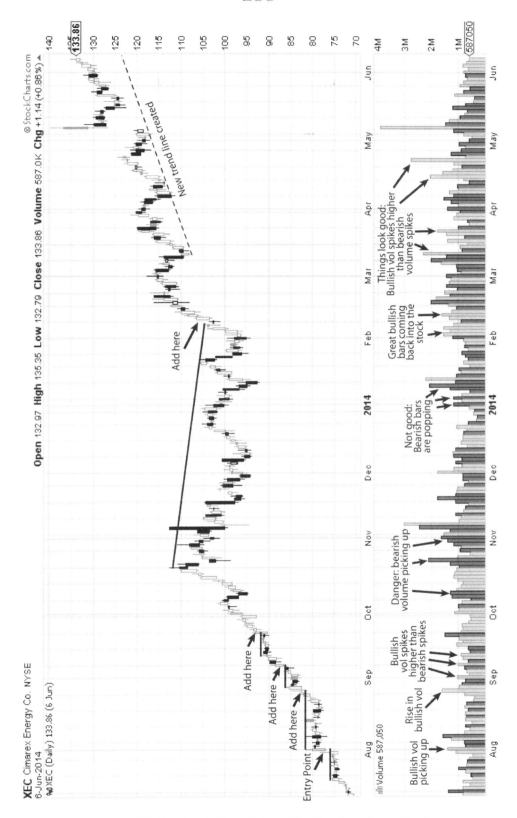

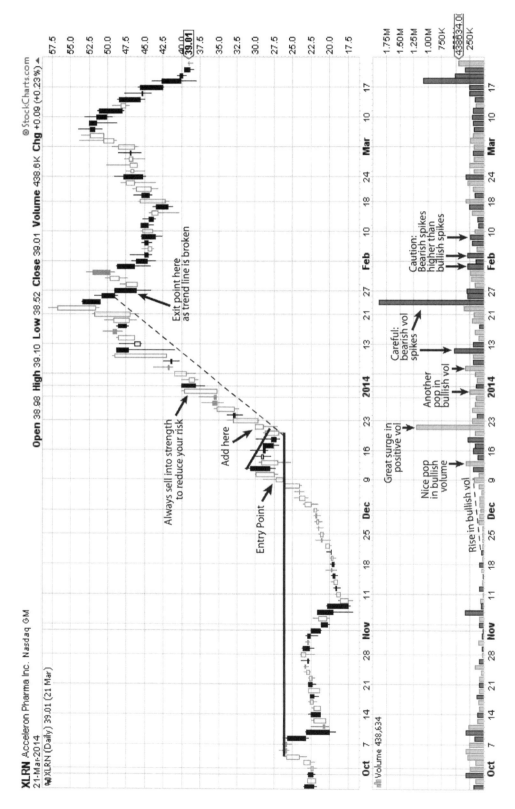

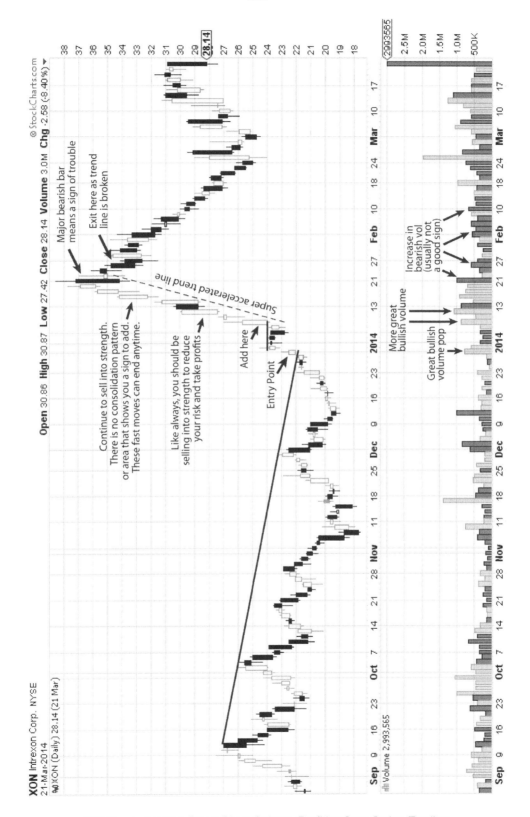

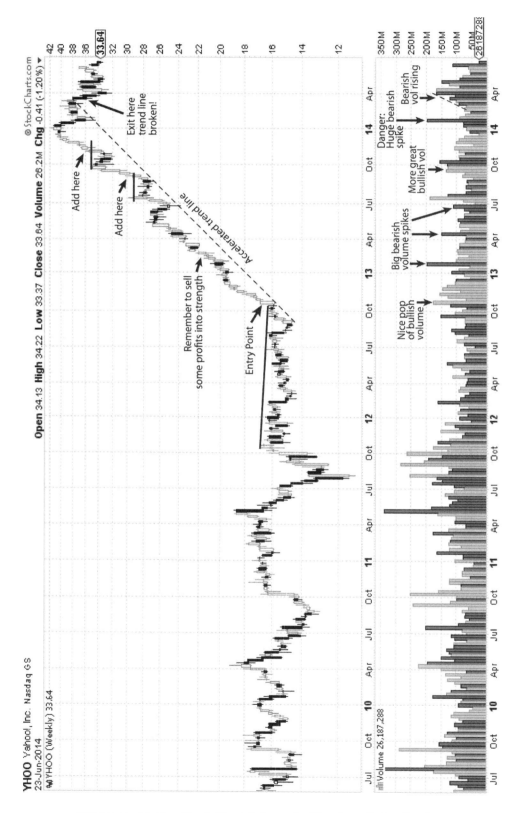

245 Money Making Stock Chart Setups: Profiting from Swing Trading

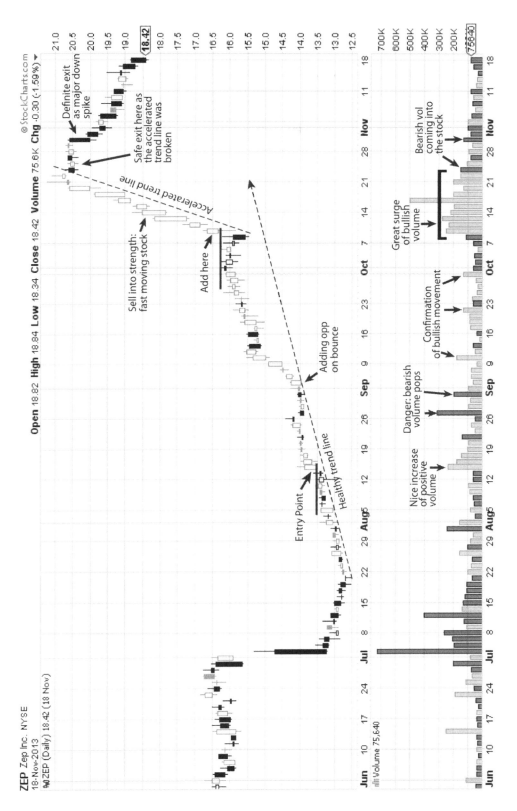

Conclusion and wrap up

Thank you so much for joining me and I appreciate you sticking with me. I know that some of the things I mentioned in this book could have you scratching your head as the concepts may be new, different, or just theories you are not used to.

Remember that this is just the start and the beginning of your stock market journey. The journey can be a difficult one if you're trying to be a full-time stock trader. Nevertheless if you have the patience, determination, and willingness to make changes in your personal actions then I know you can be successful!

Success in this business doesn't happen overnight or even over a one year period. It takes multiple years to understand how the market works and how to put all the pieces together of this business.

Just like it takes four years to get a degree at a college until you are able to work at a regular job expect the same type of concept in the stock market. However there won't be anyone nagging you to take any classes or courses. You have to be self-disciplined to do studying and homework on your own. The more studying and effort you put in the quicker you will learn this business. Unfortunately if you don't have the self-discipline to evolve your education and do your own homework then you just won't understand the business, it will take you a very long time to put things together, and more than likely you won't be successful.

A person is not likely to understand the stock market or how to make money with stocks if they study the wrong material or if they aren't willing to do what's necessary to evolve their craft.

Always be mindful and patient in this business. It takes time to get it just like anything else in the world, but when you do it makes it all worth it! Remember to constantly improve your education and invest in yourself. Investing in yourself should be your biggest priority.

So where should you go next with your education? I highly recommend that you take a look at some of my stock market educational video courses if you haven't already.

Stock Trading Foundation

The green course is a great course to continue your education. It has over three hours of in depth knowledge and includes a study guide with charts of looking at healthy price movements in a stock. It also shows you when to get in and out of stocks. The course is a bit more technical and focuses on charts, stock movement, and volume, but I know you can handle it!

Critical Charts Online

If you want to see more charts similar to the ones in this book, but during the current market conditions then you may want to visit www.tradersfly.com and look at getting access to my critical charts membership.

I typically try to post a few times a month to show you stocks that are moving, support or resistance lines to watch, or stocks that may breakout or breakdown. It is a great resource to study more charts in the current markets.

Final Note:

Continue to push yourself and be better. Don't wish that things were easier for you; instead wish that you were better and constantly work to improve.

Before I sign off I want to share with you some helpful resources to help you evolve your trading. Thanks again for sticking with me and reading this book. Always remember that there is more to life than trading.

Do what you love, contribute to others, and most importantly live life abundantly!

Sasha Evdakov

Resources

Tradersfly.com: My personal stock trading website. Signup to the newsletter and get my rapid recap videos to see the stocks I am watching

Tradersfly.com/resources/ : Get a bunch of great stock market resources from FAQ's, to broker reviews, tools, trading tips, etc.

Twitter.com/tradersfly/ : Follow me on Twitter to see real-time charts of the stocks I am watching along with some little advice on trading for that day.

Rise2Learn.com : My primary company where you can see all the courses and material I offer from stock trading to business education.

SashaEvdakov.com : My personal website. Get news on various courses I have coming or read my personal blog and get some business tips.

19067711R10148

Made in the USA
San Bernardino, CA
11 February 2015